The Concept of Just War in Judaism, Christianity and Islam

Key Concepts in Interreligious Discourses

Edited by
Georges Tamer

In cooperation with
Katja Thörner

Volume 5

The Concept of Just War in Judaism, Christianity and Islam

Edited by
Georges Tamer and Katja Thörner

DE GRUYTER

ISBN 978-3-11-073805-6
e-ISBN (PDF) 978-3-11-073313-6
e-ISBN (EPUB) 978-3-11-073326-6
ISSN: 2513-1117

Library of Congress Control Number: 2021936324

Bibliographic information published by the Deutsche Nationalbibliothek
The Deutsche Nationalbibliothek lists this publication in the Deutsche Nationalbibliografie; detailed bibliographic data are available on the Internet at http://dnb.dnb.de.

Printing and binding: CPI books GmbH, Leck

www.degruyter.com

Preface

The present volume in the book series "Key Concepts in Interreligious Discourses" (KCID) presents the results of a conference on the concept of just war in Judaism, Christianity and Islam held at the Friedrich-Alexander-University Erlangen-Nuremberg (FAU). The conference, which was generously funded by the Evangelical Church in Germany (EKD) and the Dr. German Schweiger Foundation at the FAU, took place in Erlangen on September 19–20, 2019. We wish to thank both institutions for their invaluable support.

The Research Unit KCID was replaced in October 2020 by the Bavarian Research Center for Interreligious Discourses (BaFID). The main aim of the Bavarian Research Center for Interreligious Discourses is the investigation of the fundamental ideas and central concepts in Judaism, Christianity and Islam in order to uncover their reciprocal connections and reveal similarities and differences between these three religions. Thus, BaFID is committed to deepening mutual understanding between religious communities by communicating research results.

The conference and book series KCID is one of the main activities of BaFID. It organizes conferences dedicated to the exploration of key concepts in Judaism, Christianity and Islam. A renowned set of researchers from various disciplines come together to study concepts from the viewpoint of each of the three religions. The results of each conference are published in a volume appearing in the above-mentioned book series. Particularly salient selections from each volume are made available online in Arabic, English and German on BaFID's website.

In this fashion, BaFID fulfills its aspirations not only by reflecting on central religious ideas amongst a small group of academic specialists, but also by disseminating such ideas in a way appealing to the broader public. Academic research which puts itself at the service of society is vital in order to counteract powerful contemporary trends towards a form of segregation rooted in ignorance, and to strengthen mutual respect and acceptance amongst religions. Such a result is guaranteed due to the methodology deployed by the research center, namely the discursive investigation of the concepts, as documented in the present volume on the concept of just war.

We wish to thank Dr. Albrecht Döhnert, Dr. Sophie Wagenhofer and their assistants at the publisher house De Gruyter for their competent caretaking of this volume and the entire book series. We would also like to thank Dr. Samuel Wilder for his language assistance in preparing the volume.

Georges Tamer and Katja Thörner
Erlangen, March 2021

https://doi.org/10.1515/9783110733136-001

Table of Contents

Daniel F. Polish
Just War in Jewish Thought — 1

Heinz-Gerhard Justenhoven
The Concept of Just War in Christianity — 43

Suleiman A. Mourad
The Concept of Just War in Islam — 93

Georges Tamer and Katja Thörner
Epilogue — 149

List of Contributors — 159

Index of Persons — 161

Index of Subjects — 165

Daniel F. Polish

Just War in Jewish Thought

1 Preface

Any paper that purports to offer a presentation of Jewish perspectives on just war requires a preface. Such a paper cannot be a long, detailed excursus on the various traditional theories on the subject, or a history of the discussion of this idea in Jewish thought, for the simple reason that there are precious few examples of discussions that could be so characterized in foundational texts or among Jewish thinkers. The notion of just war is an innovation of modern thought, and, as a result, not a category or concept in Jewish traditional thought. In the first instance neither the Hebrew Bible nor rabbinic texts express themselves primarily in terms of abstract concepts. Both strata of Jewish scripture are given to the concrete and specific. Jews did not engage in philosophy until well into the Middle Ages. Even beyond that, there are hardly any texts that touch on the themes that would be included in the category of just war. In this regard Jewish religious tradition is markedly asymmetrical from the Christian and Muslim religious traditions. Those two traditions do have developed theories about the validity of the fighting of wars in general, and about assessing the appropriateness of any individual war in particular, and about proper conduct during battle. Jews have no Augustine.

The reason for this asymmetry needs to be recognized before any reflection on the theme can begin. The reason is rooted in the history of the Jewish people. Unlike Christians and Muslims, Jews have not had to engage with the issue of war and warfare, because between the year 72 BCE and 1948, they existed in a diasporic condition. They lacked political sovereignty and had neither the need nor the opportunity to wage war. Admittedly, various settlements of Jewish life could be affected by wars waged by others, and could even be the victims of wars and warlike attacks. But the agency to wage wars did not exist for the collective Jewish community.[1] As a result, any conversation about waging war

1 Of course, there are rare instances where individual communities of Jews did have some sort of political cohesion and the capacity to exert military power. An example of this is the Himyarite kingdom, which converted to Judaism for the relatively brief period of the fourth to the sixth centuries and exercised political power as an independent political entity in the southern Arabian Peninsula. Yet the more consequent reality is that such communities were never the predominant reality of the Jewish historical experience, nor incorporated into the collective self-presentation of the Jewish people. More importantly, such peripheral communities were not

https://doi.org/10.1515/9783110733136-002

among Jewish thinkers could only be theoretical and speculative. Jewish thought tended toward the concrete reality of the lived experience of the Jewish people, and that of the Jewish thinkers; the issue of wars waged by them was marginal at best. Given that significant caveat, what a Jewish discussion of the issue of just war can consist of, is a presentation of the precious few instances in which that subject was explicitly addressed, and an attempt to extrapolate some kind of theory out of those descriptions and discussions of war and warfare that are presented in Jewish foundational texts.

1.1 "No War is Just"

It is, of course, possible for one to presume that the normative Jewish worldview rejects war outright—any war and all war—as if the injunction "seek peace and pursue it" (Ps. 34:15) were the totality of Jewish thought on the subject. Or one could assume that the prophets Isaiah and Micah taught the only lesson about war:

> They shall beat their swords into plowshares
> And their spears into pruning hooks
> Nation shall not lift up sword against nation
> Neither shall they learn war any more
> (Isa. 2:4; Mic. 4:3)

If one's only encounter with Jewish life was exposure to the liturgy, it might appear that peace was a Jewish *sine qua non*. The word *shalom* runs through the Jewish worship service like a leitmotif. In every service we encounter such sentiments as:

> Spread over us the shelter of Your peace
> We praise You, O God who makes peace and creates all things
> Grant great peace to Israel Your people forever, for You O ruler are the Lord of all peace ....
> We bless You O Lord who blesses His people Israel with peace

The words that conclude every section of the service similarly invoke the theme of peace:

in a position to contribute to the formulation of the shared Jewish intellectual storehouse of ideas.

> May the One who made peace on high[2] make peace for us and for all Israel[3]

This is noted even among the rabbis themselves. Leviticus Rabbah 9:3 notes that there is not a blessing or prayer in the standard liturgy that does not conclude with a prayer for or encomium to peace. An early prayer book of the Reform movement includes a more recently composed prayer in English which states

> Grant us peace, Thy most precious gift, O Thou eternal source of peace, and enable Israel to be its messenger unto the peoples of the earth. Bless our country that it may ever be a stronghold of peace, and its advocate in the council of nations.[4]

In concluding our consideration of the presence of the theme of peace in the Jewish liturgy, we would be remiss not to take note of a significant absence. It must be noted that nothing in that liturgy presents war as a desirable or even, at times, a necessary thing. We cannot avoid reflecting on the implications of the complete lack of any such sentiments.

Similarly, a casual reading of rabbinic literature might reinforce the impression that Jewish thought is pacifistic. A few examples out of many will have to suffice. Pirkei Avot 1:18 asserts, "the world is sustained by three things: truth, justice and peace". Elsewhere in Pirkei Avot, Hillel admonishes us, "be among the disciples of Aaron[5], seeking peace and pursuing it"[6] (1.12) The Tanhuma to Torah portion Shoftim 18 teaches that everything written in the Torah is written to promote peace. In the Talmud B. Shabbat 10b goes so far as to claim that God's very name is peace. The rabbis' estimation of *shalom* is exemplified in a refrain that is found with great frequency throughout the Talmud: "great is peace..." Clearly, peace is a primary value to the rabbis.

And yet despite the frequency with which we encounter encomia to peace, several caveats are in order. The first is etymological. The reality is that despite the desirability of an absence of military conflict, the word *shalom* does not nec-

2 This refers either to the act of creation itself or to the familiar rabbinic trope that at the time of creation various camps of angels fell into intense disagreement which, in the end, necessitated divine intervention and mediation

3 More recently the liberal movements of Judaism have added the words, "and on all the dwellers on earth".

4 *Union Prayer Book*, Cincinnati, Central Conference of American Rabbis, 1947, 22.

5 The rabbis offer various explanations of how Aaron came to be regarded as an embodiment of peace.

6 The conventional commentary on this statement says that the verse teaches us not to be passive or inactive in our desires for peace; but must be energetic and forceful in our exertions to bring it about.

essarily refer to that state of affairs. Rather, it derives from the word *shalem* which alludes to perfection, wholeness. It most often connotes a state of well-being without reference to military conflict. In this it resonates with the Sanskrit term *Sukkha*, the antonym to the Buddhist concept *Dukkha*, usually mistranslated as suffering but better translated as ill-being. Thus, aspirations for, and celebrations of, *shalom* most usually pertain to a generalized sense of well-being or wholeness rather than to an absence of armed conflict. Indeed, we can recall how Jews greet one another on the Shabbat: with the words "Shabbat Shalom". It is safe to assume that the salutation is not an expression of hope that the recipient will be spared from international conflict, but rather that they will enjoy a sabbath of tranquility or contentment.

1.2 Shalom Can Mean Peace

This is not to suggest that *shalom* in the liturgy and *shalom* in rabbinic discourse can never mean peace. But the peace most often sought is not cessation of military hostility, but rather more homely absences of conflict: in the home, between individuals, within the community, or even inner tranquility. When *shalom* is invoked it is in reference to the kind of peacefulness all of us seek in our everyday lives. The common way of inquiring about someone's well-being is the phrase *ma sh'lom* ... [so-and-so]. It does not imply a concern that so-and-so may find himself in the midst of armed conflict, but merely suggests what we would say in colloquial English, "how is he doing?"

There are, of course, instances when the peace that is prayed for, or talked about, is the sort of peace that we associate with military engagement. Yet even here the focus is not always on the current, this-worldly conflicts that we associate with issues of just war. There is an undertone in rabbinic thought that the cessation of war was, in the end (quite literally), not a subject of human agency but one of the qualities of the end of time. The end of inter-personal conflict and war are part of what will characterize the arrival of the Messiah and will be the stuff of the Messianic age. From this perspective prayers for *shalom* are less about what people can do to avoid battle than about longing for the onset of the 'world to come.' And indeed, the Isaiah and Micah pronouncements that we noted earlier are couched not in terms of any immediate future. Rather, both of them are presented in the context, "It shall come to pass in the end of days". (Isa. 2:1; Mic. 4:1)

As we move toward a discussion of just war, we will note that the Bible, the rabbis, and later Jewish thinkers all seem reconciled to the reality that peace—in the sense of the absence of military conflict—is not always possible; and indeed, that war is sometimes necessary. Significantly, the very words of Isaiah and Micah that we have noted are sardonically countered by another prophet, Joel, who at his particular moment in history, wrote:

> Proclaim this among the nations
> Prepare for battle
> Rouse the warriors
> Let all the fighting men come and draw near
> Beat your plowshares into swords
> And your pruning hooks into spears ...
> (Joel 4:9 – 10)

None of this is to suggest that a Jew cannot be a pacifist. Many have been. One example of such thinking (one which anticipates the subject of this paper) is a resolution placed for consideration, albeit not adopted, before the Central Conference of American Rabbis, the Reform Rabbinical group, in 1935:

> The time has come to change the traditional attitude of our faith toward war. We realize to the full the seriousness of this change we propose, and we adopt it because of our belief that the spirit of Israel, the first faith and people to love peace and pursue it necessitates such a vital change in the text and letter of our historic attitude. In the past Israel has made the distinction between righteous and unrighteous wars. In the light of the foregoing, we believe that this distinction has no reality for our day. And we are now compelled to adopt as our belief, and as the basis for action of our religious followers and ourselves, the principle that war is an unmitigated evil, and that we should abstain from all participation in it.[7]

Nor do we even suggest that one could not construct a pacifist position from elements and aspects of the Jewish tradition. This, too, is not unknown. It is simply to assert that the tradition, in itself, is not pacifist. The dispositive word is likely that of the biblical book Koheleth/Ecclesiastes:

> To everything there is a season
> And a time for every purpose under heaven ...
> A time to love, and a time to hate;
> A time for war, and a time for peace. (3:1 and 8)[8]

7 *Yearbook of the Central Conference of American Rabbis*, vol. 45 (1935), 66 – 67.
8 Unlike Pete Seeger's contemporary rendition of the text in his popular song, "Turn, Turn, Turn," the original does not conclude with the aspiration, "let's hope it's not too late".

Indeed, as Lawrence Schiffman has noted, there has always been a strand of Jewish thought which considered war to be "an instrument by which God would bring about the redemption of His people".[9] This being said, the question before Jewish thinkers, and now before us, is under what circumstances a particular war should be considered justified, and how is such a war to be prosecuted in a just way.

1.3 Qualification of the Above

Nonetheless, having asserted that the Jewish tradition is not pacifist and does recognize the necessity, under certain circumstances, of war, it would be doing a grave disservice to an understanding of Jewish values to leave the impression that this is the final articulation of Jewish attitudes. It cannot be stated strongly enough that the material reviewed in the previous section does require us to recognize that peace is regarded as a supreme value. Jewish tradition is not indifferent to peace but regards it as a desideratum—something to be sought and pursued (Ps. 34:14). Peace is the ideal condition of human society. It is the goal toward which history tends. If, to paraphrase a well-known thought, the arc of history is long, nonetheless it bends toward peace.[10] Only a serious rupture in the social fabric would necessitate the waging of war. The subject of our conversation here addresses the occasions of such rupture. In other words, from a Jewish perspective the subject that we are focusing our attention on in this volume is what must be regarded as a social aberration, a deviation from the most highly sought human condition.

2 War and Warfare in the Hebrew Bible

As in the reflection on any issue in Jewish thought, a discussion of just war in Jewish tradition must necessarily begin with the Bible. Those whose knowledge of Hebrew scriptures is superficial will assume that such a discussion will, of necessity, be very brief indeed. After all, they will assume that the Ten Command-

---

9 Schiffman, Lawrence, "War in Apocalyptic Thought," in: Lawrence Schiffman/Joel B. Wolowelsy (eds), *War and Peace in the Jewish Tradition*, New York: Yeshiva University Press, 2007, 492.
10 The quotation, "The arc of the moral universe is long, but it bends toward justice" is often attributed to Dr. Martin Luther King. In fact, he borrowed it from the abolitionist preacher Theodore Parker, from whom Abraham Lincoln also borrowed the words, "of the people, by the people, and for the people."

ments instruct, "Thou shalt not kill." Of course, those whose understanding of the Hebrew Bible is even slightly deeper will recognize that Exodus 20 does not say that at all. The text reads, *lo tirtsah*. The verb too casually translated as "kill" in actuality means to slay, or murder. The verb is employed in this sense in Numbers 35:27; Deuteronomy 22:26; 1 Kings 21:19 and elsewhere. While another word altogether, *harog*, is employed to convey the sense of kill, the taking of a human life under any circumstances. We see this in places such as the narrative of Cain and Abel in Genesis 4:8, and elsewhere such as Judges 9:24; 2 Samuel 14:7; Esther 8:11 and numerous other locations. Thus, properly translated, Exodus 20:13 does not enjoin us not to *kill*. Rather, we are instructed not to *murder*. And murder is a far different matter than killing.

Killing itself seems countenanced by the Bible and is found plentifully within it. Indeed, some delicate souls revel in dismissing the Hebrew Bible as a "bloody book." Indeed, whole portions of it go unread in certain circles, and it is true that there are portions of the Hebrew scriptures from which even the most pious properly shield young children. As much as adherents of liberal religious movements may wish the contrary, capital punishment is not proscribed in scripture. On the contrary, it is depicted as virtually "natural law" in the Noahide covenant (Gen. 9:6). The Bible, though not later Jewish tradition,[11] requires the death penalty for numerous offenses such as murder (Exod. 21:21, Num. 35:27), sexual crimes such as adultery or rape (Deut. 22:20 ff.), a wide variety of sexual acts (Lev. 20:10 ff.), blasphemy (Lev. 24:16), the worship of Baal (Num. 25:1 ff), disrespect for parents (Exod. 21:17 and Lev. 20:9), and even violating the Sabbath (Exod. 31:14–15 and 35:2 and Num. 15:32–6) and numerous others.

Biblical narratives often depict significant biblical figures as engaging in actions that would not be regarded as praiseworthy by modern readers. Thus, for instance, the first human being born through natural means, Cain, is also the first murderer (Genesis 4), an act understood as wholly without justification. The patronymic ancestors of two of the tribes, Simeon and Levi, engage in wanton slaughter (Gen. 34:25 ff.).[12] More justified, but no less violent, is Moses. His first appearance as an adult involves the slaying of an abusive Egyptian overseer (Exod. 2:12). Indeed, he continues to condone and commission capital punishment throughout the exodus. Numerous other examples could be cited. In one such set of instances of this, we find both the prophet Elijah and his disciple Eli-

11 Polish, Daniel "Does Judaism Condone Capital Punishment?" *Reform Judaism*, Summer 2002.

12 For which they are admonished by their father (Gen. 34: 30) and the one condemned on his deathbed (Gen. 49:7 ff)

sha perpetrating acts that, at best, might be described as justifiable homicide. 2 Kings 9 finds them associated with a particularly grisly sequence of events. In 1 Kings 18, Elijah oversees the execution of four hundred and fifty priests of Baal and in 2 Kings 1, he is responsible for the deaths of two hosts of soldiers. For his part, Elisha brings about the deaths of insolent children. (2Kings 2: 23 ff.). All this is done in the name of maintaining proper religious practice and decorum among the people. Elisha issues a call for a violent war against Moab (2Kings 2:19). During the period of the monarchy, events get so bloody at times that even King David, on his deathbed, sees fit to express reproach—while at the same time encouraging further bloodshed (1Kings 2:5 f.).

Even the lovely, spiritually uplifting, Book of Psalms is not devoid of its share of violence. Some authors, along with the lectionaries of various Christian denominations, proscribe the reading of various of the Psalms on the grounds of their violence. At the end of Psalm 137, for instance, the otherwise compelling and plaintive song concludes with what can only be an exhortation to infanticide (Ps. 137: 9). Other Psalms call for divine judgement to exact capital punishment on evildoers, often in disturbingly graphic terms: "the righteous shall rejoice when he seeth the vengeance; he shall wash his feet in the blood of the wicked" (Ps. 58:11). "let his children be fatherless and his wife a widow" (Ps. 109:9); "If Thou but wouldst slay the wicked O God" (Ps. 139:19). It is safe to say that killing is more than countenanced in Hebrew scriptures. In some circumstances, it is prescribed.

And similarly, moving more specifically to the subject of our volume, war seems to be accepted as a natural part of the human condition. Genesis takes it as a matter of course that Abraham would be a powerful and successful military leader (Gen. 14). Joshua's prowess as a military leader is evidenced in the midst of the exodus as well as in the eponymous book that describes his putative conquest of the land of Canaan. The role of the judges in the book of that name is exclusively that of military leader. Their fame and their place in history was established by their victories on the field of battle. Kings Saul and David, as well as the lesser kings who succeeded them were all men of arms. After all, when the institution of monarch was initially envisioned, it was explicitly for the purpose "that our king may judge us, and go out before us, and fight our battles."[13] Hebrew scriptures seem to take all of this not as something meriting special comment, but as something to be regarded as a matter of course.

Indeed God in Himself is saliently depicted as a warrior. Julius Wellhausen goes so far as to suggest that:

---

13 1Sam. 8:20.

> The name "Israel" means "El does battle," and Jehovah was the warrior El, after whom the nation styled itself. The [military] camp was, so to speak, at once the cradle in which the nation was nursed and the smithy in which it was welded into unity.[14]

Most famously, the Song of the Sea exults, "The Lord, the Warrior, Lord is His name. Pharaoh's chariots and his army has He cast into the sea." (Exod. 15:3–4). The people are assured that God will engage in war on their behalf (Deut. 1:30). The same imagery is echoed in Isaiah, "The Lord goes forth like a warrior, like a fighter, He whips up His rage" (Isa. 42:13). The minor prophet Zephaniah depicts God in the same terms toward the conclusion of his brief book: "Your God, the Lord, is in your midst. A warrior who brings triumph ..." (Zeph. 3:17). God the warrior is at the heart of the Book of Ezekiel chapters 38 and 39. Similarly, in the Book of Psalms God is referred to as a warrior or depicted with warlike imagery, such as in Psalms 68 and 83 or in individual verses like 3:9; 18:35–39; 24:8; 144:2 and 6 *inter alia*. Indeed God the warrior is depicted as viewing war in a positive light. In explaining why the nation, under Joshua, merely gained entry to land but left whole swathes of it unconquered, God is depicted as having done so with a purpose:

> so that He might test by ... [the unconquered nations] all the Israelites who had not known any of the wars of Canaan, so that succeeding generations of Israelites might be made to experience war (Judg. 3:1–2)[15]

Indeed, it is likely that the image of God going forth to battle among His own armies as described in Deuteronomy 20:4 and echoed in Deuteronomy 9:3, Exodus 14:14, Judges 4:14, may be the origin of the term "Lord of hosts." We read of the "wars of the Lord" in Numbers 21:14 and in 1 Samuel 18:17 and 25:28. All these texts reflect the reality that war was not abhorred at the most fundamental level, but rather accepted and even exalted.

Robert M. Good argues that war plays a crucial role in biblical theology. It serves as the vehicle by which God's justice is acted out in the world. "Israel imagined war to represent a legal punishment from Yahweh [against] ... nations

---

14 Wellhausen, Julius, *Prolegomena to the History of Ancient Israel*, Cleveland, Meridian Books, 1957, 433.

15 In fact, the people is referred to in what may be military terms—"the army of God"—in Exodus 7:4 and 12:41. The Israelite forces are explicitly referred to in such terms when David calls them "the army of the Living God" in 1 Samuel 17:26 (though this might just be David engaging in high rhetoric for the purpose of motivating the troops).

[that] behaved wrongfully against Israel."[16] The notion that "war is a forensic business" is found in Amos 1:3–5, Joel 4: 1–3 and 9–13, 2 Chronicles 20:26, Judges 11:15–27 and 5:9–11 and 13, and Exodus 15.[17]

Nor does the Bible shrink from depicting war in all its destructive ferocity. In the midst of the exodus, the desert generation is depicted as engaging in ferocious battles that include the utter destruction of enemy peoples, as described in Deuteronomy 3. As the Hebrews anticipate entering the promised land, they are instructed to utterly eradicate the seven Canaanite nations: "When ... the Lord your God delivers them to you and you defeat them, you must doom them to utter destruction. Grant them no terms and give them no quarter." (Deut. 7:1–2); "You shall not let a soul remain alive. No, you must give them over to utter destruction." (Deut. 20:16–17).

Still later, when the Israelites are settled in their land but beset by the Amalekites, Samuel instructs King Saul that God demands the total destruction of the enemy:

> "Now, go and crush Amalek; put him under the curse of utter destruction with all that he possesses. Do not spare him, but kill man and woman, babe and suckling, ox and sheep, camel and donkey." And Samuel said to Saul, "The Lord sent me to anoint you king over his people Israel; now therefore listen to the words of the Lord. Thus says the Lord of hosts, 'I have noted what Amalek did to Israel in opposing them on the way when they came up out of Egypt. Now go and strike Amalek and devote to destruction all that they have. Do not spare them, but kill both man and woman, child and infant, ox and sheep, camel and donkey.'" (1Sam. 15:1–3)

Significantly, when Saul fails to fulfill the divine command to completely destroy every vestige of the Amalekite nation, sparing the livestock and valuables of the defeated Amalekites, Samuel condemns him for his transgression and God expresses his dismay that Saul was made king setting Samuel on his course to replace him. (1Sam. 15:7 ff.)

The violence of war is clearly depicted in the accounts of Joshua's victories at Jericho and Ai. Contrary to the popular Black spiritual, Joshua and the people did not merely cause the walls to fall down at Jericho. Rather:

> ... The people shouted when the horns were sounded. When the people heard the sound of the horns, the people raised a mighty shout and the wall collapsed. The people rushed into the city, every man straight in front of him, and they captured the city. They exterminated everything in the city with the sword: man and woman, young and old, ox and sheep and

16 Good, Robert M., "The Just War in Ancient Israel," *Journal of Biblical Literature*, 104,3 (1985), 387.

17 Ibid.

> ass. (Josh. 6: 20 – 21)
> And they burned down the city and everything in it. (Josh. 6:24)

We read much the same depiction of the utter destructiveness of war in the account of Joshua's victory at Ai:

> [The defenders of Ai] were slaughtered, so that no one escaped or got away ...When Israel had killed all the inhabitants of Ai who had pursued them in the open wilderness and all of them, to the last man, had fallen by the sword, all the Israelites turned back to Ai and put it to the sword. The total of those who fell that day, men and women, the entire population of Ai came to twelve thousand. Joshua did not ... [stop the battle] until all the inhabitants of Ai had been exterminated. (Josh. 8:22 – 26)

Indeed, the Book of Joshua almost seems to revel in what we today would frankly call the atrocities of war.

In sum, it would not be hard to argue that the Bible seems more than amenable to war, accepting it as a normal part of the course of things. It celebrates the military achievements of its heroes and even represents God as a warrior. The battles it prescribes are brutal. Victory means extermination of the enemy. And the battles it describes follow that pattern. Triumph means the total eradication of the enemy population. Such was the shared perspective of the cultural matrix from which it emerged.

And yet that is not the final word. We find a particular paradoxical movement throughout the Hebrew scriptures. While on the one hand it is accepting of, and participates in, the cultural patterns and practices of the world out of which it emerged, on the other hand, it pushed the envelope on those values that moved toward modification of these same practices, with the effect of subverting those very norms. This is manifestly the case in its treatment of slavery, land ownership, capital punishment, and the role of women. Some might argue that it is also true in its presentation of the institution of monarchy. And upon closer examination we can see this same paradoxical movement in its approach to the issue of war-making. Because as commonplace as war is in the Hebrew scriptures, we also encounter a pattern of redefining the boundaries of war. To that extent, the biblical approach to war may be seen as a primitive version of what would later be called a theory of just war. While the Bible itself makes no distinction between what we might label just and unjust wars, we may extrapolate such a distinction from a closer examination of the text.

The notion of war presented in the Bible does not seem to conform to Hobbes' vision of a perpetual war of all against all: the life of societies being defined by ongoing conflict embodied in the terrible cycle of retribution—blood feuds; revenge for wrongs done to the tribe or family, "eye for eye, tooth for tooth, life for life"[18]—the incessant raiding, property stealing, struggles for limited natural resources and battles fought for simple territorial expansion. This divergent understanding finds expression in several ways. On the subject of taking plunder, in the paradoxical move we have already discussed, the Bible both accepts the prevailing social norm and imposes limitations on it, thus subverting it. We see a stance of permitting the taking of spoils of war and booty in Deuteronomy 20:14, Numbers 31:9 and 31:25, Deuteronomy 3:7, Joshua 8:27, 1 Samuel 30:24, 1 Chronicles 26:27, 2 Chronicles 14:12 and 20:25. And yet Genesis 14:22–23 and 35:2, Deuteronomy 13:17–18, Joshua 6:18, 2 Samuel 15:3 and 19, and Esther 9:10 and 16 seem to reflect an attitude that rejects the taking of the spoils of war.[19]

Nor were wars to be fought for the purpose of expanding territory. Rather, the Biblical presentation of warfare introduces what must be considered a new element to the phenomenon of war: rationale. There is a reason for fighting. Each of the wars presented in the Bible had a specified purpose. The wars we encounter in the Bible are fought for specified reasons. Each of them is, in the first place, clearly and explicitly depicted as being mandated by God.[20] Wars were not fought at the whim of a particular leader. Nor were they fought for some ruler's private purposes. In fairness to the biblical text,[21] it presents wars as being fought at the instigation of God. It does not yield to a reading that suggests that they emerged out of human motivations with the attribution of divine mandate subsequently superimposed upon them.

Further, each of the wars depicted in the Bible was fought for a particular purpose, and the range of purposes is quite circumscribed. Wars were fought either for the purpose of fulfilling God's promise that the people of Israel would take possession of the territory promised to them (as in Deuteronomy 1:6–8); or for the purpose of retaining possession of that territory (as throughout the Book of Judges). Even the total destruction of enemy populations is explained as necessary for the purpose of keeping the Israelites themselves from falling under the political domination of those people, or under the influence of those people and their religious ideas and practices (as in Deuteronomy

18 Exod. 21:24 and 23.

19 Looking ahead, it is the latter attitude that will become normative in later Jewish thought on the subject. See the discussion of looting, in the Israel Defense Forces *Laws of War in the Battlefied* cited later in this paper.

20 For this reason, Reuven Firestone, among others, designates such wars as "Holy Wars." See Firestone, Reuven, *Holy War in Judaism*, New York: Oxford University Press, 2012, 26 ff.

21 Whether this makes the reality better or worse to modern sensibilities is a question for another setting.

20:18). Von Rad, in the process of making his own, very different, point notes that much of Deuteronomy

> … conceives of the holy wars as predominantly wars of religion, in which Israel turns offensively against the Canaanite cult which is irreconcilable with faith in Yahweh.[22]

Modern readers might be uncomfortable with this situation, and might take issue with the stated reasons for those various wars or the ways in which the goal was pursued. But no one can deny that the wars of the Israelites are depicted as having a reason for being fought, and a specific reason at that. In this, the biblical text appears to function with an ideology different from that of neighboring civilizations. Might we not therefore argue that the seeds of a theory of *jus ad bellum*—just causation of war—have thus been planted?

More explicitly in terms of the enunciation of the principles of what might be considered the rudiments of just war theory with regard to the waging of war, several sections of Deuteronomy have the effect of dramatically tempering the severity of the act of war-making itself. Deuteronomy 20, while, as already noted, demanding the total eradication of the seven Canaanite nations (verses 13 and 16–18), at the same time introduces significant innovations in war fighting. Soldiers who wish to be excused from fighting for any reason, including simple terror, are granted exemption (verses 1–9). This injunction seems to negate the possibility of random conscription, one potential source of injustice in the waging of war.

Additionally, Deuteronomy 20 requires that when a city is being besieged, its fruit-bearing trees are not to be cut down: "is the tree of the field a man, that it should be besieged by thee?" (verses 19–20). The destruction of trees constitutes an attack, not on a military target, but on the economic viability of the civilian population. In such an act, a significant source of future livelihood is being destroyed. This assault on present and future civilian populations, asserts Deuteronomy, is not a proper way to conduct battle—we might say it constitutes an unjust military strategy.

In this same chapter, we read of even more dramatic modifications in a value system that might otherwise be assumed to embrace an ideology of "total war". Israelite armies are required to offer besieged enemy cities the opportunity to sue for peace (verses 10–11). If a city surrenders peacefully, Israelite soldiers are to do its residents no harm, albeit those residents become subjects of the conquerors. Even in cities that refuse to submit peacefully, non-combatants are not to be harmed. While enemy males are put to the sword, women and children are to be

---

22 Von Rad, Gerhard, *Holy War in Ancient Israel*, Grand Rapids: Eerdmans, 1958, 118.

spared, although they, too, along with the goods of the city, become spoils of war (verses 12–14). Rather than being total, the wars espoused by Deuteronomy 20 have significant limitations, circumscribing the scope of the battle and the classes of people subject to danger and harm.

Even this practice, which allowed women of conquered nations to be included in the spoils of war, is subject to further modification. In Deuteronomy 21 we find extensive legislation that emphasizes the humanity of these collateral victims. It mandates procedures that temper the blood lust and sexual lust of battle. Thus, if a soldier desires to appropriate for himself a woman of a conquered city or nation, he must treat her not as a pillaged object, but render her her due humanity. She is to be considered as a wife (verse 11)—a human being entitled to all the appropriate considerations accorded other human beings. Further, in the wake of battle, having brought this woman into his home, he cannot simply have his way with her. Rather, he must allow her the human dignity of a proper period of mourning for the family she herself had lost in the battle. And if, after that period of cooling off, or perhaps at any point in the future, that soldier loses his desire for her, he cannot treat her like a commodity. He is not allowed to simply dispense with her. He cannot treat her as a slave, nor can he sell her. Rather, he must grant her freedom to leave at her will and chart her course for her own future (verses 10–15). In all of these practices, the unmoderated ferocity of war-making is tempered by consideration of the humanity of the enemy. An element of empathy and simple human fellow-feeling is now introduced into the conduct of battle. In this we can find an anticipation of a more systematic theory for the just conduct of war and its aftermath.

In concluding this discussion about the rules of war-making in Biblical Israel, it is worth noting that the Bible reflects a consciousness that its own practices were in marked difference from those of the surrounding peoples. The prophet Nahum condemns Nineveh's indulgence in booty and plunder (Nah. 3:1). The prophet Amos makes mention of the cruel military practices of neighboring peoples (Amos 1:3–2:3) and notes especially the sadistic treatment of non-combatants, and the perverse motivation for their fighting (1:13). 1 Kings 20: 26–34 is devoted to a narrative that turns on the fact that neighboring peoples knew that "the kings of the house of Israel are merciful kings" (verse 31) and relates how an Israelite king magnanimously spared the life of an opposing monarch and his minions. In their idiosyncratic approach to the conduct of war, the Israelites were apparently not un-self-aware.

Can we consider these constraints on the conduct of battle—the circumscription of what warriors are allowed to do—to be, if not a systematic theory of *jus in belo*/the rules of the conduct of war, at the very least, a significant move in that direction? Can we see them as representing the recognition of the necessity of such principles and a rudimentary step toward beginning the work of articulating them?

3 Attitudes to War and its Conduct in Second Temple Judaism

Let us note briefly that in the Second Temple period, Jews continued to affirm the validity of war and its necessity under certain circumstances. Three wars against foreign occupiers have continued to be viewed positively in Jewish tradition, despite the fact that two were tragic failures. The holiday of Chanukah, celebrated to this day, was instituted to commemorate the great victory of the Maccabees over the Seleucids who ruled Judea at that time. Jews continue to venerate the "Great Revolt" against Rome and the Bar Kochba rebellion also against Rome a generation after that, despite the fact that neither of these efforts achieved the goal to which it aspired, national self-determination. Indeed, they contributed to the eventual Roman termination of Jewish national life in the land of Israel and the inauguration of the diasporic condition that characterized Jewish life until the mid-twentieth century. The defeat of the first revolt continues to be commemorated in the fast day of the ninth day of the Hebrew month of Av. The defeat is mourned. But in no normative observance of this day is there any expression of doubt as to the correctness of the war, nor any censure of the Jewish leaders who initiated it. Similarly, Bar Kochba, the leader of the later failed effort, was embraced by his contemporaries, and even celebrated as a messiah. His ultimate defeat led him to fall into disregard by subsequent generations. But with the emergence of Jewish nationalism in the nineteenth century he has become, again, enshrined in the pantheon of heroic figures by Jewish conventional wisdom. In all these cases, the resort to war was evaluated as a positive act, an appropriate response to oppressive conditions. As such, all these wars would fall into the category of wars deemed to be just.

It is noteworthy, as well, to reflect on the fact that the apocryphal book of Maccabees notes that, prior to entering battle, Judah, the leader of the Maccabean army, " ... said to those who were building houses, or were betrothed, or were planting vineyards, or were fainthearted, that each should return to his home in accordance with the law." (Macc. 3:56). This action is clearly undertaken in literal fulfillment of the instructions of Deuteronomy 20:5–8 which we have discussed earlier and which we have characterized as an element of what constituted the biblical notion of the just conduct of war. The author of Maccabees, in making special note of this, appears to be going out of his way to convey the understanding that that war was to be considered just in the way it was conducted as well as just in purpose. No doubt, the same sentiments would have been expressed about the later rebellions against Rome.

4 War and Warfare in Rabbinic Literature

The rabbis who produced the next significant stratum of Jewish religious literature lived in a very different social reality from that of the Bible, and the writings that they have left us must be understood to reflect that. The casual reader might be misled into imagining that the rabbis were able to enact, impose and enforce laws. The reality was that they lacked agency. They were not sovereigns of any territory and had no access to sovereignty. Indeed, it has been argued that their approach to war was predicated precisely upon their powerlessness. Thus, anything they said about civil law was purely speculative, theoretical, or imaginary. They had no lived experience making decisions about whether or not to undertake any battle, nor about how to conduct such battles. What they could do was offer their intellectual speculation about the application or amplification of matters described in the Bible or prescribed there. No less significantly, we cannot allow ourselves the luxury of imagining that the rabbis articulated a theory about anything. What we find in rabbinic literature is a multi-century symposium—a vast collection of a widely diverse range of perspectives on all manner of subjects including some scant attention to issues that would fall under our category of just war: which wars are justly fought; what is the just manner of pursuing such a war.

One might wish that they could present an elaborate discussion of the numerous references to *jus ad bellum* and *jus in belo* by the rabbis and abstract from them some Jewish theory of just war. Unfortunately, the reality is that the issues are addressed in significantly few places in the vast corpus of rabbinic literature. Further, those discussions that do exist are so oblique and opaque that we might assume that we could not derive a definitive position on either question from them. What they do offer are subjects for interpretation—inferential, and perhaps subjective, resources for formulating attitudes toward the appropriate rationale for war and the conduct of war. But, in the interest of complete candor, I must emphasize that nothing in the rabbis can properly be considered a dispositive position on either issue.

We can, of course, extrapolate certain general perspectives from what the rabbis taught. Killing another is not absolutely forbidden. If a person is being pursued by someone who has the intent of harming or killing them, they are entitled to kill that pursuer. (b. Talmud Sanhedrin 74 a–b). Can this be extrapolated to permit wars of collective self-defense? Does such permission apply to a situation where a person sees someone else being pursued? Can one intervene in such a situation even by employing lethal force? Would that allow entering into a war to protect innocent people even if your own country was not itself invaded or attacked? The rabbis are unclear on these latter issues.

Another rabbinic perspective that might be extrapolated to serve as a basis for a discussion of defensive war is found in the midst of a discussion of the robbery of a home:

> It is assumed that a man need not hold back with regard to [protecting] his property. A thief might say "if I go [into his house to rob it] he [the householder] will resist me and prevent me from stealing. So I must kill him."
> Concerning this the Torah instructs,[23] "[I]f someone comes to kill you, get up early in the morning to kill him first."[24]

Indeed, this injunction to preemptive defense is repeated elsewhere in the Talmud: B'rachot 58a and Yoma 85b. Clearly the implication is that if we could extrapolate from the rabbis categories of war that would be considered just, statements such as this suggest that wars waged in self-defense, even pre-emptive self-defense must be considered to be included.

One other rabbinic teaching presents a perspective on the waging of war in general that might have some bearing on the question of just wars:

> Rabbi Yose the Galilean states, "... Even in time of war, Jewish law requires that one initiate discussions of peace." (Leviticus Rabbah, Tzav, 9)[25]

In the Mishna, the earliest stratum of the Talmud, in tractate Sotah, chapter 8 consists of a commentary on and elaboration of Deuteronomy 20:5–8 and its injunctions about deferments from battle—which we have discussed earlier. The Mishna chapter concludes with a Mishna/verse that introduces some perspectives on various categories of war.

> To [what kinds of war do the deferments enumerated in Deuteronomy] refer? To a *Milchemet hareshut*. But in a *milchemet mitzvah* everyone has to go, even a bridegroom from his chamber and a bride from her canopied couch.[26]

23 Although this discussion attributes this act of preemptive self-defense to the Torah, no such statement is to be found there.
24 B. Talmud Sanhedrin 72a.
25 Cited in Michael Broyde, "Just War, Just Battles and Just Conduct in Jewish Law: Jewish Law is Not a Suicide Pact," in: Schiffman/Wolowelsy, *War and Peace*, 1.
26 This terminology is borrowed from Joel 2:16

> Rabbi Judah said "To [what kinds of war do the deferments enumerated in Deuteronomy] refer?" To a *milchemet mitzvah*. But in a *milchemet chovah* everybody has to go, even a bridegroom from his chamber and a bride from her canopied couch.

First, and most consequentially, we must define the Hebrew terms employed in the text. *Milchemet hareshut* is conventionally translated as discretionary war.[27] *Milchemet mitzvah* is perhaps best translated as (divinely) commanded war. *Milchemet chovah* is a war of obligation, an obligatory war. The first problem we encounter with our text is that these terms are nowhere defined. It is conceivable that the participants in the ancient discussion understood the meaning of these terms which were likely technical terms, or terms of art. But because they left no such record for future readers, we cannot be sure about the distinctions that they were making.

A second problem is that on first reading, the two portions of the Mishna may appear redundant. Upon closer reading, however, we note that while the first part makes a distinction between *milchemet hareshut* and *milchemet mitzvah*, the second part is concerned with distinguishing between *milchemet mitzvah* and *milchemet chovah*. Are we to assume that *milchemet hareshut* and *milchemet chovah* are two terms for the same thing? This seems unlikely given that the concepts of the discretionary and the obligatory are antonymical rather than synonymous. Or are we dealing here with three separate categories? Nothing in the text itself unravels this question for us. Perhaps this is not one conversation, but two parallel and analogous conversations on the same theme.

Further, the likelihood that this is a practical conversation about the realities of combat is undercut by the notion that brides along with bridegrooms would be summoned to battle under the appropriate conditions. In the world of the rabbis, the notion of female combatants is hard to imagine, let alone the idea of brides fighting alongside bridegrooms. This suggests that whatever the conversation meant to the rabbis, it was more an exercise in fanciful speculation than a programmatic reflection on concrete realities.[28]

The next stratum of the Talmud, the Gemara, contains a few discussions about the waging of war. Babylonian Talmud Eruvin 45a is emphatic in advocating for wars of self-defense:

> Rav Yehudah taught in the name of Rav concerning a Jewish town that was besieged by gentiles. They [the Jews] may not go out to fight against them with their weapons out of

---

27 Broyde employs the translation "authorized war"

28 Indeed, it seems very much like a fanciful midrashic application of the imagery of that Joel 2:16.

> concern for desecrating the Sabbath ... [another teaching clarifies that this is the case] if they [the gentiles] came with monetary intentions [i.e. theft]. However, if they came with the intent of taking lives, or if there is concern that they have come with that intention they [the Jews] are permitted to go out against them with their weapons and they may desecrate the Sabbath because of this. Or if a town is located near a border, even if the gentiles did not come to take lives, but rather ... [with monetary intent] they may go out against them with their weapons and they may desecrate the Sabbath because of them. For the border must be carefully guarded in order to prevent enemies from gaining a foothold there.

Clearly, defensive wars are considered just wars, as are wars fought to preserve the integrity of the land.

But what of the issues raised in Mishna Sotah mentioned above? The Gemara serves to comment on, elaborate, and often explain the words of the Mishna. The Mishna we have looked at above is commented on in Babylonian Talmud Sotah 44b:

> The Mishna teaches: To [what kinds of war do the deferments enumerated in Deuteronomy] refer? They are said with regard to discretionary wars, as opposed to obligatory wars or commanded wars. Rabbi Yochanan says concerning the various categories of war: The discretionary war referenced by the Rabbis is the same as a commanded war referred to by Rabbi Judah, and the commanded war mentioned by the Rabbis is the same as the obligatory war mentioned by Rabbi Judah.
> Rava said: With respect to the wars that Joshua waged to conquer the land of Israel all agree that they were obligatory. With respect to the wars waged by the House of King David for the sake of territorial expansion, all agree that they were discretionary wars. Where they disagree is with regard to preventative wars that are waged to reduce the idol worshippers so that they will not come and wage war against them. One authority, Rabbi Judah, called this type of war a commanded war and one authority, the Rabbis, called it a discretionary war.

While Rabbi Yochanan resolves the issue of the relation of the category discretionary war to that of obligatory war, he does not help us understand why two diametrically opposite terms would be applied to the same concept. Nor does he provide a definition for either of those terms, or for commanded war. We thus remain no closer to an understanding of what is entailed by the distinctions enunciated in the Mishna.

Rava is more helpful here. By referencing events described in the Bible, he gives us a sense of the broad contours of these various terms. According to this construct, obligatory wars were those battles fought to secure the Land of Israel for the children of Israel. Discretionary wars are understood as wars of expansion that do not involve acquiring or defending the land or protecting the people. Though we must note that while reference to Joshua's wars is self-explanatory, it is unclear to which of David's wars he was referring. David fought wars of defense against the Philistines, but also wars of expansion and plunder. The latter raises issues that are in need of being addressed. We will return to that issue presently. Rava notes that where there is disagreement is in how to categorize wars that are construed by the rabbis as necessary to preserve the spiritual integrity of the people, or what we would call pre-emptive. Are such wars to be considered discretionary or commanded? Nothing in the text resolves this issue.

The answer to that question might be elucidated by the only other text in the Talmud that discusses the issue of war. Tractate B'rachot 3b presents us with a discussion of an incident in the life of King David reported in 1 Samuel 30. The rabbis enlarge upon the narrative and draw a suggestive lesson from it:

> Once dawn arrived, the Sages of Israel entered to advise him with regard to the various concerns of the nation and the economy. They said to him: Our master, the king, your nation requires sustenance. He said: Go and sustain one another, provide each other with whatever is lacking. The sages of Israel responded to him with a parable: A single handful of food does not satisfy a lion, and a pit will not be filled merely from the rain that falls directly into its mouth, but other water must be piped in (*ge'onim*). So too, the nation cannot sustain itself using its own resources. King David told them: go and take up arms with the troops in battle in order to expand our borders and provide our people with the opportunity to earn a livelihood. Rav Yosef said: Upon what verse is this *aggada* based? As it is written: "And after Ahitophel was Yehoyada son of Benayahu and Evyatar, and the general of the king's army, Yoav"[29] The individuals named in this verse correspond with the roles in the *aggada* as follows: Ahitophel is the adviser whose advice they sought first with regard to going to war, and so it says: "Now the counsel of Ahitophel, which he counseled in those days, was as a man who inquires of the word of God; so was the counsel of Ahitophel both with David and with Absalom."
> The Sages immediately seek advice from Ahitophel to determine whether or not it was appropriate to go to war at that time and how they should conduct themselves, and they consult the Sanhedrin in order to receive the requisite license to wage a war under those circumstances. And they ask the Urim VeTummim whether or not they should go to war, and whether or not they would be successful.

In this text, the rabbis discuss a biblical account of David's participation in a discretionary war—more specifically a war initiated for the purpose of plunder. Clearly, they would not consider it proper to take issue with the actions of any biblical personage, least of all King David. In this discussion they do not allow themselves to criticize this war. But, in a move not at all uncharacteristic of rabbinic decisions, while accepting a biblical action or injunction they hedge it about with qualifications and, as a result, circumscribe its post-biblical applicability.

---

29 1Chron. 27:34.

The text's reference to David consulting the Sanhedrin is significant. We can readily recognize it as clearly ahistorical. The Sanhedrin did not exist during the time of David. And it was no longer in existence as the rabbis wrote this text. But the notion of requiring David to consult that institution leaves a clear lesson. Despite the course of action that David himself may have pursued; wars of expansion, or those initiated for plunder, are clearly in a different category than the others known to the rabbis. The impression left by this text is that the king cannot undertake a war of this type on his own initiative. Such an action requires several other layers of consultation. Some have even suggested that given the reality that the Sanhedrin no longer is in existence, the rabbis are suggesting that such wars cannot, or, perhaps, should not, be entered into at all. At the very least, the rabbis are signaling a certain skepticism about such endeavors. Discretionary wars, wars for expansion or plunder, are presented as less acceptable than Joshua's wars of conquest of the land of Israel or later wars fought in defense of the land of Israel. We can say with certainty that discretionary wars are given many more layers of accountability than (divinely) commanded wars or obligatory wars.

The question that we must confront is whether these rabbinic discourses are at all useful in formulating a Jewish perspective on just war. At the very least these rabbinic conversations do have one significant thing in common with more general just war theories. They seek to make distinctions between various different kinds of war. Even if the distinctions that they make are not clear to us, and even if their being bound to a particular historical moment might make them seem irrelevant to us, the act of explicit and systematic classification and categorization itself opens to us the possibility of making such distinctions. In this, they do represent another step in the direction of formulating a just war theory.

Beyond that, one could make the case that it would be hard to abstract a particular perspective on just war from any of these rabbinic texts, nor from all of them together. They are not consistent within themselves or congruent among themselves. They are opaque in that they do not provide clear definitions of the various categories they explore. This makes it hard to state with certainty what they affirm and what they disallow.

Michael Broyde offers a provocative suggestion about this unsystematic nature of the rabbis' discussion of issues related to war. He argues, in effect, that war by its very nature involves, or demands, a suspension of conventional ethical or legal considerations.

> The conceptual reason behind this [absence of systematic discussion of war] is pointed out by Rabbi Eliezer Yehudah Waldenberg .... [who] posit[s] two points. The first is that war is different from individual ethics and has a different set of rules. The second is that govern-

> mental decisions are different from individual decisions and also follow a separate set of rules.[30]

David Shatz, drawing further implications from Broyde's observation, suggests that Broyde's basic thesis is that:

> ... the conduct of war is in fact the suspension of normative ethics of Jewish law .... [which explains t]he paucity of halakhic material on the conduct of war. Since Halakhah envisions war to entail the suspension of all violations—from the prohibition to kill downward—it permits the violation, as military need requires, of every prohibition with the single exception of ... [idolatry][31]

The same anomic nature of war is commented on in the nineteenth century by the towering authority, Rabbi Naftali Tzvi Yehudah Berlin:

> When is a person punished [for murder]? At a time when one is supposed to act with fellowship [toward others], which is not the case in a time of war and a time of hatred. In that instance, it is a time to kill, and there is no punishment for it at all, for that is the way the world was founded ....[32]

It would seem that the task of creating a system of laws for an anomic situation is a contradiction in terms, a self-defeating effort. Broyde, Shatz, and by implication Berlin, suggest that this accounts for why the rabbis do not give us a more systematic discussion of war and establish a more definitive statement of norms for its conduct. Yet the rabbis did have various discrete observations, and even prescriptions, for the waging of war. The issue is whether those statements have any bearing on situations beyond the specific ones they describe.

The rabbis refer specifically to particular times and places. One could argue that by relating the categories exclusively to events in biblical history, they make them virtually irrelevant to other situations. It would be exceedingly difficult to create general principles from such references.

On the other hand, I would argue that given the nature of the specific narratives cited, it is possible to extrapolate from them principles that apply more generally. We can discern clearly that wars of territorial integrity are considered permissible. Similarly, wars of self-defense are also regarded in a positive light. More questionable are wars fought simply for self-aggrandizement, to expand

---

30 Broyde, "Just War," 2.

31 Shatz, David, "Introduction," in: Schiffman/Wolowelsy, *Just War*, xvii.

32 *Ha'amek Davar* on Genesis 9:5 cited in Eisen, Robert, *Religious Zionism, Jewish Law and the Morality of War*, New York: Oxford University Press, 2017, 53.

territory or in pursuit of spoils. It may be possible to extrapolate from the B'rachot text that discretionary wars are viewed with less approbation, and significant skepticism. Procedures and processes need to be put in place to contain them. The rabbis not only create a typology of wars, their presentation also suggests a hierarchy of values.

Beyond that, from a single text we might also extrapolate a rabbinic rejection of the killing of non-combatants. Reflecting on the incident, described in 1 Samuel 15, when King Saul refused to obey the divine demand to slaughter of the Amalekite enemy, "man and woman, child and infant", the rabbis posit a scenario in which Saul remonstrates with God, "(even) if the adults have sinned, what is the sin of the children?"[33] Behind this midrashic elaboration of the biblical narrative may lie the presumption of what in *jus in bello* theory would be a concern for the protection of the lives of innocent civilians.

In point of fact, the rabbis had precious little to say about the subject of war, or the conduct thereof; less, for instance than they had to say about the amount of leavening that invalidated a kitchen for Passover or the appropriate time for morning prayers and a myriad of other matters pertaining to an ordered Jewish life. In the scant references they do make to the subject, the rabbis did what they did with every issue they addressed: they sought to rationalize it. They dealt with this issue, as every issue that they took under consideration, systematically, creating typologies. And in that they took a significant step beyond the Bible in the direction of articulating some perspective on just war.

5 War in Jewish Thought of Late Antiquity and the Middle Ages

With the completion of the rabbis' corpus, subsequent Jewish thought on all subjects became devoted to commentary and codification. The giants of Jewish thought addressed themselves to elucidating what was written in the Bible and rabbinic texts, or to creating systematic presentations of the rules articulated in them. Rather than branching off into new areas of speculation, Jewish thinkers dug deeper into the foundational texts that they received from earlier ages. It is also essential to recognize that during this time, Jews achieved no greater self-determination than they had had during the rabbinic period. As a result, Jews had no practical reason to reflect on whether, or how, to engage in battle. Thus, whatever Jewish thinkers wrote about war remained purely speculative

33 Yoma 22b

and theoretical. In the context of the post-rabbinic period this meant that Jewish thinkers who addressed the issue at all did so exclusively in terms of interpreting the meaning of what few references there were to the subject in the Bible and Talmud.

This is exemplified in the work of the pre-eminent commentator on the Bible and Rabbinic texts, the blind sage, Rabbi Shlomo Yitzchaki, best-known by his acronym, Rashi (1050 – 1105). Rashi begins his commentary on Genesis 1 by asking why the Torah begins with that narrative, rather than starting with the first commandment, found in Exodus 12:2, "This month shall be to you the first month". Rashi answers his own question by referring to another Biblical text, Psalm 111:6, "The power of his deeds He told His people, to give them the nations' estate."[34] Rashi interprets this as follows:

> For should the peoples of the world say to Israel, "You are robbers, because you took the lands of the seven Canaanite nations by force", Israel can reply to them, "All the earth belongs to the Holy One, blessed be He; He created it and gave it to whom He pleased. When He chose He gave it to them, and when He chose He took it away from them and gave it to us"

In this, Rashi is, by implication, justifying the wars of conquest by which Israel took possession of the land. The implications of this are important in understanding his overall attitudes toward war.

Rashi's significant contribution to an understanding of war lies in his clarification of the types of war and his definition of each of those types. In his commentary to B. Talmud Sotah 45b, Rashi limits the categories of war to two: *milchemet mitzvah*/commanded war and *Milchemet hareshut*/discretionary war. In the course of his commentaries he defines these two categories more precisely. In his commentary, to B. Talmud Sotah 44b, he defines *milchemet mitzvah*/commanded war as a war "such as the conquest of the Land of Israel in the days of Joshua". In his commentary to B. Talmud Sanhedrin 2a he presents his contrasting definition of *Milchemet hareshut*/discretionary war: "all war is to be considered *Milchemet hareshut*/ discretionary war except for the war of Joshua to conquer the Land of Israel." He makes the implication of his distinction explicit in his commentary to B. Talmud Eruvin 17a, in which he asserts, "every war is *Milchemet hareshut*/ discretionary war from Joshua's time onward. Joshua's war [alone] is [considered] *milchemet* mitzvah/commanded war."

Rashi's focus was on clarifying the foundational texts. As a result, he appears to be limiting the reality of his categories to a particular historical moment.

34 In Robert Alter's elegant translation.

But we might extrapolate from his commentary to Eruvin 17a that any war—at any time—other than that of Joshua's conquest of the land must be considered a discretionary war. If this is the case, could he be implying the negative evaluation of all those non-Joshua wars that we saw reflected in the words of the rabbis themselves? In other words, can we imply from Rashi, that all wars, with the specific exception of Joshua's war of conquest, are to be regarded with the same skepticism shown by the rabbis or even to be evaluated negatively?

Rashi's baton of intellectual leadership was picked up by the great polymath, Moses ben Maimon, Maimonides (1135 – 1204), physician, theologian, legal scholar, community leader. Like Rashi, Maimonides' project was to rationalize the received texts. Maimonides, known by his acronym Rambam, sought to organize all the rules of the rabbinic texts into a systematic form in his legal magnum opus the Mishneh Torah. The concluding section of that work is devoted to "Kings and Wars". Its placement makes it appear to be almost an afterthought. In his discussion of war, Maimonides, like Rashi before him, seeks to clarify the teaching of the Bible and the rabbis. Maimonides will not offer perspectives much different than Rashi, but they will be presented in a more structured fashion.

Though in other works Maimonides clearly demonstrates an ability for abstract thought and speculation, in the context of his legal writing, he seeks only to comment on earlier texts and to systematize the injunctions found therein. He does not add further considerations about the waging of war or offer the kind of theoretical speculation about the subject that we could label just war theory.

Like Rashi, he limits the categories of wars to commanded and discretionary. Two examples, of many, of his dichotomy:

> At first, the king may wage only a commanded war. What do we call a commanded war? [Only] a war against the seven [Canaanite] nations [or] a war against Amalek to defend Israel from an enemy who has come against them. After that he may wage a discretionary war, that is a war that is fought with various nations in order to extend the borders of [the] Israel[ite nation] and to increase his greatness and prestige. (5.1) We may besiege a non-Israelite city [even] on Shabbat and we may make war with them [even] on Shabbat ... We do battle on Shabbat whether it is a commanded war or a discretionary war (6:15)[35]

35 In this statement Maimonides seems to assert that both commanded and discretionary wars may be fought on Shabbat. In the Laws of Shabbat 2:23 he limits fighting on Shabbat to defensive wars.

Maimonides does not take a negative view toward war. Rather he recognizes the positive necessity of commanded wars. He defines commanded wars as those fought "against the seven [Canaanite] nations or war against Amalek (5.5) [the quintessential antagonist of the Hebrews in the Bible who is condemned to extirpation in Deuteronomy 28:19] or any war to save Israel from an oppressor" (5.1) He gives priority to such wars (5.1 and 5.4). In recapitulating the injunctions of the Bible, he re-iterates the various biblical legislation about the conduct of war, such as not cutting down fruit trees (6.12), offering terms of peace (6:2) allowing those non-combatant residents of besieged cities to flee (6:7), allowing various categories of soldiers to be exempt from battle and identifying those categories (7:1 ff), and a discussion of the treatment of captured enemy women (chapter 7 and 8) that is dissonant to our contemporary sensibilities.

All of these are explanations or elaborations of "legislation" from traditional texts which we have discussed earlier. Elsewhere he asserts that anyone

> Who smashes household goods, tears clothes, demolishes a building, stops up a spring, or destroys articles of food ... transgresses the command, [*Ba'al tashchit*] /*Thou shalt not destroy.* [36]

We do find two major innovations in Maimonides' approach to war. He enlarges upon what we might regard as biblical teaching, and certainly what we found in the rabbis. While giving priority to commanded wars, he is permissive of discretionary wars fought to "enlarge the borders of Israel and increase his own greatness and prestige" (5:1). Indeed:

> Any lands conquered by Israel with a king, [conducted after necessary consultation] with a Sanhedrin are lands "conquered by the populace" and are equal in status to the Land of Israel in every regard just like the lands conquered by Joshua. This being the case as long as such lands were conquered after all the land mentioned in the Torah have already been conquered (5:6)

We shall return to the second of his significant innovations below.

The great challenge in presenting the teaching of Maimonides in the context of the discussion of just war is that of relevance. Maimonides appears to limit his concern to the biblical period, already millennia in the past when he wrote. He seems to talk in the loftiest theoretical terms about wars fought by Israelite armies against nations that had not existed for thousands of years. What can be

36 *Book of Judges*, Kings 6:10. Cited in Michael Walzer, "War and Peace in Jewish Tradition," in: Terry Nardin (ed.), *The Ethics of War and Peace: Religious and Secular Perspectives*, Princeton NJ: Princeton University Press, 1996, 109.

the practical application of such instruction? It is possible to speculate about Maimonides, as we have about Rashi, that implicit in his argument is the notion that any war other than those he discusses, i. e. other than those biblical wars of the distant past, are to be adjudged negatively. Could he be saying that all post-biblical wars are bad?

We must hasten to point out that Maimonides did not understand himself to be merely clarifying issues of the past. For him, importantly, it was an article of faith that the long-awaited Messiah would come and re-establish the Davidic kingdom. At that time all the rules of the Torah would become applicable again. Thus, he was explicating the way that wars were to be conducted at the end of days, in the times of the Messiah. As a result, he is both clarifying the past and mapping the future.

And yet the problem remains. What does Maimonides have to teach us about wars fought during this intermediate period, between the end of the biblical period and the coming of the Messiah? In the second of his significant innovations, Maimonides does, himself, make one change from the conventional definitions of the subjects he addresses. He appears to expand the meaning of commanded war to refer to the elimination of idolatry. He frames this discussion in the explicit assertion that this does not necessitate conversion to Judaism, but rather the acceptance by non-Jews of the Noahide laws, entailing the affirmation of God's oneness and the abandonment of idol worship. In this formulation, commanded wars are still wars fought with a purpose—the triumph of monotheism. In such a setting, the rules of war that he propounds would have relevance in this intermediate period.

Having examined the two significant innovations in Maimonides' approach to war, we are entitled to ask where they originated from. The historical reality is that Maimonides lived much of his life in a Muslim environment, becoming physician to the caliph, and familiar with the works of Muslim thinkers. It may be possible to discern the influence of those thinkers' perspectives about the purpose and conduct of war, especially the various meanings of *jihād*, in Maimonides' writings. It may be argued that we see this influence particularly in his generalization of the meaning of commanded war to represent the struggle against idolatry, and his permissive attitude to discretionary war for the purpose of expanding the king's borders and aggrandizing his prestige.

Living and writing during roughly the same period, the biblical commentator David Kimchi (1160 – 1235) writes about two separate narratives that presume the wrong in killing, or causing the killing of, non-combatants. He discusses the issue of obedience or disobedience to kings in reference to the incident in which King David ordered the death of Uriah the Hittite (2Sam. 11), and King Saul's wanton massacre of the priests of Nob (1Sam. 22):

> Even though it is always the case that "there is no agency for wrong doing" ... the case of Uriah is different: the text calls David the killer. Similarly with Saul, who ordered the massacre of the Nob priests—it is as though he killed them. Now it is true that in such a situation he should not execute the king's orders ... but since not everyone is aware of this or knows how to construe [the relevant texts] punishment falls on the king. [37]

Maimonides's near contemporary, Moses ben Nahman, Nahmanides, known by his acronym Ramban, (1194–1270) wrote a commentary to the Mishneh Torah that is included in the standard editions of that work. Nahmanides, who, we should note, did not live in the Muslim cultural sphere, argues against Maimonides' generalization of the wars of conquest to mean the battle to defeat idolatry. Nahmanides advocates for the literal meaning of the biblical texts. The narratives of the wars that were fought, and the rules of war that may be fought again when the Messiah comes, pertain to the literal battle for the conquest of the land of Israel—and exclusively that. In this way, Nahmanides effectively reduces the implications of the biblical narrative and any laws derived from them and limits their relevance to that one particular circumstance. He insists on the historical specificity in time and place of any biblical and Talmudic discussions of *jus ad bellum* and *jus in bello.* Would this, too, imply that all wars fought in the historical period between the end of Bible and the coming of the Messiah must be considered discretionary wars and thus subject to a significant degree of skepticism, or even viewed in a negative light?

Walzer cites David Bleich's discussion of Menachem Me'iri of Provence (1249–1316), who distinguishes between preemptive and preventative war. Me'iri writes about two kinds of permitted war:

> When the Israelites fight "against their enemies because they fear lest [their enemies] attack and when it is known by them that the enemies are preparing themselves [for an attack]." [38]

Walzer continues, citing Bleich:

> The distinction does not seem to make a practical difference, but it follows from this account, as David Bleich has argued, that "absent clear aggressive design" (or at least a plausible fear that such a design exists) no military attack is permitted.[39]

37 Commentary on 2 Samuel 12:9, cited in Walzer, "War and Peace," 102.
38 David Bleich, "Pre-Emptive War in Jewish Law," *Tradition* 21, 1 (Spring 1983) cited in Walzer, "War and Peace," 100.
39 Ibid.

In touching on one aspect of what we could recognize as *jus in bello*, Bleich asserts

> There exists no discussion in classical rabbinic sources that takes cognizance of the likelihood of causing civilian casualties in the course of hostilities legitimately undertaken as posing a halachic or moral problem.[40]

Eight centuries ago, such an argument was of merely academic interest. The meaning of those ancient wars had no practical consequence—or would not until the arrival of the Messiah. In the years following, it is striking how remarkably little discussion was devoted to the subject. The Shulchan Aruch, the great compendium of *halacha*/Jewish law (1562) has nothing whatever to say on the subject of war. The exceptions to the great silence are precious few. For instance, Rabbi Judah Loew of Prague (d. 1609) in commenting on the Genesis account of the reconciliation of Jacob and Esau extracts the lesson that non-combatants are not to be injured. even in the course of an appropriate war.[41] In this he is commenting on a specific Biblical narrative and interpreting it in light of the injunction against collateral civilian harm found in Deuteronomy 20 and reiterated, as we have seen, in later texts. What he is not doing is breaking new ground in understanding or formulating a more general theory of just war.

The conversation would continue along much these same lines for hundreds of years. It would take on a different kind of significance centuries later when a Jewish nation once again had political sovereignty and the capacity to wage war—and indeed, found themselves exercising, and debating about the justice of exercising, military power.

6 Contemporary Jewish Reflections on War

This would change dramatically and consequentially at the end of the nineteenth century and into the twentieth century, as Jews began to colonize Palestine, then part of the Ottoman empire, through a dramatic increase in the Jewish population during the British Mandate, culminating in the re-establishment of Jewish political autonomy in 1948. Issues of war and its conduct ceased to be the object of abstract theoretical speculation and became the pressing subjects of literally life and death decisions.

---

40 Bleich, "Pre-Emptive War," 19, cited in Walzer, "War and Peace," 108.
41 *Gur Aryeh* on Genesis 32:18. Walzer, "War and Peace," 108.

In considering the subject of Jewish reflections on just war in the contemporary period, we must remember that the full sense of what it means to be Jewish is not perfectly analogous to what it means to be Christian or Muslim. While those traditions are exclusively religious in character, the reality of Jewish life is more complicated, in that it contains a purely religious component (though one not defined by a common creed) and also a component that we would consider to be ethnic, touching on the historic experience of a people or a cultural entity. As a result, some of the texts we would draw on in this discussion could not be considered to be strictly "religious" in nature, but very much reflective of authentic Jewish responses to the question at hand.

Unrelated to the contemporary Jewish settlement in Ottoman Palestine, Rabbi Samuel David Luzzatto, an Italian scholar of the nineteenth century, extrapolated from Deuteronomy 20 that the only permissible wars were defensive:

> The text does not specify the cause for a permitted[42] war or [say] whether Israel may wage war without cause, merely to despoil and take booty. [But] it seems to me that in the beginning of this section [20:1], in saying "when you go forth to battle against your enemy," Scripture indicates that we should make war only against our enemies. The term "enemy" refers only to one who seeks to harm us; so, scripture is speaking only of an invader who would enter our territory to take our land and despoil us.[43]

Already in the early days of Jewish settlement, the ancient formulations of the rabbis were invoked in response to the events of real life. A sense of what was just in the face of real political decisions and necessary military action is beginning to be clear. During the days of the British mandate, in response to the deadly violence of the "Arab Revolt", a newspaper of one of the Jewish religious parties, urging Jews to exercise restraint in response, invoked the concept of "Holy war" for the enterprise of Jewish settlement of the land in terms that reflected just war categories:

> This is a holy war (*milchamah qedosha*)[44]. Let us not profane it by spilling the blood of the innocent and let us not walk in the way of the nations around us. We refuse to ruin our holy war through murdering innocent people, and we will not defile the land by polluting it with [innocent] blood ... Let us not spoil the moral purity of our war. ....[45]

---

42 We would say discretionary.

43 Cited in Solomon, Norman, "Judaism and the Ethics of War", *International Journal of the Red Cross*, 87, 858 (June 2005), 303.

44 A category not employed in any of the traditional texts to which we have referred.

45 Cited in Firestone, "Holy War," 194.

Responding to the same provocations, Rabbi Moshe Avigdor Amiel, the Chief Rabbi of Tel Aviv wrote:

> In my opinion, even if we knew for certain that we could bring about the Final Redemption [by killing Arabs] we should reject such a "Redemption" with all our strength, and not be redeemed through blood. Moreover, even if we were to apprehend several Arab murderers, if there was the slightest possibility that one of them was innocent we should not touch them, lest the innocent suffer.[46]

During Israel's War of Independence in 1948 the Ashkenazi Chief Rabbi of Israel, Isaac Halevi Herzog was asked if it was appropriate for observant Jews to volunteer for military duty even though it entailed violating the Sabbath. His response to this twentieth century issue was couched in terms of millennia-old Jewish teaching

> [I]n my view this is a mandatory war[47], for because the United Nations has decided to return to us, at the very least, a portion of the land of Israel to establish an independent government, this is a war for the conquest of the land .... And indeed to wage mandatory war one does not need a court of seventy-one [i.e. a Sanhedrin], which we do not have nowadays .... And even though we do not have a king, [nowadays] the majority of the community together with its institutions, the rabbinate, etc. have the legal status of a king.... There is no doubt that this is a mandatory war to conquer the land [of Israel] ....[48]

Herzog's description of a war that he undoubtedly viewed as just hewed closely to the inherited definition of the traditional texts. It describes an appropriate war, one for which volunteering would involve desecrating the Sabbath, in terms that conformed in all its particulars to the ancient definition, while struggling to relate those received categories to the new political realities. It results in what we must call a rather constricted definition of just war.

But in response to another question, Herzog moves closer into engagement with the kind of issues that are associated with a serious discussion of just war. The question itself is lost to us, but it appears to have involved violating the Sabbath. Herzog's answer is of a more general nature:

> If it [the killing of enemy civilians] does not serve the needs of the war, it is forbidden even on weekdays, and if it does serve the needs of the war and is therefore permitted on weekdays, it is also permitted on the Sabbath. Nonetheless I would not dare to make a decision

46 Cited in Solomon, "Judaism," 305–6.

47 And as such both permits and requires the violation of the Sabbath and the abrogation of its strictures.

48 Cited in Eisen, *Religious Zionism*, 87.

> about this [issue] even regarding weekdays, not to mention regarding the Sabbath, when it comes to innocent people among the enemy. A lot depends on an examination of the issue with respect to the influence [it would have] on the progress of the war.[49]

Herzog appears here to be addressing the justice of the killing of enemy civilians. As a general rule, he forbids it, thus suggesting that a war justly fought would preclude that. He goes on to introduce a nuanced and sophisticated modification of this position, namely that the identification of who is innocent and who is a collaborator with the enemy must be taken into consideration in determining who is deserving of such protection. In this he betrays an unexpected familiarity with the complexities of actual combat that must be included in any realistic discussion of just war.

Perhaps the Jewish writer who has written the most about issues of war was Rabbi Shlomo Goren, the first Chief Rabbi of the Israel Defense Forces who had the rare combined attribute of being an authentic Torah scholar and a combat veteran. In response to those who would argue that war was not an appropriate Jewish activity, Goren offered the powerful assertion that war and matters of the spirit ought not be set in opposition to one another:

> [T]he Torah of Israel teaches us, and its prophets inculcate in us, that we do not separate between those who carry the flag of morality and spirit and those who carry the flag of physical liberation, even by means of war and conquest. All the great ones of Israel, its teachers, and its spiritual leaders in ancient times, integrated in their souls power and spirit together. The men of spirit also provided an example of independent courage in fighting on the battlefields against the enemies of Israel and its oppressors. This integration of the sword and the book is a continuous thread in Jewish history, not just in the period of the Bible, but also afterwards in the period of the Hasmoneans and after the destruction of the Second Temple in the period of the second revolt in the days of Bar Kochba, R. Akiva, R. Simeon bar Yohai and his friends[50]

Goren's project was the creation of a Jewish *halacha*—a Jewish ethic—of war. In his numerous writings on the subject, Goren virtually rules out the permissibility of discretionary wars—at least until the Messiah comes. At the same time, he argues forcefully in favor of defensive wars, and yet seems to posit a very limited definition of what would constitute such a defensive war:

> For if we are attacked by an enemy, there is certainly no need for any authority to respond with war that has arisen in order to defend ourselves, nor is it about this matter that there is need to prove that [it is a defensive war] is in effect also at the present time, for the Torah

---

49 Ibid. 93
50 Ibid., 198.

> story has said, "if someone comes to slay you, slay him first" (*Berakhot* 58 and parallel sources).[51] And the Torah did not differentiate between the time of the Temple and the present time, nor between saving many people and saving the individual, for whoever can save [another] must save [him] because of "do not stand idly by the blood of your fellow"[52] as we have explained several times ....[53]

We have already noted that traditional sources regard defensive wars as just. Goren's contribution is that he makes explicit the notion that this positive understanding applies to the present day no less than to earlier times. He also makes explicit the idea, which we posited speculatively above, that Talmudic endorsement of self-defense applies to the collectivity no less than to the individual.

In 1956, when Israel launched what it considered a pre-emptive attack on the Egyptian military, Goren broadened the definition of defensive war, arguing that this action and others like it, rather than being described as pre-emptive, should be considered under that rubric. He couches his argument that Jewish armies were entitled to do battle beyond their own borders, in terms familiar to us from rabbinic sources:

> War to save Israel[54] from an attacking enemy is not associated only with the Land of Israel, but includes every place where saving Israel from the hand of an enemy occurs, and by means of war and conquest it is possible to save them and help them; the ruling is that this kind of war is Commanded War.[55]
> Our war, therefore was really to help Israel from the hand of an attacking enemy that was coming against us, and certainly this is commanded war regarding everything relating to conquest outside the boundary of the borders of the Land according to the Torah ... Therefore, the ruling regarding this war is that of commanded war in every way.[56]

Beyond simple defense of war-making in general and defensive wars in particular, Goren sought to articulate a Jewish battlefield ethics. With this he enters into the area of *jus in bello.*

> [A]lthough the commandment to go to war is explicitly stated in the Torah, we are also commanded to show compassion to the enemy. We may not kill [the enemy] even in time of war,

---

51 We have discussed this Talmudic citation above.

52 Goren here invokes Leviticus 19:16 in building his argument.

53 Eisen, *Religious Zionism*, 213.

54 Here the term Israel is not employed to connote the contemporary political entity, but is used in the traditional sense of referring to the Jewish people, the people of Israel.

55 Cited in Firestone, "Holy War," 243.

56 Ibid., 243–4.

> except when there is a necessity to defend ourselves [and] for the purpose of conquest and victory. [We also] may not kill women and children who are not participating in war.[57]

Goren goes on to argue that "when Jews wage war, they should do their best to prevent loss of life among enemy civilians"[58] as well as to minimize loss of life among Jewish combatants.

It should be noted that Goren's positions were not the only ones articulated by contemporary Jewish religious authorities. Aviezer Ravitzky interrogates Nahmanides' "commandment" about conquest of the land, discussed above, and introduces contemporary thinkers who interpret it in a very different fashion:

> In point of fact, halakhic language has always recognized a concept of "conquest" carried out, not by military means, but by collective settlement. Some authorities, among them Rabbi Shaul Yisraeli, a scholar of the highest authority among contemporary religious Zionists, have therefore claimed that in this case [Nahmanides' "commandment" about the necessity of conquest of the land] ... one is not speaking of "a commandment of conquest through war, but of settling and inheriting the land." The commandment of military conquest was "of a singular nature. It referred to the time of Joshua only, where the master of the prophets [Moses] [had] himself expressed an explicit command." But no such command is applicable after that time.[59]

Similarly, Ravitzky cites the work of Rabbi Nahum Rabinowitz who asserts that conquest of the land is allowed only

> by permitted means, and warfare *is not permitted to us* unless enemies threaten to attack or do attack ... [One does not find in Nahmanides' writings] any basis for concluding that war is permitted [in the present era] for the sake of conquest of the land. What is worse, such a reading entails indifference towards bloodshed. Such indifference undermines the very foundations of society and endangers the entire enterprise of the beginning of our redemption.[60]

Appropriately, in a departure from the past, the most significant Jewish statements about the conduct of war came not from rabbis or theoreticians, but from an altogether different source—something the world had not seen for two thousand years: a Jewish army. This most consequential discussion of just war in modern Jewish thought had its roots in the 1930's. Already by that time the

57 Eisen, *Religious Zionism*, 225.
58 Ibid., 227.
59 Ravitzky, Aviezer, "Prohibited Wars in Jewish Tradition," in: Terry Nardin (ed.), *The Ethics of War*, 117.
60 Ibid.

Jewish leadership of the *Yishuv*, the Jewish community of then British Mandate Palestine began to consider issues involved in the rightful conduct of self-defense and *jus in bello*. From these considerations emerged the concept of *Tohar ha-nesheq*/purity of arms. With the establishment of the state of Israel this doctrine found its ultimate expression in the "Official Doctrine Statement of the Israel Defense Forces". There, purity of arms is turned into a manual of behavior in the following terms:

> IDF servicemen and women will use their weapons and force only for the purpose of their mission, only to the necessary extent, and will maintain their humanity even during combat. IDF soldiers will not use their weapons and force to harm human beings who are not combatants or prisoners of war, and will do all in their power to avoid causing harm to their lives, bodies, dignity and property.[61]

A short but dense statement, the Official Doctrine needs to be unpacked. First, we must take note of its obvious significance in representing the first time in two millennia that Jewish reflections on war had practical application. Then, we can address the implications of the contents of the doctrine. Sadly but pragmatically, it takes for granted that war is, at times, a necessary course of action. And yet it seeks to temper the barbarity of that activity. It is premised on the recognition of the common humanity of its soldiers and those, both combatants and non-combatants, in the adversarial camp. It is assertive in limiting the sphere of injury inflicted by soldiers of the IDF. It demands that non-combatants not be harmed in any way. It extends that concern even to enemy soldiers. It is explicit in asserting that those who have been rendered *hors de combat* are not to be injured. And soldiers of the IDF are instructed to do no unnecessary damage to the property of non-combatants or of captured soldiers.

The subjects of looting and spoils of war are discussed more specifically and in more precise detail in the *Laws of War in the Battlefield* of the Israel Defense Forces:

> Looting is the theft of enemy property (private or public) by individual soldiers for private purposes. In ancient times, conflicting conceptions were held. On the one hand, the Bible presents an approach that sees looting as a negative act, as, for instance, in the Akhan Affair (Joshua 7), in which Akhan was put to death because he had taken of the consecrated spoils. On the other hand, looting was permitted in other civilizations, and even served as a means for the ruler to generate motivation among the soldiers to fight, as they looked for-

61 Found online at www.idf.il

> ward to the looting.
> Today, at any rate, looting is absolutely prohibited ....[62]

The selective reading of the biblical text and the ascription of the practice of looting exclusively to "other civilizations" is reflective of the way Jewish tradition had come to understand the practice.[63] The document continues with a nuanced discussion of the spoils of war:

> One must distinguish between looting and taking spoils of war. Seized weapons, facilities, and property belonging to the enemy's army or state become the property of the seizing state. Private property that does not belong to the state is immune to seizure and conversion to booty ....[64]

Though the Official Doctrine and *Laws of War in the Battlefield* are documents of a secular state, they are self-consciously predicated on the layers of Jewish religious deliberation that preceded it. Clearly, they are consistent with many of the perspectives in Jewish religious texts from Deuteronomy through the rabbis into the Middle Ages that we have already noted: the pragmatic acceptance of war as a sometimes necessary evil; the avoidance of injury to non-combatants, and the rejection of taking of booty or inflicting unnecessary damage to the enemy's property.

Not religious documents per se, the Official Doctrine Statement and the *Laws of War in the Battlefield* obviously were written with inspiration from the millennia of Jewish reflections on the conduct of war. Their underlying spirit has been re-translated into a religious idiom by the first Chief Rabbi of the IDF, Rabbi Shlomo Goren, in his article "Combat Morality and Halakha" which appeared in a volume dealing with contemporary halachic issues. Goren writes:

> Human life is undoubtedly a supreme value in Judaism, as expressed in the *Halacha* and the prophetic ethic. This refers not only to Jews, but to all men [sic] created in the image of God.
> We see that God has compassion for the life of idolaters and finds it difficult to destroy

62 *Laws of War in the Battlefield*, Israel Defense Forces ,Department of International Law, Military Law School, (1998; Unclassified) Chapter 6, 69–70. Cited in Moshe Sokolow, "'What is This Bleating of Sheep in My Ears': Spoils of War/Wars that Spoil," in: Schiffman/Wolowesky (eds), *War and Peace in the Jewish Tradition*, 151–2.
63 It should be noted how unusual it is—and how characteristically Israeli— to find Biblical exegesis in the midst of a military legal document.
64 *Laws of War in the Battlefield*. Loc. Cit.

> them. Since we are enjoined to imitate the moral qualities of God. We too should not rejoice over the destruction of the enemies of Israel.[65]

What might we extrapolate from this excursion through thousands of years of Jewish thought about *jus ad bellum* and *jus in bello?* Clearly, the Jewish tradition would have us aspire to a time when war was a discarded relic of human activity. Its preference for peace—in all of its senses— is evident. And yet the tradition of Jewish ethics is unequivocally practical. It does not hold us to unrealistic aspirations, nor spiritualize the various conditions of the human experience. It emerged at a period of human history when war was an all-too-familiar reality of human life. Thus, rather than simply condemning war, it has sought to mitigate its most destructive aspects. Although lacking an explicit tradition of just war thought, it has given us the elements for constructing such a theory.

I would suggest that most of the aspects of that theory are already articulated in the Official Doctrine of the IDF. What is not present there is that strand of Jewish thought, expressed first in Deuteronomy 20 and explicated by all subsequent strata of Jewish commentary, that lays great emphasis on negotiating with the enemy before accepting the inevitability of battle. Jewish tradition would have us seek first to adjudicate any differences between parties. Only as a last resort, or only in a defensive mode, should one accept the heavy responsibility of combat.

Michael Broyde offers a significant caveat about any generalizations regarding Jewish perspectives on the waging of war, i.e. on issues of *jus ad bellum:*

> When one reviews the rules found within Jewish law for waging war, one grasps a crucial reality of Jewish military ethics. The moral license that "war" grants a person or a country varies from situation to situation and event to event. Jewish tradition treats different permissible wars differently. The battle for vital economic need carries with it much less of a moral license than a war waged to prevent an aggressive enemy from conquering an innocent nation. Jewish law recognized that some wars are completely immoral, some wars are morally permissible, but grant a very limited license to kill, and some wars are a basic battle for good with an enemy that is evil. Each of these situations comes with a different moral response and a different right to wage war. In sum, it is crucially important to examine the justice of every cause .... [66]

As has been suggested, the theme of the "suspension of the ethical" necessarily involved in the waging of war forces us to acknowledge that no hard and fast rules will ultimately prove germane in the realities of the lived experience.

65 Cited in Solomon, "Judaism," 307.
66 Broyde, "Just War," 30.

This matter is discussed by the contemporary Jewish philosopher Yeshayahu Leibowitz in ways that echo Michael Broyde's explanation (and David Shatz's elaboration) of the absence of a systematic discussion of issues related to war in Halachic literature:

> ... in our moral-religious soul searching, we neither justify nor apologize for wartime bloodshed per se (in which our own blood was shed more that our enemies'). The great problem arises in the manner of the conduct of the war—which continues unabated to this day—and of what follows it. The problem is great and complex. Since permission has been granted us for the "profession of Esav,"[67] the distinction between permitted and forbidden, justifiable and unconscionable, has become very fine ... and it is incumbent upon us to check and examine whether we have crossed the line or not.[68]

7 Concluding Reflections

With this in mind I would venture to offer my own synthesis of the elements we have explored in an attempt to articulate a comprehensive just war theory built out of Jewish parts. First, know that the ideal state of human affairs, and the ideal state of affairs between political actors, is harmonious relations and collaboration. And yet, the horrors of war could be brought about by two alternative situations. The first is the attack by an enemy force, the invasion of one land by another. In that case, even the most pacifistic interpretation of Jewish tradition could not fail to acknowledge that the only appropriate response is a war of self-defense. Nothing in Jewish tradition can be read as holding a negative view of self-defense. Too many instances in Jewish history could be cited where imperiled Jewish communities took drastic measures to protect themselves from attackers. The analogy drawn from individual human experience is the situation of someone threatening mortal injury to a person. The attacked persons would be regarded as fully within their rights to defend themselves, even at the risk of inflicting grave, even mortal, damage to the attacker. In such situations,

---

67 The rabbis and subsequent Jewish tradition saw Jacob's brother Esau as the embodiment of violence and warfare. His association with edom/red is emblematic of this bloody-mindedness. Esau was, in addition, the ancestor of—and thus associated with—Amalek, the quintessential enemy of Israel condemned to extirpation. And finally Esau/Edom was identified with Rome, remembered in Jewish thought, for its violence and brutality and the horrors attendant to its suppression of the Jewish rebellion and the destruction of the Temple.

68 Leibowitz, Yeshayahu, "After Kibiya" (Hebrew) in *Torah u-Mitzvot ba-Zeman ha-Zeh*, Tel Aviv, 1954, 170. Cited in Sokolow, "What is This Bleeding," 146.

even the broadest interpretation of the often-mistranslated "thou shalt not kill" does not apply.

The second route to war is the consequence of tensions between political actors. If, like the proverbial grain of sand in an oyster shell, some irritant emerges between two political actors, every effort should be made to ameliorate the problem peacefully and in a way found to resolve the differences. Respectful negotiation must be the first recourse when such tensions arise. Only if it proves impossible to peacefully reduce the tensions, should we be willing to engage in the fearful enterprise of battle. The burden is on both parties of the dispute to find some solution other than war.

If war is forced upon a political entity, they must conduct the battle in such a way as to avoid dehumanizing or demonizing the adversary. As a consequence of this, fighters must be vigilant in diminishing the potential harm to non-combatants. Every effort must be made to avoid the death or injury to civilians. This concern is especially heightened with regard to non-combatant women. Soldiers must conduct themselves in battle the same way that they would conduct themselves in their non-military lives. Soldiers must be proscribed from allowing the bloodlust associated with battle to be converted into the sexual lust of the powerful over the powerless. Rape as reprisal or as a tool of war, or inflicting terror, must be forbidden. Civilians in general are to be treated with the respect due every human being.

By the same token, respect must be paid to the humanity of enemy combatants. Tragically, the killing of enemy soldiers is part of the essence of warfare. But once a soldier is rendered *hors de combat* either by injury or by capture, they must be accorded the respect due to every human being. Injuries of enemy soldiers must be attended to and medical treatment provided. An army must be vigilant in assuring that such injured or captured soldiers, once removed from the field of battle, are not to be killed in the frenzy associated with the emotional turmoil engendered by battle. They are not to be injured out of rage, nor in the process of "debriefing" or interrogation. Even subjecting them to psychological stress as part of interrogation or reprisal must be considered unacceptable.

Further, a justly conducted battle would be respectful of the humanity of non-combatant civilians. They must be allowed to flee a besieged city—referred to in *halacha* as the obligation to surround enemy cities on only three sides. And concern must be paid to the need for the enemy population to continue to maintain some quality of life, even in defeat. Thus, looting and the taking of the spoils of war must be strictly forbidden. It is recognized that a certain amount of physical destruction is inevitable in the theater of battle. But unnecessary destruction must be avoided. Battles must be conducted in such a way as to not destroy the post-war viability of the area of combat. Combatants must recognize that as part of the humanity of the enemy, the environment of those enemies must be left inviolate to the extent possible commensurate with what is necessary in the prosecution of battle.

Finally, the leaders of warring political entities must be alert to the conditions that could lead to the cessation of hostility. Those responsible for the conduct of battle must always be open to the enemy's suing for peace. Opportunities to negotiate for the cessation of hostility must be pursued earnestly and sincerely. Negotiations themselves should be conducted fairly and even generously with the goal not of prolonging the hostilities but of seeking a speedy conclusion. Once the battle is over a just war demands intentional action to restore amicable and collaborative relations between the former adversaries. Every effort must be made to assure that the circumstance that led to the war in the first place not be replicated in post-war relations. Perhaps one could say that a just war is one which renders further wars unnecessary, even unthinkable.

Bibliography

Broyde, Michael, "Just War, Just Battles and Just Conduct in Jewish Law: Jewish Law is Not a Suicide Pact," in: Lawrence Schiffman/Joel B. Wolowelsy (eds), *War and Peace in the Jewish Tradition*, New York: Yeshiva University Press, 2007, 1–43.

Eisen, Robert, *Religious Zionism, Jewish Law and the Morality of War*, New York: Oxford University Press, 2017.

Firestone, Reuven, *Holy War in Judaism*, New York: Oxford University Press, 2012.

Good, Robert M. "The Just War in Ancient Israel," *Journal of Biblical Literature*, 104,3 (1985), 385–400.

Miller, Patrick D., Jr., *The Divine Warrior in Early Israel*, Harvard Semitic Monograph 5. Cambridge, MA: Harvard University Press, 1973.

Polish, Daniel, "Does Judaism Condone Capital Punishment?" *Reform Judaism*, Summer 2002.

Schiffman, Lawrence, "War in Apocalyptic Thought," in: Lawrence Schiffman/Joel B. Wolowelsy, Joel B. (eds), *War and Peace in the Jewish Tradition*, New York: Yeshiva University Press, 2007, 477–95.

Seibert, Eric A., *Disturbing Divine Behavior: Troubling Old Testament Images of God*, Minneapolis: Fortress, 2009.

Shatz, David, "Introduction," in: Lawrence Schiffman/Joel B. Wolowelsy (eds), *War and Peace in the Jewish Tradition*, New York: Yeshiva University Press, 2007, xii–xxxviii.

Sokolow, Moshe, "'What is This Bleeting of Sheep in My Ears': Spoils of War/Wars that Spoil," in: Lawrence Schiffman/Joel B. Wolowelsy (eds), *War and Peace in the Jewish Tradition*, New York: Yeshiva University Press, 2007, 133–62.

Solomon, Norman, "Judaism and the Ethics of War," *International Journal of the Red Cross*, 87,858 (June 2005), 295–306.

Stern, Philip D., *The Biblical Ḥērem: A Window on Israel's Religious Experience*, Brown Judaic Studies 211, Atlanta: Scholars Press, 1991.

Von Rad, Gerhard, *Holy War in Ancient Israel*, Grand Rapids: Eerdmans, 1958.
Ravitzky, Aviezer, “Prohibited Wars in Jewish Tradition,” in: Terry Nardin (ed.), *The Ethics of War and Peace: Religious and Secular Perspectives*, Princeton NJ: Princeton University Press, 1996, 115–27.
Union Prayer Book, Cincinnati, Central Conference of American Rabbis, 1947.
Walzer, Michael, “War and Peace in the Jewish Tradition,” in: Terry Nardin (ed.), *The Ethics of War and Peace: Religious and Secular Perspectives*, Princeton NJ: Princeton University Press, 1996, 95–114.
Wellhausen, Julius, *Prolegomena to the History of Ancient Israel*, Cleveland, Meridian Books, 1957.
Wright, Jacob L. “Warfare and Wanton Destruction: A Reexamination of Deuteronomy 19:19–20 in Relation to Ancient Siegecraft,” *Journal of Biblical Literature* 127,3 (2008), 423–58.
Yearbook of the Central Conference of American Rabbis, vol. 45 (1935), 66–67.
Zenger, Erich, *A God of Vengeance? Understanding the Psalms of Divine Wrath*, trans. Linda M. Maloney. Louisville, KY: Westminster John Knox Press, 1994.

Suggestions for Further Reading

Eisen, Robert, *Religious Zionism, Jewish Law and the Morality of War*, New York: Oxford University Press, 2017.
Firestone, Reuven, *Holy War in Judaism*, New York: Oxford University Press, 2012.
Terry Nardin (ed.), *The Ethics of War and Peace: Religious and Secular Perspectives*, Princeton NJ: Princeton University Press, 1996
Lawrence Schiffman/Joel B. Wolowelsy (eds), *War and Peace in the Jewish Tradition*, New York: Yeshiva University Press, 2007.

Heinz-Gerhard Justenhoven

The Concept of Just War in Christianity

Is the teaching of 'just war' a Christian concept suitable for interreligious dialogue? There is no doubt that there is large tradition of deliberation on the legitimacy of war in Christian theological ethics. The early reception of ancient Greek and Latin stoic ethics, as found in Cicero's writings by the Christian bishop and influential theologian Augustine, enabled Christian theological ethics to develop arguments treating the biblical prohibition of killing and the fact of (military) violence, continuing down to the present day. Christianity is very diverse, and its answers to this challenge range from radical pacifism to the legitimization of warfare. A mainstream strain developed a critical approach to the use of military force, seeking to hedge the excesses of violence in war and war at large. There is no single 'just war theory,' but rather a diversity of attempts, varying as to the respective theological systematic of the particular church traditions or theologians, as will be discussed. Because of the multitude of theological schools, approaches and churches only several of the more influential milestones can be discussed by way of example in this article.[1] Thus we try to build a bridge over historical epochs as well as over the multitude of approaches, beginning with the early church.

1 Pacifism of the Early Church?

There is no just war teaching in the New Testament. Rather, the announcement of a 'kingdom of peace' is the essential message of Jesus Christ. The first followers of Jesus Christ, the early church, tried to treat this message within small house communities, expecting the return of the Lord and his Kingdom of Peace, living underground with a focus on brotherhood within their local Chris-

1 For a first orientation see: Regout, Robert H.W., *La doctrine de la guerre juste de Saint Augustin à nos jours*, Paris 1934; Holmes, Arthur F. (ed.), *War and Christian Ethics*, Grand Rapids/MI: Baker Book House, 1975; Johnson, James Turner, *Just War Tradition and the Restraint of War*, Princeton/NJ: Princeton University Press, 1981; Reichberg, Gregory M., *The Ethics of War: Classics and Contemporary Readings*, Maldon/MA: Blackwell, 2006; Justenhoven, Heinz-Gerhard/Barbieri,William A. (eds), *From Just War to Modern Peace Ethics*, Berlin/Boston: de Gruyter, 2012; Brunstetter, Daniel R./O'Dirscoll, Cian (eds), *Just War Thinkers from Cicero to the 21st Century*, Abington/New York: Routledge, 2018.

https://doi.org/10.1515/9783110733136-003

tian community, while at the same time preaching the gospel of Christ in public.[2] With the increase of Christian community at the beginning of the 2nd century, their relation to the Roman Empire remained ambivalent: The Roman Emperor was accepted as the necessary political authority to govern the Roman Empire and secure stability. Issues of social justice or a change of the political order were beyond their horizon, as the eschatological expectation of the coming of the Lord prevailed.[3] The two following key texts of the New Testament attest to this attitude. When asked whether or not they should pay taxes and thus accept the rule of the Roman Emperor, Jesus answered the religious leaders of the Jews: "Render to Caesar the things that are Caesar's, and to God the things that are God's" (Mark 12:17). Saint Paul wrote in his 'Letter to the Romans' the efficacious sentence: "Let every person be subject to the governing authorities. For there is no authority except from God, and those that exist have been instituted by God" (Rom. 13:1). While accepting the political authority as necessary, from the very beginning the Christians differentiated political and religious authority in line with the prophetic tradition of the Old Testament, their Jewish tradition, and in contradistinction to their pagan contemporaries. Prophets used to speak up to authorities criticizing them in the name of God almighty for committing crimes against God's law or transgressing basic issues of social justice. Acceptance of the emperor as a political authority, without the acceptance of any divine authority attributed to him, was a stance adopted consistently by the early Christian communities.[4]

An issue that remains controversial down to today, for example between Peace Churches and most mainstream churches, is whether a Christian is permitted to become a soldier and bear arms; both the positive and negative positions on this question relate back to the New Testament. Pacifists such as the Peace Churches refer to Jesus' Sermon on the Mount, with his command to love even one's enemies. Non-pacifists refer to reports about Roman soldiers: The Acts of the Apostles tell of a Roman soldier, the Centurio Cornelius of Caesarea, who converted to Christianity (Acts 10), without any report that he was asked to quit the army. Becoming a Christian was not incompatible with being an officer

2 Cassidy, Richard J., *Society and Politics in the Acts of the Apostles*, Maryknoll NY: Orbis Books, 1987, 21–50.

3 Cf. Leppin, Hartmut, *Die frühen Christen: Von den Anfängen bis Konstantin*, München: C.H. Beck, 2018, 345–415.

4 Brennecke, Hans Christof, "'An fidelis ad militiam converti possit'? Frühchristliches Bekenntnis und Militärdienst im Widerspruch?" in: Dietmar Wyra et. al. (eds), *Die Weltlichkeit des Glaubens in der Alten Kirche*, 50, Berlin/New York: De Gruyter, 1997, 50.

of the Roman occupational forces, as later witnesses attest.[5] During the 2nd century, more soldiers were baptized. Their problem was the requested cultic sacrifice to the divinized Roman emperor: could they serve the emperor and Christ at the same time? This issue is tackled by Tertullian (155–210 CE), a trained Roman jurist who became the first Christian author, and a fierce defender of faith in Carthage. While having accepted the reality of Christian soldiers in his "Apologeticum",[6] he later refused the possibility of Christians becoming soldiers mainly because of the cultic sacrifice for the divinised Roman Emperor required as sign of loyalty,[7] but also because of their participation in excecuting martial law and torture.[8] Tertullian is often adduced as a proof for a pacifist position of the early Church.[9] But most church historians refer to the fact that his position did not prevail at the turn of the 2nd century, as Tertullian himself turned to the radical and marginalized position of Montanism.[10] More and more soldiers became Christians and the Christian communities seem to have accepted these conversions. It was bishop Augustine who at the end of the 4th century thoroughly treated the question whether a Christian could remain a soldier.

2 Just War in Antiquity: Cicero and Augustine

The beginning of Christian just war thinking is usually dated to Augustine (354–430 CE), bishop of Hippo Regius in North Africa. Augustine was not only a theologian and bishop of the 5th century, but also a citizen of the late Roman Em-

5 Cf. Harnack, Adolf von, Militia Christi: Die christliche Religion und der Soldatenstand in den ersten drei Jahrhunderten, Darmstadt: Wissenschaftliche Buchgesellschaft, 1963 (Original: 1905), 46–92.

6 The 'rain miracle' in the war with the Quades (a Germanic tribe) with which Christians soldiers of the Melitenic legion saved the Roman army is considered as evidence of Christians soldiers, documented in Tertulian, *Apologeticum* Cap. V.; see also Apologet. Chap 37. http://www.tertullian.org/articles/mayor_apologeticum/mayor_apologeticum_07translation.htm (accessed 9. April 2020).

7 Cf. Tertullian, *de idolatria* 19, in: http://www.tertullian.org/works/de_idololatria.htm, (accessed 9. April 2020).

8 Cf. Tertullian, *de corona militum* 11, in: http://www.tertullian.org/works/de_corona.htm, (accessed April 9, 2020).

9 Roland Bainton and Jean Michel Hornus argue for a radical pacifism in early Christendom which is incompatable for Christians being soldiers. Cf. Bainton, Roland H., *The Early Church and War*, The Hardvard Theological Review 39 (1946), 189–212; Hornus, Jean Michel, *It is Not Lawful for Me to Fight. Early Christian Attitudes Towards War, Violence and the State*, Scottdale, PA: Herald Press, 1980.

10 Cf. Brennecke, 'An fidelis ad militiam converti possit'?, 85 f.

pire, trained in classical philosophy and rhetoric. He found himself confronted with the search for advice from Bonifatius. The Roman officer and newly converted Christian approached Augustine for advice as to whether a Christian might be allowed to use military force against the Germanic tribes attacking the Roman border, destroying settlements and killing their citizens. It is no wonder that Augustine had to make recourse to the Roman philosopher Cicero's *De Officio*, which best addressed such controversial ethical matters. The writings of the Church fathers were of no help, as they did not include any systematic ethical reasoning on this political issue. We will turn now, therefore, to shedding some light on Augustine's important resource for ethical deliberation.

Cicero (106–43 BCE), philosopher, advocate, author and Roman statesman, was the first to use the term 'just war' (*bellum iustum*), but he did not develop a just war theory. In his extensive writings, Cicero deliberated on various questions related to the justice of warfare.[11] He followed the stoic principle that there can be no contradiction between the moral good and the useful in the long run. Hence it would be senseless to seek only one's own advantage: according to Cicero, to do harm to others for one's own benefit will in the end do harm to the actor as well.[12] This moral insight is transferred to warfare: Cicero believed that even the defense of one's own political community (*res publica*) does not allow committing injustices to offenders; he prefers non-military, juridical means to solve conflicts. But this is only to defend oneself against injustice suffered. Hence any war other than one for compensation of injustice is not right.

Cicero then deliberates—with reference to ancient Roman wars[13]—how to conduct a war justly. As a legitimate war will serve a future peace, there are moral limits on what is allowed in warfare: only what is absolutely necessary against the injustice and serves to regain peace in the long run.[14] Cicero's arguments, here only briefly scetched, proved an important resource for Augustine and Thomas Aquinas, who incorporated them in their own theological frameworks, as we will demonstrate now. Modern receptions of the 'just war tradition' or 'just war theory' quite often reduce the tradition according to normative crite-

11 Most relevant are his writings *De republica* II,17.31 and III,23.35 and *De officiis* I,11.34–13.40.
12 Cf. Schockenhoff, Eberhard, *Kein Ende der Gewalt? Friedensethik für eine globalisierte Welt*, Freiburg i.Br.: Herder, 2018, 106.
13 Cicero, Marcus Tullius, *On Duties* (*De officiis*) I,34–40, A new translation by P.G. Walsh, Oxford World's Classic, Oxford: Oxford University Press 2000, 13–16.
14 Cf. Keller, Andrea, *Cicero und der gerechte Krieg: Eine ethisch-staatsphilosophische Untersuchung*, Stuttgart: Kohlhammer, 2012, 37 f.

ria or even project the final form of this theory back to its very beginning[15] and search for confirmation in a classical text like the ones of Augustine. In contrast, I hold the position that it is important to understand the systematic concept and the historicity of political ideas.

Augustine did not develop a systematic just war theory, but rather treated single aspects of the issue in different writings. A systematic reconstruction should embed these individual statements into his systematic theology of peace, which he developed in *The City of God* (*De civitate dei*) for example. This theology of peace was written in times of great turbulence: Rome was declining, borders had become insecure, and in 410 CE the Gothic King Alarich had conquered Rome and devastated the city. The blame for the mortal danger of *Roma Aeterna*, the eternal city, was put on the Christians for their new teaching of love and non-violence and their disrespect of the ancient guardian deities of Rome. Augustine's book *De civitate dei* is a defense of the Christian faith explaining the difference between the kingdom of God and a worldly empire like that of the Romans.

As already stated, Augustine's various statements on just war are embedded in a theology of peace: this theology includes a cosmological view of all creatures, living and nonliving, which God has created according to the eternal law (*ius aeterna*), a hierarchical order of being.[16] The cosmos as a whole, and each being, strives for peace, which according to Augustine is to be understood as *tranquilitas ordinis*, the tranquility or peacefulness of the order of the cosmos. The highest degree of peace for which human beings can strive lies with God, the *summun bonun.*[17] Following ancient philosophy, Augustine "relates the moral distinction between good and bad to the distinction between goods that produce happiness and those goods that fail to do so."[18] If one aspires to the true goods, he finds peace and happiness, ultimately in God.

According to Augustine, the human nature is spoiled and inclined to the evil since the fall of man, when humans turned their back on God. In the fallen man the passions take control, as for example in the *libido dominandi*, the desire to dominate, causing the human desire to destroy and to conquer. War and destruction are therefore a reality and humankind is not able to rid itself from bad de-

---

15 Cf. Schockenhoff, Eberhard, *Kein Ende der Gewalt? Friedensethik für eine globalisierte Welt*, 118.

16 Here I follow Brachtendorf, Johannes, "Augustine: Peace Ethics and Peace Policy," in: Justenhoven/ Barbieri (eds), *From Just War to Modern Peace Ethics*, 50 f.

17 CF. Augustine, *De Civitate Dei* XIX 11, in: Sancti Aurelii Augustinei, *De Civitate Dei*, Libri I-XXII, Tournhout 1955, 674 f.

18 Brachtendorf, "Augustine" 51.

sires, but needs redemption from their own evil desires through Christ. Whereas the Kingdom of God holds no such evil desire, i.e. no sin, according to Augustine the world is full of evil. In any human community, from the family to the state, a minimum order is required to overcome the anarchy of that nature. The penal power of the state according to Augustine is indispensable in the hands of the legitimate authority to provide the legal orderenabling a minimal peaceful coexistence in any human society.[19] Augustine is aware of the "monstrous, horrifying, disastrous evil" of wars[20], which should be avoided. He therefore distinguished unjust wars form just wars: unjust wars are a result of the *libido dominandi*, when warriors are striving for worldy commodities as the Romans did according to Augustine in expanding their empire and subjugating neighboring peoples.

Augustine's deliberation on just war should be seen in realtion to two contemporary contexts: there was the Roman accusation that Christian teaching, especially the sermon on the mount, was useless for politics or political consideration. Secondly, against the Manichaens and their pacifism, Augustine had to defend the Old Testament and its offensive wars lead by God. Other then the Manichaens, Augustine sees the Old Testament as a harbinger of the New Testament, "which contains the secrets of salvation in disguised form"[21].

Violence in the world is a consequence of the sin, the *libido dominandi*, and needs to be repelled. A war is just if and when it is oriented at overcoming a sin or to better a sinner. The legitimate authority of a *res publica* has to maintain the external peace. This authority alone is allowed to use penal force against a sinner to uphold the natural order. Only by command of this autority, and if unavoidable, can lethal force be used without offending the prohibition of killing: "Thou shalt not kill."[22] Augustine uses the term *necessitas*, which today might be translated as "last resort." A soldier who obeys the legitimate authority and executes their commands promotes natural peace as the basis of social coexistence in this world, if he accomplishes his task with benevolence (*benevolentia*). Here again, Augustine's just war theory aims at overcoming sin; with his benevolence the soldier invites the sinner to repent and reverse. Not hatred nor the desire for harm should direct a soldier, but rather the wish to overcome the evil and convince the perpetrator to abandon the sin.

---

19 Cf. Weissenberg, Timo, *Die Friedenslehre des Augustinus. Theologische Grundlagen und ethische Entfaltung*, Stuttgart: Kohlhammer, 2005, 127 ff.
20 Augustine, *De Civitate Dei* XIX 7, 672.
21 Brachtendorf, "Augustine," 56.
22 Cf. Weissenberg, *Friedenslehre des Augustinus*, 382 f.

3 Ancient Orthodox Theology on Warfare

While Augustine's teaching had become very influential for the next centuries in the Western Latin Church, this was not so much the case for the Eastern Orthodox Churches, i.e. for the Christian Churches in the Hellenistic or Greek orbit from Alexandria in Egypt to Byzantium. Before the Latin and Greek Churches drifted apart and split off in a centuries-long process that reached its culmination in the disastrous conquest of Byzantium by Latin crusaders in 1204, the unity of the Christian Churches was maintained by the seven ecumenical councils, one of which was the council of Chalcedon (451). Not only was the Creed of Chalcedon adopted, but so too was the denial of military service for priests and monks:

> Those who have entered the clergy or have been tonsured into monastic state may no longer serve in the army or accept any civil charge; otherwise those who have dared to do so, and have not repented and returned to their prior occupation for the love of God, shall be anathemized.[23]

This requirement has remained as common teaching in East and West. According to Alexander Webster there is a strong pacifist stance mostly in the monasteries and in the ranks of the clergy of the Eastern Christian churches. This tradition is also upheld by the 'passion-bearers': Christians identifying with Christ's non-violent reaction to his crucifixion and giving a non-violent response to any aggression.[24]

Nevertheless, war remained a reality in the Eastern and Western part of the Roman Empire, and the idea of overcoming war was only to be expected in the day of Christ's reign. Therefore, the Church Fathers had to deal with this reality as soldiers were Christians and members of the church. An important distinction between killing and murdering was made by Athanasius the Great, bishop of Alexandria (296–373) as he points to the relevance of the circumstances of an action:

---

23 Concilium Chalcedonense, Canon 7, in: Joseph Alberigo (ed.), *Conciliorum Oecumenicorum Decreta*, Basel et. al.: Herder, 1962, 66. English translation in: Hildo Bos/Jim Forest (eds), *For the Peace from Above: An Orthodox Resource Book on Peace, War and Nationalism*, Rollinsford/NH, 2011, 41.

24 Cf. Webster, Alexander F. C., *The Pacifist Option: The Moral Argument against War in Eastern Orthodox Theology*, San Francisco: International Scholars Publications, 1998.

> For in other matters also that go to make up life, we shall find differences according to circumstances. For example, it is not right to kill, but in war it is lawful and praiseworthy to destroy the enemy; accordingly, not only are they who have distinguished themselves in the field held worthy of great honors, but monuments are put up proclaiming their achievements. So that the same act is at one time and under some circumstances unlawful, while under others, and at the right time, it is lawful and permissible.[25]

It was especially Basil the Great (330 – 379), bishop of Caesarea in Cappadocia (in todays eastern Turkey), whose position influenced the Orthodox mainstream. Even though it seems common teaching in the post-Constantinian Church that wars are sometimes unavoidable, and thus soldiers inevitably will kill and shed human blood, Basil assumes it necessary for soldiers to repent in this case and to abstain from holy communion even though their service seems unavoidable: "Our fathers did not think that killing in war was murder; yet I think it advisable for such as have been guilty of it to forbear communion three years."[26] According to Basil's influential teaching, killing an enemy even as a defensive action leads to guilt on the part of the soldier who did the killing, who thus required repentance before he could return to full communion.

In the Western Latin Church a more elaborated just war teaching was developed mainly by Thomas Aquinas, while the

> Byzantines had retained from the Roman past the idea that wars have to be just, and the idea that a defensive war, and a war for recovery of things lost, was a just war; this was incorporated in their legal system, as was the maxim that only the public authority, namely the Emperor, may declare war.[27]

This became true mainly after the Byzantine Empire was first threatenned and then conquered by Muslim invaders. "The Byzantines were talking about the recovery of their own territories from the infidel invaders, so that behind the emotional religious symbolism there lurked the old Roman concept of just war."[28]

---

25 Athanasius the Great, "Epistle to the Monk Ammun," in: Bos/Forest, *For the Peace from Above*, 46.

26 Basil the Great, Canon 13, in: Bos/Forest, *For the Peace from Above*, 45.

27 Laiou, Angeliki, "The Just War of the Eastern Christians and the Holy Warfare of the Crusaders," in: Richard Sorabji/David Rodin (eds), *The Ethics of War: Shared Problems in Different Traditions*, Aldershot: Ashgate 2006, 34.

28 Laiou, "Just War of the Eastern Christians," 33.

4 Just War in the Middle Ages: "Decretum Gratiani" and Thomas Aquinas's *Summa Theologia*

The first systematic collection of statements on *bellum iustum* (just war) is the collection of the Canonist Gratian from Bologna, who used Ivo of Chartres' canonist collection to form his own famous collection known as "Decretum Gratiani"[29] in 1140: Gratian compiled statements of the Church Fathers, the Christian theologians from antiquity and early Middle Ages, into a systematic framework. With regard to Augustine, Roland Kany has pointed out that Augustine never wrote a 'just war theory.' What became known as Augustine's just war theory is the result of Gratian's compilation of Augustine's statements from different letters and writings in the *Secunda Pars, Causa XXIII* of his "Decretum."[30] Gratian "assembles the tradition known up to that point and serves as the foundation for diverse theories of just war."[31] Kany points out that the selection for thematic purposes (ethics, dogmatics, spirituality) from Augustine's works dates back to the 5th century. "In this manner, the gradual reception of Augustine in the form of excerpts developed, divorced from Augustine's original arguments and from the original context of his writings."[32] Thomas Aquinas' reception of Augustine on just war relies completely on Gratian's collection, as it had become prevalent in Middle Age Christian theology.

The most influential Christian just war theory is Thomas Aquinas' treatise "De bello" in his "Summa Theologia II II questio 40." In many cases the questio 40 "De bello" is taken out of the context of the *Summa Theologia* and treated as an independent treatise ignoring its theological and historical context. As the title describes, Thomas presents a systematic theology and treats the question "De bello" in his treatise "De caritate" (on love), asking: does waging war defy Christ's command to love you neighbor and not to kill?

Besides the theological context of the treatise "De bello", the historical context should be taken into consideration again. Thomas' theology reflects the socio-cultural reality of the Middle Ages from the persepctive of a devoted

---

29 Cf. "Decretum Magistri Gratiani," in: *Corpus Iuris Canonici, Editio Lipsiensis Secund post Aemilii Friedberg Richteri*, Graz: Akademische Druck- und Verl.-Anst., 1959 (Reprint of Leipzig 1879).
30 Cf. *Decretum Gratiani, Secunda Pars Causa XXIII*, 889–965.
31 Kany, Roland, "Augustine's Theology of Peace and the Beginning of the Just War Theory," in: Justenhoven/Barbieri (eds), *From Just War to Modern Peace Ethics*, 34.
32 Ibid., 35.

monk in the *orbis christianus:* the supremacy of the pope as the spiritual power over the temporal power of the princes, the unity of the (Western Latin) Church—for Thomas, the Eastern Byzantine Church was schismatic after the final break from Rome in 1054—and the orientation of the terrestrial life towards achieving eternal salvation meaning a never ending life with God. For Thomas, there was no question that only by following Jesus Christ could eternal life be obtained, and that no reasoning could prove otherwise. Once confronted with the Christian faith, only the evil could abstain from the creed. In this context the temporal authority of the princes as heads of their political community matter: it is their main task to govern their community[33] in accordance with natural law. Individuals should find circumstances within the community that neither mislead them into sin nor prevent them from living a devoted life and achieving eternal life.

The prince may have to use penal force (*bellum*) to "rescue the poor and deliver the needy out of the hand of the sinner," as Thomas writes with reference to Psalms 82:4. Here, it already it becomes clear that the translation of *bellum* with 'war' as understood in the 21st century is misleading. Thomas is not talking about a war between sovereign states when he refers to *bellum iustum*. The context clearly indicates that the use of lethal force by command of the legitimate authority against perpetrators is more to be understood in the sense of police force. But there is another meaning of *bellum iustum* as well: Gerhard Beestermöller has proven that Thomas engages the *principes* as legitimate authorities in another, rather different case. To grasp it, one needs to look at his understanding of *res publica*, which usually is translated as "state," indicating that in Thomas's world there were different 'states' that would be waging war for different reasons. As Beestermöller shows, Thomas never uses the plural of *res publica:* it is a singular unity. *Res publica* for Thomas is the *orbis christianus*, the political unit of all faithful, the *res publica fidelium.*[34] Within this community the pope has the supreme spiritual power, the princes serve with their temporal power the same end in their way in governing their respective communities: their kingdoms, princedoms, dukedoms etc.

This was the only way to conceive the temporal authority in the *res publica fidelium*, since the emperor was weak in the 13th century and lacked the means to fight injustice and restore peace in cases of feuds between princes, or in cases of princes not preventing crimes in their community.

33 The notion "state" is misleading in this context, as it appeared only in the early modern era.
34 Cf. Beestermöller, Gerhard, "Thomas Aquinas and Humanitarian Intervention," in: Justenhoven/ Barbieri (eds), *From Just War to Modern Peace Ethics*, 78.

But in case of a grave injustice and the failure of the responsible authority to vindicate it, according to Thomas some authority is definitely needed: if a grave injustice were not repelled this would encourage the weak to commit further injustices to such an extent that the spiritual health of the faithful could be endangered by the bad example. In this case Thomas engages the *princeps* to use the sword against the perpetrators in a neighboring community:

> And just as it is lawful for them (the *principes*) to have recourse to the sword (*materiali gladio*[35]) in defending that common weal against internal disturbances, when they punish evildoers, according to the words of the Apostle (Rm. 13:4): "He beareth not the sword in vain: for he is God's minister, an avenger to execute wrath upon him that doth evil"; so too, it is their business to have recourse to the sword of war (*gladio bellico*) in defending the community (*rem publicam*) against external enemies. Hence it is said to those who are in authority (Ps. 81:4): "Rescue the poor and deliver the needy out of the hand of the sinner"; and for this reason Augustine says (Contra Faust. XXII, 75): "The natural order conducive to peace among mortals demands that the power to declare and counsel war should be in the hands of those who are principes."[36]

The key statement is Psalms 81:4: "Rescue the poor: and deliver the needy out of the hand of the sinner." According to Beestermöller, Thomas is not talking about a war between states when he speaks of "external enemies" (*hostes exteriores*). His concerns are attacks on the *respublica fidelium*, the church. According to Thomas, the external enemies were the Cathars (or Albigenses) who had threatened the unity of the church in building up a radical protest movement and profound alterations to the church in southern France, spreading out to Italy, Germany and Spain from the 11th to the 14th century. The regional lord, the count of Toulouse, was their mighty protector. In 1209 Pope Innocence III called for a crusade against the Cathars that lasted 20 years. In Thomas understanding the Christian *principes* had to rescue the Christian population in these areas "out of the hand of the sinner" because the Cathars, refusing to be subjugated under the head of the church, had led the faithful away from the true belief the church was teaching.[37] With regard to the Muslim authorities in Palestine, Thomas judged likewise: as long as these *principes* allowed the Christian popu-

35 *Materialis gladio* refers to the worldly sword of the church; cf. Beestermöller, "Thomas Aquinas and Humanitarian Intervention," 81.

36 St. Thomas Aquinas, *The Summa Theologica*, Benziger Bros. Edition, 1947, II-II q.40 a.1 in: https://dhspriory.org/thomas/summa/SS/SS040.html#SSQ40OUTP1 (accessed 1. August 2019). Some key terms are translated different; in this case I follow Gerhard Beestermöller's translation.

37 Cf. Thomas Aquinas, *Summa Theologiae* II-II q.39, a.4. respondeo.

lation to practise their faith he considered them legitimate authorities. Only when they did not were Christian princes permitted to fight against them.

Now Thomas' intention with regard to the second criterion becomes clear: "Secondly, a just cause is required, namely that those who are attacked should be attacked because they deserve it on account of some fault."[38] A just case according to Thomas is an injustice hindering the faithful to live a devoted life. And thirdly, Thomas continues, "it is necessary that the belligerents should have a rightful intention, so that they intend the advancement of good, or the avoidance of evil."[39] Good and evil according to Thomas are moral categories, and should be judged in the light of the eternal destination of humankind. It is obvious that in many respects Thomas's 'just war theory' has been misunderstood or misused to legitimate the use of military force in many regards.

5 Just War in Early Modern Age: Francisco de Vitoria, Martin Luther and John Calvin

Three hundred fifty years later, in the 16th century,[40] under very different historical and intellectual circumstances, Francico de Vitoria[41] reflected on just war. Reformation was about to end the unity of Latin Christendom. Furthermore, the age of discovery and colonization brought about the questions of whether and why the Spanish king and Emperor were the legitimate rulers of the New Indies, and whether the Spanish colonists were allowed to exploit the continent and its indigenous inhabitants. Confronted with the 'uncivilized Indians' of the Carribeans, the position of Juan Ginés de Sepúlveda was amenable to the legitimizing of colonization: With reference to Aristotle he stated that these Indians were slaves by nature and needed to be civilized by the Spanish Christians—and of course they had to rightfully labor for them.

That position was challenged by Dominican missionaries, who had baptized many Indians and pointed to the Christian King's responsibility to protect his Indian subjects. Some of them had already become Christians, others were yet to

---

38 Thomas Aquinas, *Summa Theologiae* II-II, q.40 a.1.

39 Ibid.

40 This paragraph is a brief summary of my article: Justenhoven, Heinz-Gerhard, "Francisco de Vitoria: Just War as Defense of International Law," in: Justenhoven/Barbieri (eds), *From Just War to Modern Peace Ethics*, 121–35.

41 Francisco de Vitoria (1483–1546), Dominican theologian and founder of the *School of Salamanca*, the peak of Catholic theology in the Early Modern Age.

be confronted with the Gospel of Christ. But how could missionaries bring the message of the Savior's love, as long as Christian soldiers and colonizers were only interested in conquest, gold and slaves, and therefore slaughtered and suppressed the Indian population, the Dominican missionary Pedro de Montesinos asked in his famous sermon in 1511 the Spanish slaveholders. Bartholomé de Las Casas, a slaveholder himself at that time, attended the sermon and some time later converted to become the fiercest defender of the rights of the Indians.[42]

For Vitoria, the Indian question was a theological one: The fact that quite a number of the Indians had professed their faith in Christ is the starting point of Vitoria's deliberation. The Indian people were obviously able to believe in Christ. This could only be possible, Vitoria concluded, as the Creator had furnished the Indians with the ability to do so. From here, Vitoria made recourse to Aquinas' and Augustine's theology of a cosmos in complete harmony that the Creator had set in alignment to himself. Within the order of the cosmos, it is the destination of humankind to respond to God's call to salvation. Being an image of God, every human being is able to understand and accept faith by reason, once the Gospel is preached to him or her. As images of God, the Europeans were able to respond to the call to salvation; likewise, some Indians had already responded to God's call and confessed the Christian faith, as Dominican missionaries had reported. Here, the Thomistic distinction between nature and grace comes to be of great value. According to Aquinas, grace does not change but rather fulfills nature, while being based on it. The fact that the Indians are able to convert to Christianity, Vitoria concludes, shows that by creation God has given the Indians the same nature as the Europeans that is open for his grace as they obviously are gifted with sufficient reason to understand the sense of the gospel. As humankind is gifted with reason by its nature, not by civilization, Vitoria concluded, there can be no difference between Spaniards and Indians in this regard. Being created to respond to God's call and therefore being images of God constitutes the Indians' human dignity and fundamental rights.[43] With this thesis, Vitoria could negate claims that the Indians, for spiritual reasons, were to be made subject and civilized by the Spanish conquerors. The question then surfaced: what were the rights the Indian people could claim against the Spanish King and his colonizers? Vitoria's problem was that there

---

42 Cf. Delgado, Mariano, "Mit welchem Recht ...? Die Kontroverse über die Legitimation der Unterwerfung der Indios durch die Spanier im 16. Jahrhundert", in: Mariano Delgado (ed.), *Das Ringen um die Wahrheit*, Stuttgart: Kohlhammer, 2011, 157–87.

43 Cf. Justenhoven, Heinz-Gerhard, *Francisco de Vitoria zu Krieg und Frieden*, Köln: Bachem, 1991, 60f.

was no generally accepted moral and juridical foundation covering the Old continent and the New World.

From the knowledge of the highly civilized cultures like the Aztec and Inca Empire, both conquered and destroyed by Spanish conquerors, Vitoria drew the argument that "they have some sort of rules in their affairs, since they have states (*civitas*) in which rules exist and they have ... administrations, authorities and laws"[44]. Reason as a prerequisite to organize states is obviously given to the Indian people by nature, in the same way that it is given to the European people. Stating the dignity of the Indian nature and the existence of political communities, Vitoria made the fundamental argument to reject papal or imperial claims for world sovereignty, arguments that enabled the subjugation of Indian peoples.

As an early representative of the doctrine of the sovereignty of the people, Vitoria stated that the prince is not originally the bearer of political power, but rather political power has its foundation in the people. Following the Aristotelian tradition, Vitoria argues that wherever human beings live, they have to meet their necessities and therefore build states. If this is so, Vitoria concludes, the Indian and European states are based on natural law in the same way and therefore enjoy equal rights. But by which causes could the Spanish have waged wars against the legitimate Indian states? Vitoria's deliberation includes the rejection of papal or imperial supremacy as well as the rejection of the Christian faith as legitimate causes for warfare. Most interesting and influential was Vitorias deliberation of international law. In fact, he introduced the modern notion of international law, changing the classical definition of *ius gentium* as "what natural rationality constitutes among all men" (*inter omnes homines*)[45] into "what natural rationality constitutes within all nations (*inter omnes gentes)* is called law of the peoples (*ius gentium*)."[46]

According to Vitoria, *ius gentium* includes the law that is common to all peoples or nations and originates in reason. Vitoria includes the right to hospitality, freedom of travel and trade between nations and states, into the *ius gentium*, as

---

44 "... habent ordinem aliquem in suis rebus, postquam habent civitates, quae ordine constant, et habent ... magistratus, dominos, leges, ..." Francisco de Vitoria, "De indis" I,1,15, 402, in: Francisco de Vitoria, *Vorlesungen II. Völkerrecht, Politik, Kirche*, Ulrich Horst/Heinz-Gerhard Justenhoven/Joachim Stüben (eds), Stuttgart: Kohlhammer, 1997 (eng. translation HGJ).

45 Cf. Digesten I,1,9, in: Okko Behrends et. al. (eds), *Corpus Iuris Civilis*, Vol 2 Heidelberg: C.F. Müller, 2007.

46 De indis III,2, in: Vitoria, *Vorlesungen II*, 460. According to Johannes Thumfart Vitoria relies with this new interpretation of *ius gentium* on his contemporate Miguel de Ulzurrun, Catholicum opus imperial regiminis mundi (1525), cf. Johannes Thumfart, *Die Begründung der globalpolitischen Philosophie. Francisco de Vitorias Vorlesung über die Entdeckung Amerikas im ideengeschichtlichen Kontext*, Berlin: Kulturverlag Kadmos, 2012, 127.

they are common to all peoples. Vitoria enumerates further norms of the *ius gentium:* most of them are consequences of his idea of a fundamental unity and communication between the peoples of the world: free access to all countries of the world (*ius peregrinandi*), free trade (*ius negotiandi*), the right to become a citizen of another state and diplomatic immunity. Vitoria faces much criticism from some of his modern interpreters who presume that he opened the door wide for the justification of the conquest of the Indian states with this argument.[47] Instead of putting forward my own argument regarding this, I would like to quote Vitoria himself:

> ... if the barbarians attempt to deny the Spaniards in these matters which I have described as belonging to the law of nations (*ius gentium*), that is to say from trading and the rest, the Spaniards ought first to remove any cause of provocation by reasoning and persuasion, and demonstrate with every argument at their disposal that they have not come to do harm. But wish to dwell in peace and travel without any inconvenience to the barbarians. And they should demonstrate this not merely in words, but with proof ... But if reasoning fails to win the acquiescence of the barbarians, and they insist on replying with violence, the Spaniards may defend themselves, and do everything needful for their own safety ... Hence, if war is necessary to obtain their rights (*ius suum*) they may lawfully go to war.[48]

Vitoria's position was voiced publicly after the fall of the Indian states through the hands of men like Cortés and Pizzaro, whose cruelties were made public by the vocal criticism of Bartolomé de Las Casas.[49] On the background of the Dominican friar's criticism, Vitoria's words sound almost ironic, as the very facts were well known: while the Spanish could of course have made use of the right to travel and trade, they had shown a very different behavior than Vitoria demanded and therefore no right to go to war.

Vitoria added another most interesting argument, which remains at stake in international law even today. The rulers of the modern era consider themselves to be defenders of *ius gentium*, as it is the basis of coexistence in the 'globalized' world of the early 16th century. Very similar to our situation five hundred years later, there was a plurality of sovereign states with no supreme judge to decide conflicts between the rulers and their political communities. In Vitoria's understanding each ruler had to protect the rule of law, i.e. the *ius gentium* as "the

---

47 Cf. Muldoon, James, "Francisco de Vitoria and the Humanitarian Intervention," *Journal of Military Ethics* 5 (2006), 139.

48 Francisco de Vitoria, "On the American Indians" 3,1, in: Francisco de Vitoria, *Political Writings*, Anthony Pagden (ed.), Cambridge: Cambridge University Press 1991, (short: Edition Pagden) 281 f.

49 Cf. Gillner, Matthias, *Bartolomé de Las Casas und die Eroberung des indianischen Kontinents*, Stuttgart: Kohlhammer, 1997, 31 f.

whole world somehow is a political community."[50] In a very similar way to the individual, *res publica* could not exist in peace, the "orbis could not exist, if there were not some who had the power and authority to deter and punish the wicked, so that they would not do any harm to the good."[51] Each ruler (*princeps*) according to Vitoria should consider himself as judge of the whole world and not only his own political community: politics should be oriented towards the global common good, not only towards national interests.

At the same time, Vitoria realized that his concept evolves an unsolvable problem: As each *princeps* shall be equally responsible for the common good of the global *res publica,* two princes may judge differently on the same issue. Therefore it is necessary to deliberate, "whether war can be just on both sides."[52] Differently than the earlier tradition, Vitoria realizes that diverging judgments emerge from a different knowledge or interpretation of an issue, or simply by an error. Therefore, two *princeps* may believe to have a just cause and send their soldiers to war. Vitoria's solution to this dilemma makes recourse to probabilism[53]: the obligation of the *princeps* to be most careful in their judgment. Acknowledging the subjectivity of any judgment, the *princeps* is obliged to consult "reliable and wise men who can speak with freedom" and "also listen to the arguments of the opponents."[54] While the head of the state and his counselors bear this responsibility, the simple citizen or soldier is responsible for the cause of the war (only) in as much as they are able to oversee the case. Vitoria concludes that a soldier may run into a situation where he believes himself to fight for a just cause without understanding the injustice of the war he is fighting—with insurmountable ignorance from his side.[55]

Vitoria's treatise "De iure belli" has become famous, as he deliberates the *ius in bello* at greater length than Thomas Aquinas. Thomas requests that a war should be fought with the right intention (*intentio recta*). Vitoria translates the

---

50 "totius orbis ... aliquomodo est una respublica." Francisco de Vitoria, "de potestate civili" 21, in: Vitoria, *Vorlesungen I*, 156.

51 "... orbis stare non posset, nisi esset penes aliquos vis et auctoritas deterrendi improbos, ne bonis noceant." Francsico de Vitoria, "de iure belli" IV,5 in: Vitoria, *Vorlesungen II*, 564.

52 Francisco de Vitoria, "On the law of war," in: Edition Pagden, 312.

53 Gabriel Vázquez further developed this idea, cf. Scattola, Merio, " Wie der König im Krieg nach der wahrscheinlichen Meinung handeln soll: Die Kriegslehre des Gabriel Vázquez im Horizont des Probabilismus," in: Norbert Brieskorn/Markus Riedenauer (eds), *Suche nach Frieden: Politische Ethik in der frühen Neuzeit*, Vol 3, Stuttgart: Kohlhammer, 2003, 119–153.

54 Francisco de Vitoria, "On the law of war," 307.

55 Cf. Hamilton, Bernice, *Political Thought in Sixteenth Century Spain*, Oxford: Claredon Press, 1963, 147.

criterion 'right intention' into the criterion "not to harm out of greed."[56] Since the end of the 15th century, cannons had emerged on the battlefield and were used to besiege cities, while killing innocent civilians at the same time. The reference to the right intention was therefore insufficient, "Thomas' sixteenth and seventeenth century successors insisted on more externalized, objective standards," as LeRoy Walters noted.[57] The starting point of his reasoning is Augustine's axiom of "peace and security of the commonwealth being the aim of any war."[58] Any action taken in a war must be seen in relation to this final goal of a just war, peace and security. According to Vitoria, any military action can only be serving peace and security if it is adequate to this ultimate goal.

The tradition from Augustine to Thomas Aquinas and Vitoria can be considered the classical mainstream tradition. We find recourse to these theologians not only in the Catholic but also in the Anglican Church tradition.[59] In the Lutheran and Reformed Churches, Martin Luther and John Calvin play a decisive but not exclusive role. Martin Luther (1483–1546), Vitoria's contemporary, did not make recourse to the just war debates of the scholastic tradition, even though he was acquainted with it, having been a Catholic monk of the Augustine order before becoming the initiator of the Reformation. Similarly to Augustine, Luther responded to contemporary questions with regard to the legitimacy of using military force.[60] To understand Luther's approach one has to consider his 'doctrine of the two kingdoms' with the distinction of the two authorities: the political and the spiritual. Luther's aim was the reform of the church, the spiritual realm, not a political and social reformation. The spiritual authority of the church according to Luther should be exclusively used to preach the word of

---

56 Cf. "Et ita Sanctus Thomas ponit ... quod non (fiat) nocendi cupiditate." Francisco de Vitoria, *Comentarios a la Secunda Secundae de Santo Tomás*, vol. 2, Vicente Beltrán de Heredia (ed.) Salamanca: Spartado, 1932, 279.

57 Walters, LeRoy, *Five Classic Just-War Theories: A Study in the Thought of Thomas Aquinas, Vitoria, Suarez, Gentili and Grotius*, Ann Arbor: University Microfilm International, 1971, 354.

58 Anthony Pagden translates "finis" as purpose, but in ethical reasoning the finis indicates the aim of an act. Cf. Francisco de Vitoria, "On the law of war," in: Edition Pagden 309 ff.; see the Latin text: "finis belli est pax et securitas reipublicae," Francisco de Vitoria, "de iure belli," in: Francisco de Vitoria, *Vorlesungen II*, 546.

59 Cf. Reed, Charles, *Just War? Changing Society and the Churches*, London: Society for Promoting Christian Knowledge, 2004. For a brief overview of the modern Anglican debate cf. Biggar, Nigel, "Between Development and Doubt: The Recent Career of Just War Doctrine in the British Churches," in: Charles Reed/David Ryall (eds), *The Price of Peace: Just War in the Twenty-First Century*, Cambridge/UK: Cambridge University Press, 2007, 55 f.

60 Cf. Stümke, Volker, *Das Friedensverständnis Martin Luthers: Grundlagen und Anwendungsbereiche seiner politischen Ethik*, Stuttgart: Kohlhammer, 2007, 326–31.

God. Against the practice of the Catholic church of his time, Luther taught to rely only on God's grace with regard to salvation: the sinner would only be justified through Christ's sacrifice at the cross. Good deeds or anything a believer tries to do is of no value for his salvation. All Luther requested from the state with regard to religion was religious freedom and schooling to enable the believers to read and understand the gospel of Christ. Following Christ's command, true Christians would not need a "worldly sword" nor law within their Christian community (the Church), and thus did not need military force.[61] Political authority and the sword are needed only because Christians are living in this world together with non-believers (or those who only pretend to follow Christ), like sheep among wolves. It is therefore the task of the government, the political authority, to protect the state against interior or exterior threats—as last resort also with military force. The feud, the attempt of minor princes trying to pursue their interest with military force, is absolutely forbidden and to be suppressed by the legal government. The authority of the state should aim at order, security, monopoly of the legitimate use of force and law to maintain peace. Being citizens of the state, the Christians obey the state and support it in fighting evil and injustice. This position led Luther to justify military force against the peasants' revolution, a social uprising of peasants in Southern Germany, Switzerland and Austria, for which he was heavily criticized.[62] In occasional writings such as "Whether Soldiers, Too, Can Be Saved"[63], Luther deliberated more in depth on when and how to use military force legitimately. The use of military force by the worldly authority can be justified only in defense and as last resort after having made attempts to solve the conflict peacefully through negotiations or arbitration.[64] While obviously not taking up the scholastic just war thinking, Luther follows this teaching even in using this non-theological argument, as found for example in Francisco de Vitoria's writings: "it is allowed to repel force by force."[65]

The French-born theologian and ecclesiastical statesman John Calvin (1509–1564) is considered one of the most efficacious figures of the Reformation, having inspired or founded the reformed churches in Switzerland, the Netherlands,

61 Luther, Martin, *Von weltlicher Obrigkeit*, in: Martin Luthers Werke, Kritische Gesamtausgabe (WA), Weimar: Böhlau, 1883 ff., WA 11, 252,20.

62 Cf. Crossley, Robert N., *Luther and the Peasant's War: Luther's Actions and Reactions*, New York: Exposition Press, 1974.

63 Luther, Martin, *Whether Soldiers, Too, Can Be Saved*, in: Hans J. Hillerbrand (ed.), Annotated Luther: Christian Life in the World, vol. 5, Minneapolis MN; Fortress Press, 2017, 183–233.

64 Stümke, *Das Friedensverständnis Martin Luthers*, 398 f.

65 For Luther cf. Stümke, *Das Friedensverständnis Martin Luthers*, 405; cf. Francisco de Vitoria, De iure belli, in: Vitoria, *Vorlesungen II*, 546.

Scotland and the Puritan Movement in England. Calvin follows Luther's 'Doctrine of the Two Kingdoms'. This is of relevance in view of Calvin's controversy with the Anabaptists, some of whom attempted to erect the reign of Christ in the city of Münster in the 1530s.[66] According to Calvin both realms are to be distinguished and not to be mixed—an argument against any form of theocracy. On the other hand, they are not to be separated, but rather to be understood from their defined relationship—an argument against a dualistic understanding of the 'Doctrine of the Two Kingdoms' of some Anabaptists. Thus he argues very similarly to Luther with regard the Sixth Command ('Thou shall not kill') and the duty of the political authority in protecting the population: An individual Christian shall avoid violence and shall not revenge an injustice suffered. But it is the duty of the political authority to protect the neighbor by enforcing the law according to Paul's Letter to the Romans 13:1–7.[67] Still, killing a human being even when unavoidable and necessary while protecting others, according to Calvin does not leave the soldier inculpable but foul and with a macula and thus in need of repentance;[68] in this argument, reformation theology follows Basil the Great's position as shown above.

Hence Calvin speaks rather of a legitimate or rightful war than of a just war. For the determination of the legitimacy of a war, he follows the classical teaching to be found in Augustine and Thomas Aquinas, not in the sense that he developed a systematic just war theory but rather, as in Augustine we find the criteria scattered over his extensive writings.[69] According to Calvin it is the natural office of the princes who hold the *legitimate authority* to decide about the necessity of the use of military force as *last resort*, meaning the prince shall do everything to find ways of peaceful conflict resolution before calling war a necessity. The only reason Calvin accepts as *just cause* for a war is the defense against exterior or interior offenders. And the prince or municipal authorities like the magistrate of Geneva waging war with the *right intention* should aim at reaching peace as the ultimate goal of the defense of their state or city. Even though it is legitimate to start a defensive war against an aggressor having invaded one's land, not ev-

---

66 Calvin is often blamed for having created the theocratic rule in Geneva, cf. Ernst Troeltsch, *Protestantisches Christentum in der Neuzeit*, 1906, (Reprint: Berlin/New York: de Gruyter, 2004), 288. Critical to this reading: cf. Hofheinz, Marco, *Johannes Calvins theologische Friedensethik*, Stuttgart: Kohlhammer, 2012, 177–91.

67 Cf. Hofheinz, *Johannes Calvins theologische Friedensethik*, 132.

68 Cf. in Calvin's sermon to Deuteronomy 5:17: "... tant y a neantmoins que encore est-il dit que c'est une macule, que l'homme est souillé." quote in: Hofheinz, *Johannes Calvins theologische Friedensethik*, 137, footnote 3.

69 Cf. Hofheinz, *Johannes Calvins theologische Friedensethik*, 140–48.

erything is allowed: the means for fighting back have to be *proportionate*. The background of Calvin's deliberations is his own experience with the wars of the French Catholic kings and clergy against his protestant brothers, known as Huguenots, since the 1530s, he himself having been expelled from his home country and a protestant refugee. Other than Luther, Calvin argues that the subjects bear a (partial) responsibility for the legitimacy of the war, minor magistrates less than higher ones.[70]

Luther and Calvin reflected on matters of warfare from the point of view of their Lutheran or Calvinist theology, and thus shaped their church's approach to this matter.[71] At the same time, it is interesting to see the recent reception of Augustine, Thomas Aquinas and Vitoria by the Russian Orthodox Church.

6 Just War Teaching of the Russian Orthodox Church

The first systematic just war teaching of an Orthodox Church was issued by the Russian Orthodox Church in 2000 as a brief chapter in *The Social Doctrine of the Russian Orthodox Church.*[72] It borrows heavily from the Catholic just war tradition without adopting its global perspective. War is understood as an evil "caused by the sinful abuse of the God-given freedom," therefore "Christians involuntarily come to face the vital need to take part in various battles,"[73] of which war is one. The Church shall contribute to solving conflicts, but sometimes war may occur as last resort. While the Catholic Church in the 20th century developed a universalist orientation to the global common good *inter alia* with regard to war, as will be shown later, the Russian Orthodox orientation remains a national one: "From the Christian perspective, the conception of moral justice in international relations should be based on the following basic principles: love one's neighbour, people and fatherland; understanding the needs of other nations ..."[74] This argument is maintained as there is no further debate on the legitimate authority; it

70 Faber, Eva Maria, "Verantwortung für den Frieden bei Johannes Calvin," in: Brieskorn/ Riedenauer (eds), *Suche nach Frieden*, 114.
71 Saying this, I would still agree to Volker Stümke's point, that Luther has inspired peace ethics at large; cf. Volker Stümke, "Krieg und Frieden in der Reformation: Martin Luther," in: Ines Werkner/Klaus Ebeling (eds.), *Handbuch Friedensethik*, Wiesbaden: Springer VS, 2017, 265–75.
72 *The Social Doctrine of the Russian Orthodox Church*, Chapter VIII, in: www.mospat.ru/en/documents/social-concepts (accessed 24. September 2019).
73 *The Social Doctrine of the Russian Orthodox Church*, VIII,2.
74 Ibid., VIII,3.

seems to be without question that this is the national government. This is a remarkable fact, since at the same time in Western Christian theology the most virulent debates deal with this issue: is the legitimate authority the national government, or should it be an international authority like the UN Security Council?[75]

With regard to the just war criteria, the Russian Orthodox Church borrows openly from the Western Christian tradition, without reflecting the systematization of the criteria. While in the Catholic tradition since Thomas Aquinas the criterion of the legitimate authority is listed first, the Russian Orthodox Church document lists the just cause first. This difference is of systematic relevance: putting the criterion of the just cause first leaves unanswered the question of who is entitled to decide the justice of the cause– silently indicating that the national government does so. This position leads to endless wars with each side claiming to lead a just war: the problem of the 'just war from both sides' has been discussed and rejected in the Catholic tradition, as Francisco de Vitoria states: "except in ignorance, it is clear that this cannot happen."[76]

Attention is drawn to the fact that waging war can and will endanger the spiritual health of the warring soldiers: "War should be waged with righteous indignation, not maliciousness, greed and lust (1John 2:16) and other fruits of hell."[77] Being rather nationally orientated, the Russian Orthodox Church "seeks to carry out her peace service both on national and international scale, trying to help resolve various contradictions and bring nations, ethnic groups, government and political forces into harmony."[78] While struggling to overcome hostilities and supporting negotiations between hostile parties, the Russian Orthodox Church does not discuss the structural causes of war in the international system.

7 From Just War to Peace Ethics in Contemporary Catholic Peace Teaching

While the European states adhered to nationalism and heedlessly made a path toward World War I, the papacy gave Catholic just war thinking a radical turn. The founder of modern Catholic peace ethics was an Italian Jesuit, Luigi Taparelli d'Azeglio (1793–1862). During the 1820s he became teacher of Vincenzo

75 Cf. Beestermöller, Gerhard, *Krieg gegen den Irak – Rückkehr in die Anarchie der Staatenwelt?* Stuttgart: Kohlhammer, 2003, 53–67.

76 Francisco de Vitoria, "On the Law of War," in: Edition Pagden, 313.

77 The Social Doctrine of the Russian Orthodox Church, VIII, 5.

78 Francisco de Vitoria, "On the Law of War," in: Edition Pagden, 313.

Pecci, later elected Pope Leo XIII. Taparelli understood the necessity of a functioning international law and the creation of a true global community in times of the globalizing economy of the late 19th century. As sovereign and equal members, the states should form a community (*ethnarchia*) and create a functioning international law. To be effective, according to Taparelli, this law needs instruments of jurisdiction, a court of law and law enforcement. War was only to be legitimized against an aggressor; it should be authorized by the 'ethnarchy'—the organized community of states.[79] In Taparelli's thinking we find some key ideas of Woodrow Wilson's "League of Nations," as well as of Pope Benedict XV.'s quest of for effective international law as prevention aganist any aggression.

The elected pope at the eve of World War I, Pope Benedict XV, was confronted with the claims of Catholics in Germany, Hungaro-Austria and France to fight a just war against each other with disastrous consequences, cheered by their bishops on different sides of the trench. Benedict's various attempts to arbitrate between the warring parties as well as his appeals to stop the fighting all ended in vain. In 1917 he finally launched a diplomatic peace initiative called "Dès le début." He suggested a completely new international organization to overcome war once and for all. Key was his suggestion to create a "federation of nations" (*nationes foederatae*). Benedict demanded that the material force of violence should be replaced by the "moral power of law."[80] In accordance to Taparelli he saw an effective and mandatory international jurisdiction as crucial; with this quest he went far beyond the authority of the Permanent International Court of Law, created in 1919 as part of the new League of Nations. Benedict asked for sanctions without determining them precisely, when he stated: "... sanctions (should) be set against the state that refuses either to submit the international issues under arbitration or to accept the decisions" of this court.[81] Within such a functioning international legal system, arms should be reduced dramatically.

One generation later, it was again the experience of a horrid war that forced a pope to rethink the Church's position. Eugenio Pacelli, who had lobbied for Benedict XV.'s peace plan in 1917, was elected pope in 1939 and immediately

---

79 Cf. Schrage, Marco, "Luigi Taparellis Entwurf einer weltweiten Friedensordnung," *Theologie und Philosophie* 94 (2019), 367–402.

80 "qu'à la force matérielle des armes soit substituée là force morale du droit": Benedict XV., "Dès le début," in: http://w2.vatican.va/content/benedict-xv/fr/apost_exhortations/documents/hf_ben-xv_exh_19170801_des-le-debut.html (accessed 2. Aug. 2019); originally in French, translation HGJ.

81 Ibid.

challenged by Hitler's war. While arguing along the way that was paved by his predecessors, on Christmas 1944 Pope Pius XII. (1939–1958) deliberately dropped the traditional idea of just war as legitimate means to restore law. To the contrary, he requested that the nascent United Nations Organization should "do everything possible to proscribe and ban once and for all the aggressive war as legitimate solution of international controversies and as instrument of national aspirations."[82] His successor Pope John XXIII (1958–1963) was even more clear, and challenged the international community to enhance the UN to become an effective and global political authority:

> Today the universal common good presents us with problems that are world-wide in their dimensions; problems, therefore, which cannot be solved except by a public authority with power, organization and means co-extensive with these problems, and with a worldwide sphere of activity. Consequently, the moral order itself demands the establishment of some such general form of public authority.[83]

This global public authority shall not "be imposed by force" but rather "be set up with the consent of all nations." Criteria of this authority are "fairness, absolute impartiality" and "dedication to the common good of all peoples." Ever since, the popes have repeated this quest—without clarifying the shape of the public authority for the international common good.[84]

It has become clear that the papacy of the 20th century has undergone what could be called a Copernican revolution in just war thinking. The focus has shifted to a more constructive peace thinking, with enormous skepticism against any form of legitimization of war.[85] This becomes obvious with Pope John Paul II., who as a young man in Poland suffered under the German occupation and was well aware that peoples and states have a right to self-defense. Still, he remained sceptical of hasty calls for armed resistance and encouraged the search

---

82 "… di fare cioè tutto quanto possibile per proscrivere e bandire una volta per sempre la guerra di aggressione come soluzione legittima delle controversie internazionali e come strumento di aspirazioni nazionali." Pius XII, "Radiomessagio di sua Santità Pio XII ai popoli del mondo interno 24.12.1944", in: http://w2.vatican.va/content/pius-xii/it/speeches/1944/documents/hf_p-xii_spe_19441224_natale.html: (accessed 2. August 2019) Originally in Italian.

83 John XXIII, *Pacem in Terris* Nr. 137, in: http://www.vatican.va/content/john-xxiii/en/encyclicals/documents/hf_j-xxiii_enc_11041963_pacem.html (accessed 1. April 2020).

84 Cf. Justenhoven, Heinz-Gerhard/O'Connell, Mary Ellen (eds), *Peace through Law: Reflections on Pacem in terris from Philosophy, Law, Theology, and Political Science*, Baden-Baden: Nomos, 2016.

85 Nigal Biggar, Anglican Professor of theology at the University of Oxford, notes with regret the same attitude for the Anglican Church and theology: cf. Biggar, Nigal, "Between Development and Doubt," 59–61.

for peaceful means of resistance. At the same time, one of his focusses had become reconciliation. He understood how historical experience of injustice bears new hatred and violence. Thus, he challenged his own church to do the first step: with regard to the Orthodox Church, Evangelical Churches, the Jewish and the Muslim community and indigenous inhabitants of Latin America for example.[86]

8 Integration of the Just War Criteria Into the Guidelines of a 'Just Peace'

The Catholic and Evangelical Churches, especially in Germany, have been struggling to redefine their position after the horrors of World War II and with the beginning of the Cold War.[87] There are different trends ranging from pacifism to just war advocates, that struggle to define common ground. One position that emerged in the debates of the diverse academic and church deliberations is the transformation of the 'just war theory' into what is now called the 'guidelines for just peace.'[88] While the term 'just peace' is much older, it came into more general use in church documents of the 1980s[89] and has been used by the 'Ecumenical Assembly for Justice, Peace and Integrity of Creation' in the (East) German Democratic Republic (GDR) in Dresden 1988.[90] Being a term of church documents at the beginning, 'just peace' found a broader reception in theological literature thereafter, being cited as a normative idea that guided politics. Its components are first of all the "insoluble interdependence of justice and peace"[91] in a normative sense, mostly explained with regard to the biblical term *shalom*.[92]

---

86 Cf. Justenhoven, Heinz-Gerhard, "The Peace Ethics of Pope John Paul II.," in: Justenhoven/ Barbieri, *From Just War to Modern Peace Ethics*, 313–433.

87 Cf. Kronenberg, Ulrich, *Gerechter Frieden – Gerechter Krieg? Chancen und Grenzen zweier friedensethischer Denkmodelle*, Leipzig: Evangelische Verlagsanstalt, 2019, 17–48.

88 Cf. Eine Denkschrift des Rates der Evangelischen Kirche in Deutschland, *Aus Gottes Frieden leben – den gerechten Frieden denken*, Gütersloh: Gütersloher Verlagshaus 2007, Nr. 1; and: The German Bishops, *A Just Peace*, 27. September 2000, Bonn 2000, Nr. 59, in: https://www.dbk-shop.de/media/files_public/cgnjfnbo/DBK_1166001.pdf, (accessed 1. April 2020).

89 Cf. United Methodist Bishops, "In Defense of Creation: Nuclear Crisis and a Just Peace," *Origins* 16 (1986/87), 16–20.

90 See full text: http://oikoumene.net/home/regional/dresden/dmd.3/textsearch/index.html, (accessed 1. April 2020).

91 Reuter, Hans-Richard, "Was ist gerechter Friede? Die Sicht der christlichen Ethik," in: Hans-Richard Reuter, *Recht und Frieden. Beiträge zur politischen Theologie*, Leipzig: Evangelische Verlagsanstalt, 12 (engl. translation HGJ.)

92 Cf. Huber, Wolfgang/Reuter, Hans-Richard, *Friedensethik*, Stuttgart: Kohlhammer, 1990, 35.

The second aspect is the reliance on (international) law and the respective institutions (such as the United Nations) to secure peace between states and within states. This aspect is also strongly emphasized by Richard Harries, Anglican Bishop of Oxford (1987–2006), in his criticism of the British government regarding the legitimacy of the 2003 Iraq war.[93] A third aspect is post-conflict care, mostly called peacebuilding. The Catholic and the Evangelical position are in close correspondence with regard to this determination.[94] The just peace concept has largely determinated the work of the ecumenical World Council of Churches during the last decades.[95] Through the Council's work, the concept of just peace was formally endorsed by the Anglican Church of Canada in 2004,[96] to cite just one example of how the idea spread throughout the ecumenical world, even in Orthodox Churches.[97]

The biblical reference and eschatological dimension of the term 'just peace' should enable the churches to be a critical voice vis-à-vis the ruling order in anticipation of the messianic peace, as the German Catholic bishops summarized:

> the peace of the messianic people of God presupposes the miracle that man has implicit trust in God and his fellow man and is in a position to renounce the use of violence. Only faith can perceive a miracle that transcends reason such as this. However, reason can admit that the attitude born of this miracle can help overcome the limitations of an order protected by the threat of violence. Thus, faith can help reason to surpass itself without abdicating reasonableness. Faith encourages and propels reason to take the initial steps towards a messianic peace within the existing system in order to create a more reasonable and humane world.[98]

Ending violence and initiating political and social justice as indispensable prerequisite to bring about political peace is the ethical demand resulting from eschatological hope.

---

93 Harries, Richard, "The Continuing Crucial Relevance of Just War Criteria," in: Timothy Blewett/Adrian Hyde-Price/Wyn Rees (eds), *British Foreign Policy and the Anglican Church*, Aldershot: Ashgate Publishing, 2008, 32f.

94 Cf. The German Bishops, *A Just Peace*, Chapter II.

95 Cf. *An Ecumenical Call to Just Peace*, World Council of Churches (ed.), Geneva 2011; http://www.overcomingviolence.org/fileadmin/dov/files/iepc/resources/ECJustPeace_English.pdf (accessed 3. April, 2020); largely documented also through the work of it's Secretary Generals Willem Vissert Hofft and Konrad Raiser.

96 Cf. Ingham, Michael, *No War, Just War, Just Peace: Statements by the Anglican Church of Canada 1934–2004*, https://ploughshares.ca/pl_publications/no-war-just-war-just-peace-statements-by-the-anglican-church-of-canada-1934–2004/, (accessed 3. April 2020).

97 Cf. Asfaw, Semegnish/Chehadeh, Alexius/Simion, Marian G. (eds), *Just Peace: Orthodox Perspectives*, Geneva: World Council of Churches Publications, 2012.

98 The German Bischops, *A Just Peace*, Nr. 56.

Human security in a broad sense has to be the focus of politics and therefore the constitutional factor of a "qualitatively contentful peace."[99] It is to be realized first of all in the constitution of a functioning national as well as international legal order. In doing so, the idea of a just peace can be transferred into internationally agreed rules—the international law and the legal institutions. Hans Richard Reuter defines three aspects that the national and international legal order must achieve: protection against physical violence, promotion of liberty and reduction of poverty.[100] As international law is agreed on by all UN-member states, complying with international law to promote peace becomes a moral duty. However, the problem of conflict as a sociological data remains wherever human beings live together. The moral challenge is not to avoid conflict, but rather the solution of conflicts in a humane and civil manner.[101] Citizens obey the law as long and insofar as they understand the moral foundation of law in guaranteeing the citizen's freedom and security; and as long as law is binding impartially all citizens. In cases of severe conflicts or statutory violations, the ultimate means is to bring a case to court. Conflict resolution on the basis of law is the precondition for a minimum political peace, assuming functioning legal institutions and law enforcement. The church documents struggle with the challenge of ineffective conflict resolution in the international arenas as well as in fragile states. On the one hand one must see the reality of sovereign states, on the other hand all UN-member states have signed the UN-Charter agreeing to solve their conflicts without recourse to force. Out of the perspective of just peace, the 'Peace Memorandum of the Evangelical Church in Germany' argues for a cooperative global order on the basis of international law without a world government. The means of this cooperative global order are regional and global institutions, as well as global policy. "Through enhanced policy coordination and juridification, they promote substantial interdependence between states."[102] Within this framework, the Peace Memorandum argues, matters of the use of force to prevent aggression and protection against severe human rights violations have to be dealt with. The presupposition of this is the independent and willing cooperation of all relevant actors. But what about spoilers cancelling cooperation and dismissing international juridication? In this case—and this is

99 Huber, Wolfgang, "Rückkehr zur Lehre vom Gerechten Krieg? Aktuelle Entwicklungen in der Evangelischen Friedensethik," *Zeitschrift für Evangelische Ethik* 49,2 (2005), 120 (engl. translation HGJ).

100 Cf. Reuter, "Was ist ein gerechter Friede?" 16 f.

101 Cf. Overbeck, Franz Josef, *Konstruktive Konfliktkultur: Friedensethische Standortbestimmung des Katholischen Militärbischofs für die Deutsche Bundeswehr*, Freiburg i.Br.: Herder, 2019, 67–81.

102 *Aus Gottes Frieden leben – den gerechten Frieden denken*, 58 (translation: HGJ).

the reality of today's international system—the guidelines of just peace leave us without systematic answer. The issue of impartial and effective international law enforcement to structurally overcome war has yet to be dealt with.[103]

From the beginning, the most fiercely debated issue has been, and remains, the issue of the use of military force. While the pacifist wings in both churches advocate conscientious objection, nonviolent resistance and the dissolution of armies even in times of the Cold War[104], the majority tried to integrate the individual as well as the collective right of self-defense into just peace thinking. The nuclear strategy of NATO and the Warsaw Pact threatening each other with nuclear destruction resulted in a moral dilemma: while most theologians in the West justified NATO's nuclear strategy of threatening with a nuclear war to prevent it, there was a consensus at the same time that any nuclear war was disproportionate and non-discriminatory, i.e. killing civilians and combatants without differentiating.[105] While reverence for collective security within the UN system was more of a theoretical nature until 1989, after the end of the Cold War the idea of peace enforcement through UN mandated military missions became more of a reality. In particular the cruel violence against civilians, war crimes and humanitarian catastrophes in Northern Kurdistan, Somalia, Bosnia and Kosovo inflamed the public cries for military or humanitarian intervention even in reluctant societies such as in Germany. The systematic position as in the Peace Memorandum of the Evangelical Church in Germany integrated the use of military force into the perspective of a global legal order: military force can only be morally acceptable if it aims to enforce or maintain international law as "law preserving force," und thus serves human security at large.[106] Within this systematic framework the traditional just war criteria could be integrated, now called "criteria of an ethics of law preserving force."[107] The Peace Memorandum of the Evangelical Church in Germany summarized this position in 2007:

> Modern international law has abolished the concept of a just war. The doctrine of *bellum iustum* no longer has a place within the framework of the ideal of a just peace. It does

103 Cf. Overbeck, *Konstruktive Konfliktkultur*, 80.
104 Cf. Die Feuersteiner Erklärung der Pax-Christi-Delegiertenversammlung 1986: "Gewaltfrei widerstehen – Kriegsdienste verweigern – Abschreckung überwinden," *Junge Kirche* 48 (1987), 350–54.
105 See the discussion in Schockenhoff, Eberhard, *Kein Ende der Gewalt. Friedensethik für eine globalisierte Welt*, 332–91.
106 *Aus Gottes Frieden leben – den gerechten Frieden denken*, 70. The text was drafted by Hans-Richard Reuter: compare with: Reuter, "Was ist ein gerechter Friede?" 15–25.
107 Cf. *Aus Gottes Frieden leben – für gerechten Frieden sorgen*, 68 (engl. translation HGJ).

> not follow, however, that the moral criteria that were contained in the bellum iustum doctrines must therefore be abolished—or that it is permissible to abolish them.[108]

While the Evangelical and the Catholic Churches in Germany developed their 'just peace' teaching, the debate in the Anglo-Saxon realm undertook a recovery of the just war tradition, initiated by Paul Ramsey.

9 The Anglo-Saxon Revival of the 'Just War Theory'

Just war reasoning had become prominent in Europe again during World War I, as bishops, clergy, army, civilians and intellectuals argued for the just cause of their side[109] without contemplating the fact of the moral dilemma of a 'just war on both sides.' Most of them had an apologetic character. A systematically more interesting just war debate occurred in the 1960s in the United States.[110] Its beginning is indebted to the Methodist theologian Paul Ramsey, Professor at Princeton University. He re-introduced the just war criteria in the emerging debate on nuclear weapons to bridge the pacifist anti-nuclear position with the purely political arguments of the proponents of the nuclear strategy.[111] Using just war criteria, Ramsey intended to fill the gap in both debates: to his understanding, the pacifist debate lacked political realism, while the political debate was largely led without moral arguments. On the pacifist side, the prospect of a nuclear war causing the annihilation of humankind and any life on earth had led some to argue that any alternative would be preferable, including the submission to Russian tyranny. At the same time, official US security policy was to threaten 'massive retaliation' with nuclear weapons if needed.Ramsey

---

108 *Aus Gottes Frieden leben – für gerechten Frieden sorgen*, 102. English translation quoted from: Lienemann, Wolfgang, "International Peace as legal Order," in: Ad de Bruijne/Gerard den Hertog (eds), *The Present "Just Peace/Just War" Debate*, Leipzig, Evangelische Verlagsanstalt, 2018, 44.

109 Cf. Missalla, Heinrich, *Gott mit uns. Die deutsche katholische Kriegspredigt 1914–1918*, München: Kösel, 1968; Fuchs, Stephan, *"Vom Segen des Krieges": Katholische Gebildete im Ersten Weltkrieg*, Stuttgart: Steiner, 2004.

110 Wolfgang Lienemann sees a continuous pro just war argumentation in the Anglo-Saxon world from Reinhold Niebuhr to Paul Ramsey, Nigel Biggar, David Fischer and James Turner Johnson. Cf. Lienemann, Wolfgang, "International Peace as Legal Order," 37.

111 Cf. Ramsey, Paul, *War and Christian Conscience: How Shall Modern War Be Conducted Justly?* Durham: Duke University Press, 1961.

saw the need to find a responsible moral position grounded in Christian ethics between unlimited nuclear warfare and the total abolition of force in face of the political threat.[112] With recourse to Augustine's just war thinking and Father John Ford's 1944 article on "The Morality of Obliteration Bombing"[113], Ramsey introduced the traditional criteria of non-combatant immunity (criterion of discrimination) and proportionality into the debate on nuclear weapons. In so doing he delivered moral arguments for the limitation of modern warfare. Later, Ramsey developed the highly critized argument that nuclear deterrence served to prevent war and could be understood as a result of Christian love: "It is no part of the work of charity to allow this [oppression] to continue to happen. Instead, it is the work of love and mercy to deliver as many as possible of God's children from tyranny ..."[114] This position was fiercly criticized by peace groups and activists like Pax Christi, the International Catholic Peace movement.[115]

With his recourse to the just war tradition, Paul Ramsey certainly contributed to the moral debate on security policy.[116] On the other hand, it is striking that he referred only to the *ius in bello* criteria (discrimination and proportionality), while completely disregarding the *ius ad bellum* criteria that had played an important role throughout the history of just war thinking. For classical authors like Thomas Aquinas or Francisco de Vitoria, the justice of a war depended on the right authority and the just cause, as well as on the adequacy of force i.e. proportionality in relation to the intended end of the war, peace and tranquility.

10 Moral versus Juridical *ius ad bellum* Arguments

The debate on *ius ad bellum* emerged at the end of the 20th century under very different circumstances. After the end of the Cold War, a short period of renewed cooperation within the United Nations Organization had begun. The idea of enforcing international law against aggressive regimes under the umbrella of the

---

112 Cf. Ramsey, *War and Christian Conscience*, 134.

113 Ford, John C., "The Morality of Obliteration Bombing," *Theological Studies* 5 (1944), 261–309.

114 Ramsey, Paul, *The Just War. Force and Responsibility*, New York: Saribner, 1968, 143.

115 Cf. McNeil, Particia F., *Harder than War: Catholic Peacemaking in Twentieth-Century America*, New Brunswick/NJ, Rutgers University Press, 1992,

116 Cf. Johnson, James Turner, "Paul Ramsey and the Recovery of the Just War Idea," *Journal of Military Ethics* 1 (2002), 136–44.

United Nations received broad acceptance. In January 1991 the UN Security Council issued UN-resolution 678 to mandate the US-led coalition to force Saddam Hussein's army out of Kuwait, which his army had conquered some month earlier. The mainstream of intellectuals referring to the just war theory argued the UN-Security Council to be the right authority to decide on the justice of the cause. Others found it more plausible that the US government should be seen as the right authority "as the country's lawful political leaders of the nation held the responsibility for choosing to use force for the common good."[117] While the mainstream position could refer to the United Nations' responsibility for the international common good, the later position voted for a national government to take the responsibility of defending (international) common values or even the common good. In doing so they left the door open for a moral dilemma: in any war the opposing sides could each claim to fight a just war when the respective government had decided to do so, as happened at the beginning of World War I in Europe. If so, the dilemma of a "just war on both sides" is unsurmountable, as Francisco de Vitoria had already stated in his famous lecture "De iure belli" in 1539. Vitoria excluded this possibility, warning the governments against hastily claiming the righteousness of their case.[118] There is no real proof on who is right here. Even if the argument is striking that the violations of international law by Saddam Hussein were obvious, given his intervention into a sovereign state in order to acquire Kuwait's oil reserves, the systematic problem remains as to who has the right to decide legally and morally about the use of military force in the interest of the international common good, and not only in partial interest: national governments first of all are entitled to make decisions in the interest of their people, not for the international common good. And exactly this has happened with regard to the Gulf War. Anthony J. Coates argued that "even when an individual state acts ostensibly on his own behalf, if it acts in defence of its legitimate interests or in vindication of its rights, it acts at the same time as the agent and representative of the international community."[119] But he himself points to the fact that this did not happen:

> Far from upholding the authority of the United Nations, the United States and its allies (principally Britain) did their best to undermine the efforts of the Secretary General Javier Pérez de Cuéllar to maintain U.N. control and to achieve a diplomatic solution to the crisis.

---

117 Cole, Darrell, "The first and the Second Gulf Wars," in: Mark David Hall/Daryl Charles (eds), *America and the Just War Tradition: A History of U.S. Conflicts*, Notre Dame, Indiana: University of Notre Dame Press, 2019, 253.

118 Cf. Francisco de Vitoria, "De iure belli," in: *Vitoria, Vorlesungen II*, 577.

119 Coates, Anthony J., *The Ethics of War*, Manchester: Manchester University Press, 1997, 128.

> The aim, and the reality, was one of autonomous action by the United States and its subordinates.[120]

The cooperation in the Security Council was tested during the following years simply due to the fact that even UN mandated wars were executed by armies under national command without any effective control by the UN. It is not surprising that the strategic goals of national governments deploying troops have a decisive impact on the outcome of a war. Even though the (more or less) impartial authority of the UN Security Council mandated the use of military force, it was left to the UN member states to realize the military action and thus to persue their partial interests at the same time. At the moment, there is no solution to this moral dilemma within the UN system. and it weakens the credibility of the just war argumentation. Even though the UN Charter has provided the establishment of a UN Military Staff Committee (UN Charter Art 47[121]), it was never institutionalized, due to the unwillingness of the UN member states. The problem of arguing in favor of a national government as the rightful authority is that in this case the just war theory has no criterion to counter its misuse by partial interests, as the debate on the Kosovo intervention has shown.

The at times fierce debate on NATO's Kosovo intervention has brought up a new issue: What if the "just authority," the Security Council, is in disagreement and thus does not come to a conclusion even in case of a grave humanitarian catastrophe. Most political observers expected in 1999 an "ethnic cleansing" against the Kosovar Albanians by Serbian militias and regular troops in Kosovo similar to the one that occured some years earlier in Bosnia. The public debate in most Western countries expected their politicians to act to prevent a second "Srebrencia," when Serbian militias killed thousands of Bosnian men in view of the world without being hindered by an effective intervention.[122] The German philosopher Otfried Höffe argued that legal authority—the UN Security Council—had dropped out and a state of emergency had to be declared, meaning that a humanitarian intervention was morally required. He argued that emergency relief in the sense of defense of a third person or party is morally required from whomever is able to provide it. Höffe presents his argument by way of an analogy be-

---

120 Coates, Anthony J., "Just War in the Persian Gulf?" in: Andrew Valls (ed.), *Ethics in International Affairs: Theories and Cases*, Lanham et. al.: Rowman & Littlefield Publishers, 2000, 35.
121 Cf. https://treaties.un.org/doc/publication/ctc/uncharter.pdf (accessed 6. March 2020).
122 Cf. the collection of church documents of this debate in: Buchbender, Ortwin/Arnold, Gerhard (eds), *Kämpfen für die Menschenrechte: Der Kosovo-Konflikt im Spiegel der Friedensethik*, Baden-Baden: Nomos, 2002.

tween an individual's defense of another person and the collective defense of states, peoples or minorities in imminent danger.[123]

Jean Bethke Elshtain couches the argument for authority in this debate somewhat differently. While being a political scientist, Elshtian relies with her just war reasoning on St. Augustine's *De civitate dei.* Elshtain makes recourse to Augustine's argument to save "the innocent from certain harm," and relates it in the first instance to the duty of governments to protect their people, and secondarily to the need to help "a nation or people incapable of defending themselves against a determined adversary."[124] The just cause according to Elshtain exists when the "ill treatment–killings, rapes, torture, displacement–adds up to a humanitarian catastrophe."[125] The rightful authority, in lack of unity and therefore a mandate of the UN Security Council, seems at hand: "NATO makes up a legitimately constituted concert of states and therefore, has authority to act, if need be, for humanitarian reasons and in a collective self-defense, protecting the whole idea of a European community of nations."[126] According to Elshtain, the morality of the case is given and therefore whoever is willing to act in defense of the moral values at stake, is morally entitled to do so. The crucial aspect of Elshtain's argumentation is that she uses a moral argument to buttress the legal system, as opponents of the intervention like Dieter S. Lutz or Jürgen Habermas have pointed out.[127] Morality is used to disqualify objections: "If we have to use force, it is because we are America. We are the indispensable nation. We stand tall. We see further into the future," as former Secretary of State Madeleine Albright stated in 1998 in the context of the Iraq crisis.[128] This position of moral exceptionalism heralds the end of international law as a rule-based order accepted by the consent of the community of states, all the more so as the moral exceptionalism is not free from partial national interests, as the 'humanitarian wars' since the 1990s have proven.

---

123 Cf. Höffe, Otfried, "Humanitäre Intervention? Rechtsethische Überlegungen," in: Gerhard Beestermöller (ed)., *Die humanitäre Intervention – Imperativ der Menschenrechtsidee? Rechtsethische Reflexionen am Beispiel des Kosovo-Krieges*, Stuttgart: Kohlhammer, 2003, 11–28.

124 Elshtain, Jean Bethke, "Kosovo and the Just-War Tradition," in: William Joseph Buckley (ed.), *Kosovo. Contenting Voices on Balkan Interventions*, Grand Rapids, MI: William B. Eerdmans Publishing, 2000, 363.

125 Elshtain, "Kosovo," 364.

126 Elshtain, "Kosovo," 354.

127 Cf. Lutz, Dieter S., "Wohin treibt (uns) die NATO?" in: Dieter S. Lutz (ed.), *Der Kosovo-Krieg: Rechtliche und rechtsethische Aspekte*, Baden-Baden: Nomos, 1999/2000, 111–28. Habermas, Jürgen, "Von der Machtpolitik zur Weltbürgergesellschaft," in: Jürgen Habermas, *Zeit der Übergänge*, Frankfurt/M: Suhrkamp, 2001, 27–39.

128 Herbert, Bob, "War Games," in: *New York Times*, February 2, 1998

The opposing position was articulated juridically: the UN Security Council had admittedly determined a threat to world peace, without however agreeing on military measures due to the Russian refusal. NATO's air attack on Serbia to stop its army and Serbian militias in Kosovo was considered illegal according to a majority of international lawyers,[129] and UN Secretary General Kofi Annan reminded NATO of the requirement of a mandate of the UN-Security Council.[130] Furthermore, the opponents of NATO intervention pointed to the fact that partial interests—of the West—were at the forefront, misusing the humanitarian argument to overrun the international legal order and pursuing goals counterproductive to the international common good.[131] The argument was made that NATO and the US, in particular, were more interested in reducing Russia's and Serbia's influence on the Balkans and installing a government in Kosovo with friendly ties to the West than in human rights.[132]

The terrorist attacks on the World Trade Center in New York City on September 11, 2001, marked a turning point, not only with regard to the perception of an unknown threat but also for the just war debates.[133] In her 2003 study *Just war Against Terror. The Burden of American Power in a Violent World*, Jean Bethke Elshtain elaborated her thesis of American exceptionalism having the authority to wage war in the common interest, this time against jihadist terrorism in Afghanistan. The systematic point of Elshtain's argument once more is the security of the individual. While in the Kosovo case the responsible Serbian government in Belgrade not only neglected the security of their Kosovar Albanan citizens but in fact were the originator of their suffering, in the case of the terror attacks of 9/11 it was now up to the US government to protect the American people from further harm and thus provide security, which Elshtain—again with recourse to Augus-

---

129 Cf. Charney, Jonathan I., "Anticipatory Humanitarian Intervention in Kosovo," in: *American Journal of International Law* 93 (1999), 834–41.

130 Simma, Bruno, "Die NATO, die UN und militärische Gewaltanwendung: Rechtliche Aspekte," in: Reinhard Merkel (ed.), *Der Kosovo-Krieg und das Völkerrecht*, Frankfurt/M: Suhrkamp, 2000, 9–50.

131 Cf. Grube, Falko, *Menschenrechte als Ideologie: Die Rolle der Menschenrechte bei der Legitimation militärischer Interventionen*, Baden-Baden: Nomos, 2010, 210–49.

132 Kurt Gritsch gives an excellent analysis of the arguments in favor of the intervention; cf. Gritsch, Kurt, *Inszenierung eines gerechten Krieges: Intellektuelle, Medien und der "Kosovo-Krieg,"* Hildesheim: Olms, 2010.

133 Cf. for example the analysis of (mostly German) church documents by: Kirchschlager, Bernd, *Kirche und Friedenspolitik nach dem 11. September 2001 Protestantische Stellungnahmen und Diskurse im diachronen und ökumenischen Vergleich*, Göttingen: Ruprecht, 2007.

tine—proves to be the "primary responsibility of government,"[134] as it is without "civic peace—a basic framework of settled law and simple, everyday order—human life descends to its most primitive level".[135] Thus following Augustine, Elshtain argues that it is in accordance with the Christian message of Jesus, the Prince of Peace, who resisted in taking up arms on his own behalf, that governments have to take up arms on behalf of those that need protection and security.[136] Elshtain sees the world in a situation where international law exists only in theory but not in practice, and argues for the tragic duty of governments to use force against jihadist terrorists, protecting those who want to live in peace. "The right authority criterion was met," Elshtain states, "when both houses of the U.S. Congress authorized statutes and appropriated monies for the war effort." An additional argument is the US government's recourse to UN Charter Article 51, the right of self-defense, which was approved by the UN Security Council. Unfortunately, one does not read any suggestions from Elshtain about what to do to enhance international institutions beyond describing their deficits.[137]

Regarding the just cause, Elshtain interprets the terror attacks of 9/11 as "an act of aggression aimed specially at killing civilians."[138] As it aimed at disrupting peace and tranquility, it is up to governments to enact justice: "Preventing further harm and restoring the preconditions for civic tranquility is a justifiable *casus belli.*"[139] A supportive argument for the *jus ad bellum* against the Taliban, according to Elshtain, is their irresponsible government under which the Afghan people had to suffer: a comparably high degree of hunger, child and motherhood mortality, lack of basic health service and education amount to the conclusion: "Examining the evidence, we can see that the U.S. military response in Afghanistan clearly meets the just cause criterion of being a war fought with right intention—to punish the wrongdoers and to prevent them from murdering civilians in

---

134 Elshtain, Jean Bethke, *Just War Against Terror. The Burden of American Power in a Violent World*, New York: Perseus Books, 2003, 46.

135 Elshtain, *Just War against Terror*, 48.

136 The American Calvinist theologian Darrell Cole argues similarly without mentioning the development in international law: "For a war to be just, it must be declared and waged by someone who truly has the authority to do so. No matter how large a following you may have behind you, if you aren't the sovereign leader of the land, you cannot declare war – at least not a just war." Cole, Darrell, *When God Says War is Right: The Christian's Perspective on When and How to Fight*, Colorado Springs/CO: Waterbrooks Press, 2002, 78.

137 Cf. Elshtain, Jean Bethke, "International Justice as Equal Regard and the Use of Force," in: Gerhard Beestermöller/Michael Haspel/Uwe Trittmann, *"What we are fighting for ... ". Friedensethik in der transatlantischen Debatte*, Stuttgart: Kohlhammer, 2006, 31 f.

138 Elshtain, *Just War Against Terror*, 59.

139 Ibid.

the future."[140] Elshtain's idea behind her just war reasoning is that all human beings have equal rights. Whenever human rights are violated, this "constitutes a *prima facie* justice claim."[141] Elshtain argues that there may be no difference with regard to the justice claim between a state's own citizens and the citizens of a foreign country and labels it the "equal regard" criterion. Thus she also calls for "the use of force as a remedy under a justice claim based on equal regard and inviolable human dignity."[142] According to her theory, depending on the circumstances someone who has the power should respond to this justice claim considering prudential and consequential concerns.

Even the criterion of last resort seems evident for Elshtain: "What is to do with the likes of bin Laden and Al Qaeda? ... They are not parties to any structure of diplomacy and thus cannot be negotiated with; in any event, because what they seek is our destruction, there is nothing to negotiate about."[143] If "there is nothing to negotiate about," what else than violence will prevail in international relations? It is exactly this position that is convincingly refuted by the Anglican Archbishop Rowan Williams of Canterbury. Assuming the identity of national interests to the international common good, according to Rowan Williams, leads to the misperception of the fundamental idea of Thomas Aquinas's just war teaching: "violence is not to be undertaken by private persons. If a state or administration acts without due and visible attention to agreed international process, it acts in a way analogous to a private person. It purports to be judge of its own interest."[144] With her position, Elshtain in fact legitimizes the Bush government's policy of undermining the prohibition of force of the UN Charter (Article 2,4) and heading to war if it is in the national interest without considering the consequences:[145] If it is allowed to one power, it is allowed to all who wish to do so; the result is less security rather than more. Elshtain's reading of the just war tradition not only helps to destroy collective security but also diminishes international security.

140 Elshtain, *Just War Against Terror*, 61.
141 Elshtain, Jean Bethke, "International Justice as Equal Regard and the Use of Force," 28.
142 Ibid.
143 Elshtain, *Just War against Terror*, 61.
144 Williams, Rowan, *Just War Revisited.* A Lecture by the Archbishop of Canterbury, Dr. Rowan Williams, to the Royal Institute for International Affairs, Chatham House 14. October 2003, 2, in: aoc2013.brix.fatbeehive.com/articles.php/1827/just-war-revisited-archbishops-lecture-to-the-royal-institute-for-international-affairs (20. April 2020).
145 Cf. Krisch, Nico, "The Rise and Fall of Collective Security: Terrorism, US Hegemony, and the Plight of the Security Council," in: Christian Walter et. al. (eds), *Terrorism as a Challenge for National and International Law: Security versus Liberty?* Berlin: Springer, 2004, 879.

11 The *ius in bello* Discourse of the Revisited Just War Theory

The revisionist just war discourse[146] did not occur explicitly within Christian ethics, but it has influenced it. Its most outspoken representative is the US-American moral philosopher Jeff McMahan. In contrast to Michael Walzer, he holds the position that war does not have its own moral rules. According to McMahan war and killing in civilian life are governed by the same ethics:

> ... the justifications for killing people in war are of the same form as the justifications for the killing of persons in other contexts. The difference between war and other forms of conflict is a difference only of degree and thus the moral principles that govern killing in lesser forms of conflict govern killing in war as well. The state of war makes no difference other than to make the application of the relevant principles more complicated and difficult because of the number of people involved ...[147]

McMahan's pivotal moral concern is the permission to attack and probably kill an opponent in war given the basic proposition of the immorality of killing a human being.

To explain when and why a person may be attacked and as consequence be killed, McMahan borrows the term "liable" from civil law into ethics: "Liable to attack" refers to a person who has committed an act in violation of a moral norm and in consequence is morally responsible for the imminent damage. McMahan's idea is that the doer himself bears the responsibility for the damage: if one overturns a valuable piece of art—on purpose or unintentionally—, he is liable for the damage. This legal figure is the basis for McMahan's moral consideration of a person committing an aggression for example and thus being liable to attack, i.e. bearing the moral responsibility for the damage he may suffer from being rightfully repelled by force.[148] According to McMahan there is no difference in the first place whether the person is liable to attack because of a damage committed on purpose or unintentionally when a risk is approved. But the "extent to which a person is excused for posing a threat of wrongful harm affects the degree of his moral liability to defensive harm, which in turn affects the stringency

146 With regard to McMahan's argumentation, I largely follow Bernhard Koch: Koch, Bernhard, *Der Gegner als Mitmensch: Michael Walzer, Jeff McMahan und die ethische Kritik am Humanitären Völkerecht*, Habil., Albert-Ludwigs-Universität Freiburg, 2020.
147 McMahan, Jeff, *Killing in War*, Oxford: Clarendon Press 2009, 156.
148 Cf. Ibid., 32f.

of the proportionality restriction on defensive force."[149] The stronger the reasons for the excuses are, the weaker is the liability to attack. McMahan differentiates three categories of reasons for excuses: duress, epistemic limitations and diminished responsibility. Without any excuses there is full liability to attack, in case of complete excuse the liability to attack is omitted. Stating this, McMahan leaves no room for retaliation or revenge.

Who then is liable to attack in a just war? According to McMahan, a war is only justified as defense: against an imminent attack of a foreign military aggression or against an imminent attack of whatever forces against the civilian population; a humanitarian intervention. In any other case the combatants are unjustified; McMahan calls them "unjust combatants." They constitute a threat for the attacked and thus McMahan calls unjust combatants "threats". Nonetheless, unjust combatants may be excused in different regards and therefore are differently liable to attack. To investigate the different degrees of liability and thus the different degree of justified defense, McMahan distinguishes five types of threats:[150] 1.) "Culpable Threat" is one who intentionally and fully consciously attacks another person. 2.) "Partially Excused Threat" are usually those combatants who are not fully aware of the injustice of the war they are fighting.

3.) "Excused Threat" is a combatant with a higher degree of ignorance or similar excusable reasons such as combatants who were forced to fight or similar hardships. 3a.) "Innocent Threat" could be someone who had no intention to harm and could not foresee any harmful consequence, which in reality hardly ever happens to a combatant. 4.) "Nonresponsible Threat" is one who poses a threat to another person without being responsible for the act that produces the threat. 5.) "Justified Threat" finally is the justified combatant who fights for the just cause. He may pose a proportionate threat to the unjustified combatant; proportionate is the threat that is adequate and indispensable to overcome the unjust threat. These distinctions are relevant for soldiers not only to measure the counterforce but also with regard to the risk that they have to shoulder for themselves. With regard to the risk a soldier has to take for himself, there is a considerable difference when fighting a "culpable threat" in comparison to fighting an "innocent threat" like a child soldier, for example. In the latter case the soldier ought to bear a much higher risk to himself to spare the life of the "innocent threat" or lessen unavoidable harm.

With his differentiated approach Jeff McMahan creates awareness of the complicated consideration for the sparing of life even in cases of unavoidable

---

149 Ibid., 156.
150 Cf. Ibid., 159–75.

use of military force as defense. McMahan's deliberations have influenced ethical reasoning to limit the use of force in war a great deal.[151] Against the justification of a limited use of military force, John Howard Yoder has stood up all his life, representing the Historic Peace Churches as one of their most influential theologians of the present age.

12 A Pacifist Dispute of Just War

The Mennonite theologian John Howard Yoder (1927–1997) was the most influential and well-known representative of the Peace Churches' theology of the 20th century.[152] Yoder denied the possibility of a just war for a Christian theology at all. The starting point of Yoder's ethical reasoning is ecclesiology: The community of the believers, the church, lives what they believe: believing in Christ according to Yoder means to follow the path of Jesus who lived a nonviolent life that ended with his crucifixion.[153] As such, he showed a way of life with consequences for human interaction: "Jesus was, in his divinely mandated ... prophethood, priesthood and kingship, the bearer of a new possibility of human, social, and therefore political relationship."[154] Following Jesus on this path forms the believers into the church in the sense that they are "ecclesia," the called or chosen people believing in his kingdom, ready to live a nonviolent life, meaning ready to bear the cross: "The believer's cross must be, like his Lord's, the price of his social nonconformity. It is not, like sickness or catastrophe, an inexplicable, unpredictable suffering; it is the end of a path freely chosen after counting the cost."[155] Yoder's ecclesiology is to be understood in opposition to the mainstream churches. He criticizes state churches, for example, as being intertwined with political society, lacking critical distance to the violent rules that govern the world. Or he criticizes the Pietist Churches as spiritualizing the mes-

---

151 Cf. Koch, Bernhard, "Diskussionen zum Kombattantenstatus in asymmetrischen Konflikten," in: Ines Werkner/Klaus Ebeling (eds), *Handbuch Friedensethik*, Wiesbaden: Springer VS, 2017, 843–54.

152 While acknowledged as a theologian, it should be noted that Yoder has been accused of sexual harassment at the Anabaptist Mennonite Biblical Seminary and Notre Dame University, cf. National Catholic Reporter June 25, 2015 https://www.ncronline.org/news/accountability/allegations-sexual-harassment-against-john-howard-yoder-extend-notre-dame (accessed 22. April 2020).

153 Yoder, John Howard, *The Politics of Jesus*, Grand Rapids: William B. Eerdmanns Publishing, 1972,

154 Ibid., 62.

155 Ibid., 97.

sage of Jesus depriving it from its critical potential for the social reality.[156] Yoder's idea of church is its *Sein* (being) as the new creation. The 'old creation' is the fallen world, fallen against God's intention. The state and all powers are part of the fallen creation, of the 'old eon.' The church, the followers of Christ, are the 'new eon.' They are not part of this world, of the 'old eon,' but have to be a sign of the new eon for this world. Thus the church has no power, nor does it participate in ruling this world. It is up to the church to point to Christ, the ruler of the world.[157] Jesus preached the beginning of the Kingdom of God changing the reality of human life towards brotherly love, equality of human beings and, thus, challenging the orders of society. The church's mission is to witness without any compromise Christ's message in constant opposition to the powers that govern the world; this is her prophetic witness: messianic hope according to Yoder leads to messianic ethics. This nonconformity provokes rejection from the powers; sorrow and grief are results of following the path of Jesus. In doing so, the church as a community of believers shows its willingness to bear the cross. This evangelical nonconformity of the church allows it to speak prophetically to the world while putting its hope in Christ.[158] In Max Weber's terminology, Yoder advocates a *Gesinnungsethik* no matter what the immediate consequences. Fernando Enns, in his interpretation of the Yoderian position, points out that the Peace Churches reject a teleological or utilitarian *Verantwortungsethik.*[159] Asked if this is not irresponsible, Yoder points to the responsibility of the community of the believers, who could only be a church in following consequently the nonviolent path of Jesus to overcome violence. Its mission is the confession of this nonconformity in opposition to the world and its logic.

The just war theory according to the Peace Churches and Yoder follows a very different, non-Christian rationality: their logic is political rather than Christian when asking for the legitimate authority, just cause, last resort or right intention. The key argument is that the just war theory is based on human rationality and may be in opposition to the revealed truth. With reference to Thomas Aquinas, Fernando Enns explains the Peace Church's position: as the state is responsible for the common good and a just war is only legitimate in defense of the common good, this war is understood to be just in a political sense, implying that fighting this war is not a sin. The classical authors of the just war theory like Thomas Aquinas based their thesis on Saint Paul's Letter to the Romans, Vers

156 Yoder, *Politics of Jesus*, 157 ff.
157 Cf. Enns, Fernando, *Friedenskirche in der Ökumene: Mennonitische Wurzeln einer Ethik der Gewaltfreiheit*, Göttingen: Vandenhoek & Rupprecht, 2003, 159.
158 Cf. ibid., 174–6.
159 Cf. ibid., 217.

13:4: "... it is not for nothing that the symbol of authority is the sword: it is there to serve God, too, as his avenger, to bring retribution to wrongdoers." Romans 13:4 became the classical biblical topos to legitimize the use of force by Christian authorities. In their 1953 declaration "Peace is the Will of God," the Historic Peace Churches denounced that Romans 13 could be interpreted this way.[160] Furthermore most Peace Churches reject the argument of a just war being the lesser evil, as it insinuates that evils were comparable. However it is argued that a warring party always pursues its own interests. The Peace Churches denounce that an evil suffered has any moral legitimization. Fernando Enns rightly points to the problem that this position of his church might justify the suffering of a third party: is 'pacifism for others morally justifiable?,' Enns asks.[161]

13 Just Policing to Replace Just War?

The deliberations on 'humanitarian intervention' are the systematic starting point to deliberate 'just policing' as a possible position for the Peace Churches: the use of an international police force for the protection of those who suffer under severe aggression such as genocide or ethnic cleansing. Others like Gerald Schlabach discuss the possibility of replacing military forces by international policing after the 9/11 attacks and President Bush's announcement of the "war on terror."[162] Finally the discussions on just policing have played an important role during the Mennonite-Catholic dialogue (1998–2003), more precisely the first international dialogue between representatives of the Mennonite World Conference and the Pontificial Council for Promoting Christian Unity as a third option between pacifism and just war thinking.[163] And from there on the idea was taken up by the World Council of Churches in 2006.[164] What's behind just policing?

160 Historic Peace Churches, "Peace is the Will of God," in: Douglas Gwyn et. al. (eds), *A Declaration on Peace. In God's People the World's Renewal Has Begun*, Appendix A, Scottdale/Pa.: Herald Press, 1991, 53–78.
161 Cf. Enns, *Friedenskirche*, 213.
162 Schlabach, Gerald W., "Warfare vs Policing: In Search of Moral Clarity," in: Gerald W. Schlabach, *Just Policing, not War. An Alternative Response to World Violence*, Collegville/MI: Liturgical Press, 2007, 73 f.
163 Cf. *Called to Be Together to Be* Peacemakers: Report of the International Dialogue Between the Catholic Church and the Mennonite World Conference 1998–2003, in: www.vatican.va/roman_curia/pontifical_councils/chrstuni/mennonite-conference-docs/rc_pc_chrstuni_doc_20110324_mennonite_en.html (22.4.2020).
164 Cf. World Council of Churches, "Vulnerable Populations at Risk: Statement on the Responsibility to Protect," *The Ecumenical Review* 58 (2006), 172.

According to Gerald Schlabach, the Mennonite John Howard Yoder "was prepared to affirm the legitimacy of the state, with its police function, as God's provision to limit evil in a world estranged from God."[165] The police force can be acceptable to Peace Churches insofar as they serve to protect the innocent and punish the guilty. As such, they are part of the legal order. Even though Mennonites reject the exercise of lethal force themselves as Christians as a result of the biblical prohibition of killing, the state's police force can be accepted as last resort. This very limited permission of the use of lethal force by the state in acknowledgement of the sinful world leads to the concession that "limited police action within society or by the United Nations could not be condemned in principle,"[166] while war as expression of a state pursuing its self-interest by military means is not acceptable.

'Just policing' was brought into discussion to bridge Catholic just war thinking and Mennonite pacifism, the idea being that a rigid interpretation of just war criteria would lead to something like 'international policing' aimed at the international common good. Over this bridge those pacifists—and Peace Churches—could walk with regard to the need to protect civilians against massive human rights violations or ethnic cleansing, as in Rwanda in 1999. 'Just policing' is thus less a concept than a compromise formula still in need of being systematically clarified; and it seems unclear what 'just' adds to 'policing.' A concept of international policing as a replacement of the use of military force presupposes a functioning international law with respective international institutions and international policing as instruments of law enforcement. The development of international law has made impressive progress in the 20th century, but the ability of international adjudication is yet to be developed to the point of being mandatory and able of dealing with all political issues, including the interdiction of the use of force to pursue national interests.[167] The idea has been discussed for example by Carl Friederich von Weizsäcker and his idea of "Weltinnenpolitik" (world interior politics).[168]

For the time being international police missions are more suitable to uphold post-conflict security than military missions. But experience has shown that the success of police missions depends on the consensus of the population and those in power including warlords or militias. If they should decide to oppose

---

165 Schlabach, "Warfare vs Policing," 82.

166 Ibid.

167 Cf. Justenhoven, Heinz-Gerhard, *Internationale Schiedsgerichtsbarkeit: Ethische Norm und Rechtswirklichkeit*, Stuttgart: Kohlhammer, 2006, 231–5.

168 Cf. Ulrich Bartosch (ed.), *Weltinnenpolitik: Zur Theorie des Friedens von Carl Friedrich von Weizsäcker*, Berlin: Duncker & Humblot, 1995.

the international attempt to secure peace and security some time later and continue to fight for their partial interests, police missions very quickly either fail or need to be armed up to the level of military forces. Policing is a good option in post-conflict situations in which the political conflict is basically settled or when warlords agree to the status quo to preserve their power.[169] In case the political conflict remains unsettled, or relevant power brokers are unsatisfied with the status quo, there is a likelihood of one player taking up arms again; depending on the level of violence, police missions may be able to do little about it. Nevertheless, from a Christian point of view, it is morally required to develop international policing as an instrument to repel unjust violence and protect those who suffer without ignoring its limits. But this implies a solution to the open question of international adjudication and law enforcement.

14 Conclusion

There is not one just war theory or tradition in Christianity, but rather a diverse debate: on whether military force might be entirely unavoidable and thus legitimized, or whether Christians may not apply military force killing other human beings. Theological and philosophical arguments are invoked; recourse to the Bible, the Holy Scripture, plays a role as well as Greek stoic philosophy in the beginning. The integration of Greek philosophy into theological reasoning in Thomas Aquinas' *Summa Theologica* has become a standard in the Western Latin Churches.

It is debated whether or not Christians and the churches have to be part of the struggle in this world to overcome violence through the reign of law, or whether Christians should rather live as counter-societies beyond the realm of the 'kingdoms of this world.' What unites pacifists and just war theorists is the claim to change societies for the better and overcome anarchical violence in this world. It is a specific quality of the just war theorists that there is an advancing differentiation with regard to the criteria, if one takes a look at the development from antiquity to the 21st century, from Augustine to Jeff McMahan. At the same time, the danger of misusing just war criteria to legitimize partial interest can hardly be overcome. The criteria must be understood as guidelines for

---

169 Cf. Lederach, John Paul, "The Doables: Just Policing on the Ground," in: Gerald W. Schlabach (ed.), *Just Policing, Not War – An Alternative Response to Worlds Violence*, Collegeville/ MI: Liturgical Press, 2007, 175–91.

political decision making; they would be misunderstood if used to legitimize political action.

Bibliography

Asfaw, Semegnish/Chehadeh, Alexius/Simion, Marian G. (eds), *Just Peace: Orthodox Perspectives*, Geneva: World Council of Churches Publication, 2012.
Augustine, *De Civitate Dei* XIX 11, in: Sancti Aurelii Augustinei, *De Civitate Dei*, Libri I-XXII, Tournhout, 1955.
Bainton, Roland H., "The Early Church and War," *The Harvard Theological Review* 39 (1946), 189–212.
Beestermöller, Gerhard, *Krieg gegen den Irak – Rückkehr in die Anarchie der Staatenwelt?* Stuttgart: Kohlhammer, 2003.
Beestermöller, Gerhard, "Thomas Aquinas and Humanitarian Intervention," in: Heinz Gerhard Justenhoven/William A. Barbieri (eds), *From Just War to Modern Peace Ethics*, Berlin: De Gruyter, 2012, 71–97.
Benedict XV., "Dès le début", in: *Actes de S.S. Benoît XV*, Libreria Editrice Vaticana; 1917, in: http://w2.vatican.va/content/benedict-xv/fr/apost_exhortations/documents/hf_ben-x-v_exh_19170801_des-le-debut.html (2. August 2, 2019).
Biggar, Nigel, "Between Development and Doubt: The Recent Career of Just War Doctrine in the British Churches," in: Charles Reed/David Ryall (eds), *The Price of Peace. Just War in the Twenty-First Century*, Cambridge/UK: Cambridge University Press, 2007, 55–75.
Brachtendorf, Johannes, "Augustine: Peace Ethics and Peace Policy," in: Heinz-Gerhard Justenhoven/William Barbieri (eds), *From Just War to Modern Peace Ethics*, Berlin-Boston: De Gruyter, 2012, 49–70.
Brennecke, Hans Christof, "'An fidelis ad militiam converti possit'? Frühchristliches Bekenntnis und Militärdienst im Widerspruch?" in: Dietmar Wyra et. al. (eds), *Die Weltlichkeit des Glaubens in der Alten Kirche*, Berlin-New York: De Gruyter, 1997, 45–100.
Brunstetter, Daniel R./O'Dirscoll, Cian (eds), *Just War Thinkers from Cicero to the 21st Century*, Abington-New York: Routledge, 2018.
Buchbender, Ortwin/Arnold, Gerhard (eds), *Kämpfen für die Menschenrechte: Der Kosovo-Konflikt im Spiegel der Friedensethik*, Baden-Baden: Nomos, 2002.
Cassidy, Richard J., *Society and Politics in the Acts of the Apostles*, Maryknoll NY: Orbis Books, 1987.
Charney, Jonathan I., "Anticipatory Humanitarian Intervention in Kosovo," in: *American Journal of International Law* 93 (1999), 834–41.
Cicero, Marcus Tullius, *On duties (de officiis) I*, A new translation by P.G. Walsh, Oxford World's Classic, Oxford: Oxford University Press, 2000, 34–40.
Coates, Anthony J., *The Ethics of War*, Manchester: Manchester University Press, 1997.
Coates, Anthony J., "Just War in the Persian Gulf?" in: Andrew Valls (ed.), *Ethics in International Affairs. Theories and Cases*, Lanham et. al.: Rowman & Littlefield Publishers, 2000, 33–47.

Cole, Darrell, "The First and the Second Gulf Wars," in: Mark David Hall/Daryl Charles (eds), *America and the Just War Tradition. A History of U.S. Conflicts*, Notre Dame, Indiana: University of Notre Dame Press, 2019, 251–70.

"Concilium Chalcedonense, Canon 7," in: Joseph Alberigo (ed.), *Conciliorum Oecumenicorum Decreta*, 66, Basel et. al.: Herder, 1962, 66.

Crossley, Robert N., *Luther and the Peasant's War: Luther's Actions and Reactions*, New York: Exposition Press, 1974.

"Decretum Magistri Gratiani," in: *Corpus Iuris Canonici, Editio Lipsiensis Secund post Aemilii Friedberg Richteri*, Graz: Akademische Druck- und Verl.-Anst., 1959.

Delgado, Mariano, "Mit welchem Recht ...? Die Kontroverse über die Legitimation der Unterwerfung der Indios durch die Spanier im 16. Jahrhundert," in: Mariano Delgado (ed.), *Das Ringen um die Wahrheit*, Stuttgart: Kohlhammer, 2011, 157–87.

Die Feuersteiner Erklärung der Pax-Christi-Delegiertenversammlung 1986: "Gewaltfrei widerstehen – Kriegsdienste verweigern – Abschreckung überwinden," *Junge Kirche* 48 (1987), 350–4.

Eine Denkschrift des Rates der Evangelischen Kirche in Deutschland, *Aus Gottes Frieden leben – für den gerechten Frieden sorgen*, Gütersloh: Gütersloher Verlagshaus, 2007.

Elshtain, Jean Bethke, "Kosovo and the Just-War Tradition," in: William Joseph Buckley (ed.), *Kosovo: Contenting Voices on Balkan Interventions*, Grand Rapids, MI: William B. Eerdmans Publishing, 2000, 363–70.

Elshtain, Jean Bethke, *Just War Against Terror: The Burden of American Power in a Violent World*, New York: Perseus Books, 2003.

Elshtain, Jean Bethke, "International Justice as Equal Regard and the Use of Force," in: Gerhard Beestermöller/Michael Haspel/Uwe Trittmann, *"What we are fighting for ...": Friedensethik in der transatlantischen Debatte*, Stuttgart: Kohlhammer, 2006, 22–37.

Enns, Fernando, *Friedenskirche in der Ökumene: Mennonitische Wurzeln einer Ethik der Gewaltfreiheit*, Göttingen: Vandenhoek & Rupprecht, 2003.

Ernst Troeltsch, *Protestantisches Christentum in der Neuzeit*, 1906, Reprint: Berlin-New York: De Gruyter, 2004.

Faber, Eva Maria, "Verantwortung für den Frieden bei Johannes Calvin," in: Norbert Brieskorn/Markus Riedenauer (eds), *Suche nach Frieden: Politische Ethik in der Frühen Neuzeit*, vol. 1, Stuttgart: Kohlhammer, 2000.

Ford, John C., "The Morality of Obliteration Bombing," *Theological Studies* 5 (1944), 261–309.

Francisco de Vitoria, *Comentarios a la Secunda Secundae de Santo Tomás*, vol. 2, Vicente Beltrán de Heredia (ed.) Salamanca: Spartado, 1932.

Francisco de Vitoria, *Political Writings*, Anthony Pagden (ed.), Cambridge: Cambridge University Press, 1991.

Francisco de Vitoria, "De potestate civili", in: *Francisco de Vitoria, Vorlesungen I, Völkerrecht, Politik, Kirche*, Ulrich Horst/Heinz-Gerhard Justenhoven/Joachim Stüben (eds), Stuttgart: Kohlhammer 1995, 114–61.

Francisco de Vitoria, "De indis," in: *Francisco de Vitoria, Vorlesungen II. Völkerrecht, Politik, Kirche*, Ulrich Horst/Heinz-Gerhard Justenhoven/Joachim Stüben (eds), Stuttgart: Kohlhammer, 1997, 371–541.

Francisco de Vitoria, "De iure belli", in: *Francisco de Vitoria, Vorlesungen II. Völkerrecht, Politik, Kirche*, Ulrich Horst/Heinz-Gerhard Justenhoven/Joachim Stüben (eds), Stuttgart: Kohlhammer, 1997, 543 – 605.

Fuchs, Stephan, *"Vom Segen des Krieges": Katholische Gebildete im Ersten Weltkrieg: Eine Studie zur Kriegsdeutung im akademischen Katholizismus*, Stuttgart: Steiner, 2004.

Gillner, Matthias, *Bartolomé de Las Casas und die Eroberung des indianischen Kontinents*, Stuttgart: Kohlhammer, 1997.

Gritsch, Kurt, *Inszenierung eines gerechten Krieges: Intellektuelle, Medien und der "Kosovo-Krieg"*, Hildesheim: Olms, 2010.

Grube, Falko, *Menschenrechte als Ideologie: Die Rolle der Menschenrechte bei der legitimation militärischer Interventionen*, Baden-Baden: Nomos, 2010.

Habermas, Jürgen, "Von der Machtpolitik zur Weltbürgergesellschaft," in: Jürgen Habermas, *Zeit der Übergänge*, Frankfurt/M: Suhrkamp, 2001, 27 – 39.

Hamilton, Bernice, *Political Thought in Sixteenth Century Spain*, Oxford: Claredon Press, 1963.

Harnack, Adolf von, *Militia Christi: Die christliche Religion und der Soldatenstand in den ersten drei Jahrhunderten*, Darmstadt: Wissenschaftliche Buchgesellschaft, 1963.

Harries, Richard, "The Continuing Crucial Relevance of just War Criteria," in: Timothy Blewett/Adrian Hyde-Price/Wyn Rees (eds), *British Foreign Policy and the Anglican Church*, Aldershot: Ashgate Publishing, 2008, 31 – 6.

Herbert, Bob, "War Games," in: *New York Times*, February 2, 1998.

Hildo Bos/Jim Forest (eds), *For the Peace from Above. An Orthodox Resource Book on Peace, War and Nationalism*, Rollinsford/NH: Orthodox Research Institute, 2011.

Historic Peace Churches, "Peace is the Will of God," in: Douglas Gwyn et. al. (eds), *A Declaration on Peace. In God's People the World's Renewal Has Begun*, Appendix A, Scottdale/Pa.: Herald Press, 1991, 53 – 78.

Höffe, Otfried, "Humanitäre Intervention? Rechtsethische Überlegungen," in: Gerhard Beestermöller (ed.), *Die humanitäre Intervention – Imperativ der Menschenrechtsidee? Rechtsethische Reflexionen am Beispiel des Kosovo-Krieges*, Stuttgart: Kohlhammer, 2003, 11 – 28.

Hofheinz, Marco, *Johannes Calvins theologische Friedensethik*, Stuttgart: Kohlhammer, 2012.

Holmes, Arthur F. (ed.), *War and Christian Ethics*, Grand Rapids/MI: Baker Book House, 1975.

Hornus, Jean Michel, *It is not Lawful for me to Fight. Early Christian Attitudes Towards War, Violence and the State*, Scottdale, PA: Herald Press, 1980.

Huber, Wolfgang, "Rückkehr zur Lehre vom Gerechten Krieg? Aktuelle Entwicklungen in der Evangelischen Friedensethik," *Zeitschrift für Evangelische Ethik* 49,2 (2005), 113 – 20.

Huber, Wolfgang/Reuter, Hans-Richard, *Friedensethik*, Stuttgart: Kohlhammer, 1990.

Ingham, Michael, *No War, Just War, Just Peace: Statements by the Anglican Church of Canada 1934 – 2004*, https://ploughshares.ca/pl_publications/no-war-just-war-just-peace-statements-by-the-anglica-n-church-of-canada-1934 – 2004/, (3. April 2020).

Johannes Thumfart, *Die Begründung der globalpolitischen Philosophie. Francisco de Vitorias Vorlesung über die Entdeckung Amerikas im ideengeschichtlichen Kontext*, Berlin: Kulturverlag Kadmos, 2012.

John XXIII, *Pacem in Terris* Nr. 137, http://www.vatican.va/content/john-xxiii/en/encyclicals/documents/hf_j-x-xiii_enc_11041963_pacem.html (accessed 1. April 2020).
Johnson, James Turner, *Just War Tradition and the Restraint of War*, Princeton/NJ: Princeton University Press, 1981.
Johnson, James Turner, "Paul Ramsey and the Recovery of the Just War Idea," *Journal of Military Ethics* 1 (2002), 136–44.
Justenhoven, Heinz-Gerhard, *Francisco de Vitoria zu Krieg und Frieden*, Köln: Bachem, 1991.
Justenhoven, Heinz-Gerhard, *Internationale Schiedsgerichtsbarkeit. Ethische Norm und Rechtswirklichkeit*, Stuttgart: Kohlhammer, 2006.
Justenhoven, Heinz-Gerhard, "Francisco de Vitoria: Just War as Defense of International Law," in: Heinz Gerhard Justenhoven/William A. Barbieri (eds), *From Just War to Modern Peace Ethics*, 34, Berlin-Boston: De Gruyter, 2012, 121–35.
Justenhoven, Heinz-Gerhard, "The Peace Ethics of Pope John Paul II.," in: Heinz Gerhard Justenhoven/William A. Barbieri (eds), *From Just War to Modern Peace Ethics*, Berlin/Boston: De Gruyter, 2012, 313–433.
Justenhoven, Heinz-Gerhard/Barbieri, William A. (eds), *From Just War to Modern Peace Ethics*, Berlin-Boston: De Gruyter, 2012.
Justenhoven, Heinz-Gerhard/O'Connell, Mary Ellen (eds), *Peace Through Law. Reflections on Pacem in terris from Philosophy, Law, Theology, and Political Science*, Baden-Baden: Nomos, 2016.
Kany, Roland, "Augustine's Theology of Peace and the Beginning of the Just War Theory," in: Heinz Gerhard Justenhoven/William A. Barbieri (eds), *From Just War to Modern Peace Ethics*, Berlin/Boston: De Gruyter, 2012, 31–48.
Keller, Andrea, *Cicero und der gerechte Krieg. Eine ethisch-staatsphilosophische Untersuchung*, Stuttgart: Kohlhammer, 2012.
Kirchschlager, Bernd, *Kirche und Friedenspolitik nach dem 11. September 2001: Protestantische Stellungnahmen und Diskurse im diachronen und ökumenischen Vergleich*, Göttingen: Ruprecht, 2007.
Koch, Bernhard, "Diskussionen zum Kombattantenstatus in asymmetrischen Konflikten," in: Ines Werkner/Klaus Ebeling (eds), *Handbuch Friedensethik*, Wiesbaden: Springer VS 2017, 843–54.
Koch, Bernhard, *Der Gegner als Mitmensch: Michael Walzer, Jeff McMahan und die ethische Kritik am Humanitären Völkerecht*, Habil., Albert-Ludwigs-Universität Freiburg, 2020.
Krisch, Nico, "The Rise and Fall of Collective Security: Terrorism, US Hegemony, and the Plight of the Security Council," in: Christian Walter et. al. (eds), *Terrorism as a Challenge for National and International Law: Security versus Liberty?*, Berlin: Springer, 2004, 879–908.
Kronenberg, Ulrich, *Gerechter Frieden – Gerechter Krieg? Chancen und Grenzen zweier friedensethischer Denkmodelle*, Leipzig: Evangelische Verlagsanstalt, 2019.
Laiou, Angeliki, "The Just War of the Eastern Christians and the Holy Warfare of the Crusaders," in: Richard Sorabji/David Rodin (eds), *The Ethics of War: Shared Problems in Different Traditions*, Aldershot: Ashgate, 2006, 30–43.
Lederach, John Paul, "The Doables: Just Policing on the Ground," in: Gerald W. Schlabach (ed.), *Just Policing, Not War – An Alternative Response to Worls Violence*, Collegeville/MI: Liturgical Press, 2007, 175–91.

Leppin, Hartmut, *Die frühen Christen: Von den Anfängen bis Konstantin*, München: C.H. Beck, 2018.

Lienemann, Wolfgang, "International Peace as Legal Order," in: Ad de Bruijne/Gerard den Hertog (eds), *The Present "Just Peace/Just War" Debate*, Leipzig, Evangelische Verlagsanstalt, 2018, 35–57.

Luther, Martin, "Von weltlicher Obrigkeit," in: *Martin Luthers Werke, Kritische Gesamtausgabe (WA)*, 252,20, Weimar: Böhlau, 1883ff

Luther, Martin, *Whether Soldiers, Too, Can Be Saved*, in: Hans J. Hillerbrand (ed.), Annotated Luther: Christian Life in the World, vol. 5, Minneapolis MN; Fortress Press 2017, 183–233.

Lutz, Dieter S., "Wohin treibt (uns) die NATO?" in: Dieter S. Lutz (ed.), *Der Kosovo-Krieg. Rechtliche und rechtsethische Aspekte*, Baden-Baden: Nomos, 1999/2000, 111–28.

McMahan, Jeff, *Killing in War*, Oxford: Clarendon Press, 2009.

McNeil, Particia F., *Harder than War. Catholic Peacemaking in Twentieth-Century America*, New Brunswick/NJ: Rutgers University Press, 1992.

Missalla, Heinrich, *Gott mit uns: Die deutsche katholische Kriegspredigt 1914–1918*, München: Kösel, 1968.

Muldoon, James, "Francisco de Vitoria and the Humanitarian Intervention," *Journal of Military Ethics* 5 (2006), 128–43.

Okko Behrends et. al. (eds), *Corpus Iuris Civilis*, vol. 2, Heidelberg: C.F. Müller, 2007.

Overbeck, Franz Josef, *Konstruktive Konfliktkultur: Friedensethische Standortbestimmung des Katholischen Militärbischofs für die Deutsche Bundeswehr*, Freiburg i.Br.: Herder, 2019.

Pius XII, "Radiomessagio di sua Santità Pio XII ai popoli del mondo interno 24.12.1944," http://w2.vatican.va/content/pius-xii/it/speeches/1944/documents/hf_p-xii_spe_19441224_natale.html (accessed 2. August 2019).

Ramsey, Paul, *The Just War. Force and Responsibility*, New York: Saribner, 1968.

Ramsey, Paul, *War and Christian Conscience: How Shall Modern War Be Conducted Justly*, Durham: Duke University Press, 1961.

Reed, Charles, *Just War? Changing Society and the Churches*, London: Society for Promoting Christian Knowledge, 2004.

Regout, Robert H.W., *La doctrine de la guerre juste de Saint Augustin à nos jours d'après les théologiens et les canonistes catholiques*, Paris: A. Pedone, 1934.

Reuter, Hans-Richard, "Was ist gerechter Friede? Die Sicht der christlichen Ethik," in: Hans-Richard Reuter, *Recht und Frieden: Beiträge zur politischen Theologie*, Leipzig: Evangelische Verlagsanstalt, 2013, 12–27.

Reichberg, Gregory M., *The Ethics of War: Classics and Contemporary Readings*, Maldon/MA: Blackwell, 2006.

Report of the International Dialogue Between the Catholic Church and the Mennonite World Conference; *Called to be together to be Peacemakers*, 1998–2003: www.vatican.va/roman_curia/pontifical_councils/chrstuni/mennonite-conference--docs/rc_pc_chrstuni_doc_20110324_mennonite_en.html (accessed 22.04.2020).

Scattola, Merio,"Wie der König im Krieg nach der wahrscheinlichen Meinung handeln soll: Die Kriegslehre des Gabriel Vázquez im Horizont des Probabilismus," in: Norbert Brieskorn/Markus Riedenauer (eds), *Suche nach Frieden: Politische Ethik in der frühen Neuzeit*, Vol 3, Stuttgart: Kohlhammer, 2003, 119–53.

Schlabach, Gerald W., "Warfare vs Policing: In Search of Moral Clarity," in: Gerald W. Schlabach, *Just Policing, not War. An Alternative Response to World Violence*, Collegville/MI: Liturgical Press, 2007, 69–92.
Schockenhoff, Eberhard, *Kein Ende der Gewalt? Friedensethik für eine globalisierte Welt*, Freiburg i.Br.: Herder, 2018.
Schrage, Marco "Luigi Taparellis Entwurf einer weltweiten Friedensordnung," *Theologie und Philosophie* 94 (2019), 367–402.
Simma, Bruno, "Die NATO, die UN und militärische Gewaltanwendung: Rechtliche Aspekte," in: Reinhard Merkel (ed.), *Der Kosovo-Krieg und das Völkerrecht*, Frankfurt/M: Suhrkamp, 2000, 9–50.
Stümke, Volker, *Das Friedensverständnis Martin Luthers: Grundlagen und Anwendungsbereiche seiner politischen Ethik*, Stuttgart: Kohlhammer, 2007.
Stümke, Volker "Krieg und Frieden in der Reformation: Martin Luther," in: Ines Werkner/ Klaus Ebeling (eds), *Handbuch Friedensethik*, Wiesbaden: Springer VS, 2017, 265–75.
St. Thomas Aquinas, *The Summa Theologica*, Benziger Bros. Edition, 1947, II-II q.40 a.1, https://dhspriory.org/thomas/summa/SS/SS040.html#SSQ40OUTP1, (accessed 1. August 2019).
Tertulian, *Apologeticum*, http://www.tertullian.org/articles/mayor_apologeticum/mayor_apologeticum_07translation.htm (accessed 9. April 2020).
Tertullian, *De corona militum*, http://www.tertullian.org/works/de_corona.htm, (accessed 9. April 2020).
Tertullian, *De idolatria*, http://www.tertullian.org/works/de_idololatria.htm, (accessed 9. April 2020).
The German Bishops, *A Just Peace, 27. September 2000*, Bonn: Sekretariat der Deutschen Bischofskonferenz, 2000, https://www.dbk.de/fileadmin/redaktion/veroeffentlichungen/deutsche-bischoefe/D-B66en.pdf (accessed 1. April 2020).
Ulrich Bartosch (ed.), *Weltinnenpolitik. Zur Theorie des Friedens von Carl-Friedrich von Weizsäcker*, Berlin: Duncker & Humblot, 1995.
United Methodist Bishops, "In Defense of Creation: Nuclear Crisis and a Just Peace," *Origins* 16 (1986/87), 16–20.
Walters, LeRoy, *Five Classic Just-War Theories: A Study in the thought of Thomas Aquinas, Vitoria, Suarez, Gentili and Grotius*, Ann Arbor: University Microfilm International, 1971.
Webster, Alexander F.C., *The Pacifist Option: The Moral Argument against War in Eastern Orthodox Theology*, San Francisco: International Scholars Publications, 1998.
Weissenberg, Timo, *Die Friedenslehre des Augustinus: Theologische Grundlagen und ethische Entfaltung*, Stuttgart: Kohlhammer, 2005.
Williams, Rowan, *Just War Revisited.* A Lecture by the Archbishop of Canterbury, Dr. Rowan Williams, to the Royal Institute for International Affairs, Chatham House, 2003.
World Council of Churches (ed.), *An Ecumenical Call to Just Peace*, Geneva, 2011.
World Council of Churches, "Vulnerable Populations at Risk: Statement on the Responsibility to Protect," *The Ecumenical Review* 58 (2006), 167–74,
Yoder, John Howard, *The Politics of Jesus*, Grand Rapids: William B. Eerdmanns Publishing, 1972.

Suggestions for Further Reading

Asfaw, Semegnish/Chehadeh, Alexius/Simion, Marian G. (eds), *Just Peace: Orthodox Perspectives*, Geneva: World Council of Churches Publications, 2012.

Justenhoven, Heinz-Gerhard/Barbieri, William A. (eds), *From Just War to Modern Peace Ethics*, Berlin-Boston: De Gruyter, 2012.

Justenhoven, Heinz-Gerhard/O'Connell, Mary Ellen (eds), *Peace through Law. Reflections on Pacem in terris from Philosophy, Law, Theology, and Political Science*, Baden-Baden: Nomos, 2016.

Lienemann, Wolfgang, "International Peace as Legal Order," in: Ad de Bruijne/Gerard den Hertog (eds), *The Present "Just Peace/Just War" Debate*, Leipzig: Evangelische Verlagsanstalt, 2018, 35–57.

Luther, Martin, *Whether Soldiers, Too, Can Be Saved*, in: Hans J. Hillerbrand (ed.), Annotated Luther: Christian Life in the World, vol. 5, Minneapolis MN; Fortress Press, 2017, 183–233.

Overbeck, Franz Josef, *Konstruktive Konfliktkultur: Friedensethische Standortbestimmung des Katholischen Militärbischofs für die Deutsche Bundeswehr*, Freiburg i.Br.: Herder, 2019.

Reichberg, Gregory M., *The Ethics of War: Classics and Contemporary Readings*, Maldon/MA: Blackwell, 2006.

Webster, Alexander F.C., *The Pacifist Option. The Moral Argument Against War in Eastern Orthodox Theology*, San Francisco: International Scholars Publications, 1998.

Williams, Rowan, *Just War Revisited*. A Lecture by the Archbishop of Canterbury, Dr. Rowan Williams, to the Royal Institute for International Affairs, Chatham House, 2003.

Yoder, John Howard, *The Politics of Jesus*, Grand Rapids: William B. Eerdmanns Publishing, 1972

Suleiman A. Mourad

The Concept of Just War in Islam

1 Avant-propos

Any investigation of the topic of just war in Islam has to start with the problem of the concept itself. On the one hand, "just war" originated as a Christian concept in the period we commonly call the Middle Ages,[1] and, as such, it carries a Christian garb. On the other hand, the concept has become in the last century a major component of international law, and manifests well-defined legal parameters. The awareness of these two facts is important because, at least in theory, they help the scholar avoid serious historical anachronisms when looking for the concept in other religious traditions or cultures and across time spans. This does not mean that we cannot find quasi-similar concepts, but we need to be careful not to take the concept of just war according to its strict Christian or international law definition and look for it elsewhere. We must understand the concept broadly.

In its most basic meaning, "just war" signifies war that is considered just, which raises two problems: 1) how to define war, and 2) how to define, or who defines, justness. The great theorist of international law Lassa Oppenheim (d. 1919), for instance, defined war in his seminal work on international law in the following manner: "War is a contention between two or more States through their armed forces, for the purpose of overpowering each other, and imposing such conditions of peace as the victor pleases."[2]

One can realize a few major problems in this popular definition, which is limited to conventional war.[3] First, the definition is Eurocentric, in the sense that it restricts itself to wars between defined states and does not take into consideration other wars, including Europeans' wars outside Europe, which have been mostly waged against groups and not states. Second, peace is tied to the dictate of the victor rather than to an objective standard. But this is not the

1 It is often argued that Augustine of Hippo (d. 430 CE) was the originator of the concept of just war, when actually it was only in 1148, and mostly for legal reasons, that the canonist Gratian (d.c. 1155 CE) took Augustine's sporadic discussions of war and turned them into a theory of just war.

2 Oppenheim, Lassa, *International Law: A Treatise. Vol. II: War and Neutrality*, ed. Ronald F. Roxburgh, London: Longmans, Green and Co. 1921, 67 (§54).

3 The term "war" can also be used in a metaphorical sense, in which case it does not involve violence: e.g., war of words, war against deceases, etc. This is beyond the purview of this chapter.

https://doi.org/10.1515/9783110733136-004

venue to criticize Oppenheim. The point is that we cannot take such a definition of war—which is already facing serious challenges, especially since 2001 and the beginning of the "War on Terror"—as our starting point for the investigation of just war in Islam.[4]

Consequently, it is better to take a broader definition of war, such as the following statement about war as "organized, purposive violence, undertaken by one willful group against another."[5] Such a working definition, therefore, allows us to study "just war" as an attempt to explain war as violence launched for just causes and/or ends and requiring certain conditions of conduct.

Aside from the issue of definition, there is the additional problem of studying just war in such a complex religious tradition as Islam, which is a mosaic of beliefs. At no point did Islam have a well-defined theology or dogma on any issues around which the Muslims agreed, including on the concepts of war and justice. In other words, when we talk about Islam, we can only talk about Islamic thought as produced by Muslim groups or individuals who aspired to define a position on a given issue, albeit inherently inconclusively. It is inconclusive in that classical Muslim scholars often accepted as a premise the disagreement among them as an integral component of Islamic thought, which validated diverse opinions. Such a diversity does not allow us to impose harmonious conclusive answers about war or just war in Islam for that matter, and its conditions. Therefore, investigating just war in Islam requires either investigating the mosaic of Islamic beliefs and doctrines, which leads to many, often contradictory answers, or limiting the inquiry to a specific Muslim sect or group of scholars, in which case we only address just war according to that specific group and not just war in Islam.

There is another important issue that must also be acknowledged at the forefront, namely the fact that the concept itself comes from outside the Islamic tradition, and modern scholars have struggled to find examples in Islamic thought that resonate with it. It is not an organic discussion emanating naturally from within the tradition (this aspect will be examined in section 8 below).

These concerns do not, however, invalidate the exercise as such. In my opinion, they are important in order to properly re-center the question and the discussion. The question should be: is there something comparable in Islamic thought to the concept of "just war" broadly defined? This different way of asking the question sidelines the problems that we often come across in Islamic

4 See, for example, the remarks in Lawrence Freedman, "Defining War," in: Yves Boyer/Julian Lindley-French (eds), *The Oxford Handbook on War*, Oxford: Oxford University Press, 2012.
5 Freedman, "Defining War," 20.

studies and in comparative study of religion in general where we see constant efforts to compare concepts across religious traditions. By doing so, we tend to oversimplify things and impose a hegemony of one tradition over the others. Worse, this tendency is often interpreted to mean that on certain issues one tradition is superior to the others. No comparison is without valorization. Thus the need to be careful.

I also want to avoid the modern trap that some scholars inadvertently fall into, namely anachronism and academic dishonesty. This often takes the form of looking for examples from the Islamic tradition that might seem adequate to the concept under investigation, taking them out of their contexts, using them as proof of the existence of the concept in Islam, and ignoring the contrary evidence or the complex diversity of opinions that demonstrate disagreement among Muslims.

In what follows, therefore, I am going to look at the way Muslim thinkers across the centuries have discussed war, especially the laws and logics that explain its purpose and conduct. This discussion includes the laws about the causes of war, which correspond to *jus ad bellum*, and what is permitted to be done during war and the conduct of warriors, which correspond to *jus in bello*. It is also pertinent to include a discussion of war in the sense of the duty to fight in God's name, irrespective of causes and conducts, because in my opinion this too should be taken into consideration when talking about just war in Islam. In this respect, the discussion will focus on such themes as why and when war can be obligatory, what makes it different from other forms of violence, who calls for it, how Muslims are to treat their enemies, etc.

I will avoid giving a linear presentation of the topic because I do not believe that such a presentation is informative. When speaking of Islam, scholars tend to try to establish the position of the Qur'ān and the teachings of the prophet Muḥammad, as if these two sources can really give us the position of "true" Islam on a certain topic, and compare that with what Muslim scholars later said and did. The teachings of the Qur'ān are invariably conflicting on nearly every topic, and the only way we can make any coherent sense out of the text is if we apply the hermeneutical tools that Muslim scholars invented in order to impose certain harmony on the divine text. These tools include the notions of abrogation, general (*ʿām*) vs. specific (*khāṣṣ*) stipulations that determine whether a case is universally applicable or restricted to specific circumstances, veritative (*ḥaqīqa*) vs. figurative (*majāz*) expressions, and explicit (*muẓhar*) vs. implicit (*muḍmar*) pronouncements. Similarly, the ḥadīth of the prophet Muḥammad is a massive register of pronouncements on countless topics. We cannot assert the authenticity of most ḥadīths, and they are often contradictory. To quote a ḥadīth and say it reflects the Prophet's teaching on an issue is academically questionable, to say the least. As we will see later, the contradiction within the Qur'ān, within the ḥadīth, and between these two foundational sources was apparent to medieval scholars, and often led them to accept several contradictory views as plausible.

One should also keep in mind the circumstances that led some Muslims to develop their views about war. In other words, the context in which they were thinking and living is very important, as well as possible external influences.[6] These factors must have contributed to the way Muslims shaped and reconsidered their attitude towards war, and developed new understandings about it. I will avoid making speculations about motives unless the language and other tangible factors make it evidently clear that certain arguments were impacted by specific historical events and moods.

Finally, the examination below is divided according to genres of religious literature. Such an arrangement is one of convenience and should not be taken rigidly, due to the fact that most of the scholars examined in this chapter held expertise in different fields, and their discussion of war bridged some of them. That, for example, Ibn Rushd is discussed under "the Islamic Legal tradition" section instead of the "Philosophy" section is because his views on war were taken from his work on jurisprudence. He often argued that jurisprudence and philosophy are interconnected and that philosophy allows for a higher form of legal reasoning and knowledge to be attained.[7] Similarly, aṭ-Ṭūsī is also discussed under the same section heading, even though he was a leading theologian and his views were anchored in the theological tenets of Shīʿism.

2 The Islamic Legal Tradition

2.1 *Abū Yūsuf* and *ash-Shaybānī*

In order to show the complexity of studying just war in Islam, I will start with the earliest recorded discussion on war that we have. In a question presented to him by caliph Hārūn ar-Rashīd (r. 786–809 CE), the chief-judge of Baghdad Abū Yūsuf (d. 798 CE) wrote:

6 On the issue of external influences, see for example, Sizgorich, Thomas, *Violence and Belief in Late Antiquity: Militant Devotion in Christianity and Islam*, Philadelphia: University of Pennsylvania Press, 2009; and Tesei, Tommaso, "Heraclius' War Propaganda and the Qur'ān's Promise of Reward for Dying in Battle," *Studia Islamica* 114 (2019), 219–47.
7 See, for instance, Ibn Rushd, *Faṣl al-maqāl fī taqrīr ma bayn ash-sharīʿa wa-l-ḥikma min ittiṣal*, ed. Muḥammad-ʿĀbid al-Jābirī, Beirut, Markaz Dirāsāt al-Wiḥda al-ʿArabīyya, 1997.

> You asked, O commander of the faithful, about the polytheists: Are they to be summoned to Islam before war or are they to be fought without any summoning? What is the common practice (*sunna*) regarding their summoning and fighting, and the enslavement of their offspring? Also, what about the war against the evil dissenters from among the Muslims? Are they to be summoned to Islam and to join the community before they are fought? And how about the properties of those who are defeated?[8]

It is clear from the questions that the caliph wanted to know the position of Islamic law regarding the motive and conduct of war against the polytheists and also against errant Muslims who seek political or religious dissent, which weakens the religion of Islam and puts the Muslim community in peril. Abū Yūsuf's answers merit careful scrutiny, for they reveal how the topic of war is discussed in Islamic law and the challenges jurists faced in forming their opinion.

Abū Yūsuf started by saying that: "According to the traditions that have reached us, the messenger of God never fought a tribe until he first summoned them to obey God and his messenger."[9] He then listed a prophetic ḥadīth in support of this view. He also listed another ḥadīth, which states that when the companion Salmān al-Fārisī (d. ca. 656) led the war against the polytheists of Persia, he ordered his troops not to fight them until he summoned them to Islam, as the Prophet used to do with the polytheists of Arabia. Interestingly, this second ḥadīth describes Salmān as having summoned the Persians to either convert to Islam or pay the *jizya* (poll tax) and submit to the rule of the Muslims without conversion (the issue of the *jizya* will be discussed further below).

Abū Yūsuf continued his discussion and offered a contradictory view. He said that some jurists and Successors (companions of the Companions of the prophet Muḥammad) maintained that polytheists everywhere who were reachable by Muslim troops have already heard of the summoning to Islam, and accordingly the Muslims are at liberty to fight them without the need to summon them to Islam. He listed two reports in support of this, and added as well three prophetic ḥadīths that show the Prophet pausing his attack against a tribe until dawn to see if they make the call to prayer. If he did not hear the call to prayer, he would order his men to attack them. The import of these prophetic ḥadīths is that the Prophet did not bother to summon them to Islam. He only wanted to verify if they were Muslims or not.

Abū Yūsuf also cited a fourth prophetic ḥadīth that says the Prophet once attacked the tribe of al-Muṣṭaliq without warning them or summoning them to Islam while most of them were having an afternoon nap and the remaining

8 Abū Yūsuf, *Kitāb al-Kharāj*, ed. Iḥsān 'Abbās, Beirut: Dār ash-Shurūq, 1985, 378.
9 Ibid. 378.

few were fetching water.[10] Again, the import of this ḥadīth is that the prophet Muḥammad did not see any reason to summon them to Islam before attacking them.

The discussion by Abū Yūsuf reveals three major realizations about the laws of war:

1) Abū Yūsuf completely ignored the position of the Qur'ān on war.
2) He subtly admitted that the teachings attributed to the prophet Muḥammad about war are inconsistent and give rise to two contradictory positions: war is conditioned on the summoning of the enemy to Islam or not.
3) He plainly acknowledged that some jurists consider as no more applicable the prophetic practice of the need to summon the enemy to Islam as a condition for war (I mean the argument that war can only commence after the enemy rejects the summons).

The significance of Abū Yūsuf is that his book provides the first legal discussion about war that qualifies under the broad context of just war. This is not a theoretical and personal reflection. It is articulated in response to a question from the ʿAbbasid caliph Hārūn ar-Rashīd. Moreover, his distinction between the condition of war at the time of Muḥammad and the war after the Prophet's death is well established in Sunni legal manuals. For instance, the Shafiʿī jurist al-Māwardī (d. 1058) separated the discussion of war into three periods: before the migration to Medina, after the migration to Medina, and after the death of the Prophet.[11] In each period, al-Māwardī argued, the laws of war changed. The import is that the discussion of war is not a passive process of quoting ḥadīths and qur'ānic verses. It requires scrutiny to determine the Prophet's many positions and views, as well as those of the Companions and Successors (who are generally dubbed the founding fathers of Islam), and determine which of them remain valid. This process, however, never led to any consensus.

Abū Yūsuf's companion ash-Shaybānī (d. 805)—the two were the founders of the Ḥanafī school of Sunni law, which they named after their teacher jurist Abū Ḥanīfa (d. 767)—also expressed his thoughts about *jihād* and legitimate warfare. For instance, ash-Shaybānī argued that war is not conditioned on summoning the enemy to Islam if the enemy had already heard of Islam. It is fine if done,

10 For these discussions, see Abū Yūsuf, *Kitāb al-Kharāj*, 378–80.

11 Al-Māwardī, *al-Ḥāwī al-kabīr*, ed. ʿAlī Muʿawwaḍ and ʿĀdil ʿAbd al-Mawjūd, Beirut: Dār al-Kutub al-ʿIlmiyya, 1999, 14:102.

and fine if not done.[12] He was also asked: "Do you disapprove that the Muslims destroy the villages they cross on their way in the territory of war?" He replied: "No, to the contrary, I see that as something commendable, for God had said in his noble book: 'No palm-tree did you cut down, or leave standing on its trunk, except by God's consent, and that He may shame the insincere' (Qur'ān 59:5). I like that they do this for it rouses the enemy and makes them enraged."[13]

2.2 Ibn Rushd

This approach to treat the views of the Prophet on equal footing with those of the founding fathers is very widespread in Sunnism. In his legal manual *Bidāyat al-mujtahid wa-nihāyat al-muqtaṣid* (*The Starting Point of the Seeker, and the End Point of the Thrifty*), the famous philosopher and Mālikī jurist Ibn Rushd (1198)—also known as Averroes—discussed war under the rubric of *jihād*, which he considered as a communal duty, meaning that not every person is obliged to do it.[14] He divided his discussion into several categories, some of which fall broadly under *jus ad bellum* or *jus in bello*. I should repeat a point made earlier that I am being careful in saying that they fall broadly under the two categories because Ibn Rushd did not adopt one category for the causes and objectives of war, and another category for the conduct of war. He used many categories to discuss *jihād*, some of which are generally included in modern discussions of *jus ad bellum* and *jus in bello*.

For instance, under the category entitled "the Condition of War," Ibn Rushd contended that the pretext of war is to summon people to Islam. Thus, he argued, the Muslims cannot fight an enemy unless they summon them first to Islam. He alleged that all jurists agree on this view, which is not true, as we saw earlier in the discussion of Abū Yūsuf and ash-Shaybānī. Ibn Rushd acknowledged though that there is disagreement among jurists on whether the summoning is to be repeated if the war is halted and later resumed, explaining that the disagreement resulted from what the Prophet said about this issue which contradicted what he once did.[15]

---

12 Ash-Shaybānī, *Kitāb as-Siyar*, ed. Majid Khadduri, Beirut: Dār al-Muttaḥida li-n-Nashr, 1975, 108; idem, *The Islamic Law of Nations: Shaybānī's Siyar*, trans. Majid Khadduri, Baltimore: Johns Hopkins Press, 1966, 95.
13 Ash-Shaybānī, *Kitāb as-Siyar*, 110; idem, *The Islamic Law of Nations*, 99.
14 Ibn Rushd, *Biḍāyat al-mujtahid wa-nihāyat al-muqtaṣid*, ed. Muḥammad Ṣ. Ḥ. Ḥallāq, Cairo: Maktabat Ibn Taymīya, 1994, 2: 329.
15 Ibid., 2: 342–43.

Under two other categories—entitled "those against whom war is waged" and "who to fight"—Ibn Rushd argued that war is waged against all polytheists (quoting Qur'ān 8:39), and noted that jurist Mālik b. Anas (d. 795)—the eponym of the Mālikī school—made an exception for the Ethiopians and Turkic peoples, on the basis of a prophetic ḥadīth. The purpose of the war against the People of the Book, Ibn Rushd argued, is to compel them "to convert to Islam or pay the *jizya*." This condition is extended to the Zoroastrians, for the Prophet said they should be treated like the People of the Book. Otherwise, there is disagreement on all other groups. Some jurists, including Mālik, accepted taking *jizya* from them, while other jurists, including ash-Shāfiʿī (d. 820), insisted that the *jizya* is not applicable except to the People of the Book and Zoroastrians.[16]

There is something interesting about Ibn Rushd's argument that the People of the Book are to be fought until they either convert or pay the *jizya*. This is a matter of disagreement among Muslims, as we will see below. It must have been the context of medieval Spain that led him to take such a position that the Christians were the enemies of the Muslims and Islam. Thus, whereas in the Near East, the motive of the war against the People of the Book was generally the *jizya* only, in Spain it was more complicated due to the general atmosphere that prevailed there.

It must be noted here that there was an exception extended to the members of the powerful Christian tribe of Banū Taghlib, whom caliph ʿUmar (r. 634–644) exempted from *jizya* and decreed that they pay *zakāt* like the Muslims. This view was a point of agreement among major jurists such as Abū Ḥanīfa and ash-Shāfiʿī, the eponym of the Shāfiʿī school.[17]

With respect to *jus in bello*, the views that Ibn Rushd presented also reveal controversy and disagreement among Muslim jurists. For example, he contended that the imam (*imām*), that is the leader of the Muslims, has the authority to free, enslave or kill enemy hostages, release them on ransom, or impose on them the *jizya*, and that there is an exception made for monks, based on prophetic ḥadīths, the practice (*sunna*) of Abū Bakr and other reports. He asserted that captive enemies could not be killed if an *amān* (assurance of safety from death and not from enslavement) has been granted to them. But who can grant such an assurance? Opinions vary from exclusively the leader of the Muslims, to someone authorized by the leader, to any free Muslim man, to a woman or even a slave; the assurance issued by a slave is rejected by Ibn Rushd.[18] He then acknowl-

16 Ibid., 2:331 and 347–48.
17 Ibid., 2:6.
18 Ibid., 2:332–36.

edged that there is no agreement on who among the enemy the Muslims can kill during combat aside from enemy fighters. Some jurists banned the killing of women, children, the elderly and the handicapped, while others allowed it.[19] These disagreements, according to Ibn Rushd, are caused by the fact that the verses of the Qur'ān that deal with these matters contradict each other, that the practice of Muḥammad is inconsistent, and that the Qur'ān and Sunna are also at variance.[20]

Ibn Rushd also argued that Muslim scholars disagree regarding whether the killing of the enemy is merited because of their unbelief or their capacity to fight. Those who say it is the former (unbelief) allow the killing, irrespective of age, gender or condition. Those who say it is the latter (capacity to fight) only allow the killing of fighters.[21] Moreover, Ibn Rushd asserted that captured enemy combatants must not be tortured or maimed, but there is disagreement over burning them. There is equally a disagreement over the use of mangonels, and the type of damage the Muslims are allowed to inflict on the enemies' land, cattle and property.[22]

Ibn Rushd also discussed the topic of truce, saying that Muslim scholars disagree over the conditions for it to happen (clemency or necessity), and what it implies (paying the enemy or being paid by the enemy). The disagreement is caused by variance between Qur'ān and ḥadīth. There is also disagreement over the length of a truce; some put the maximum at three years, others at ten years.[23]

In summary, Ibn Rushd realized that Muslim scholars did not agree on the laws of war, and that this is due to serious contradictions within the Qur'ān, within the ḥadīth, between the Qur'ān and ḥadīth, and between these two foundational sources and the opinions and practices of Muslim rulers and scholars. In other words, the problem is as much a conflict within the sources, as it is in the historical practice and between the sources and the historical practice. Ibn Rushd did not prefer one group to the others, and gave them all the same level of authority. He often accepted the contradictions and did not try to resolve them. The discussion of Ibn Rushd shows us the complexity of Islamic law in terms of its multiple sources (textual and personal), its methodology, and its inconclusive position on many issues, especially war.

19 Ibid., 2:336–39.
20 Such statements are regularly repeated by Ibn Rushd: see, for example, Ibn Rushd, *Bidāyat al-mujtahid*, 2:337–38.
21 Ibid., 2:339.
22 Ibid., 2:339–41.
23 Ibid. 2:345–46.

2.3 Al-Kulaynī and aṭ-Ṭūsī

The discussion of war in Shīʿī law is largely similar to that in Sunni law. The only major difference is that Shīʿī scholars assign an exclusive role to the imam to define war and administer its execution. For instance, in his seminal work of Twelver Shīʿī jurisprudence, *Kitāb al-Kāfī* (*The Sufficient*), al-Kulaynī (d. 941) quoted a letter allegedly written by the fifth Shīʿī imam Abū Jaʿfar Muḥammad al-Bāqir (d. ca. 735) to an unnamed Umayyad caliph, in which al-Bāqir discussed *jihād*, its motives and objectives, and its conduct. For example, al-Bāqir argued that God imposed *jihād* in order to safeguard the borders of Muslim territories, to summon people to obey and worship God, or to levy *jizya* from those who do not convert.[24] In another ḥadīth attributed by al-Kulaynī to the first Shīʿī imam ʿAlī (d. 661), he allegedly said: "God imposed the duty of *jihād* ... because the world and religion cannot be straightened except by it."[25]

The two views about the purpose of war and what constitutes a rightful war are very important for our deliberation. War is a necessary tool to make the world better, but only if it intends to achieve the kind of objectives that al-Bāqir identified: to protect Muslim lands, convert others to Islam, or levy the *jizya*.

Al-Kulaynī then identified three types of wars. One applied to the past, during the time of the prophet Muḥammad: it was a war against Arab polytheists, who had no choice but either to be killed, convert to Islam or be enslaved. The second type of war is against the people of dhimma. Those among them who live in Muslim lands must, according to al-Kulaynī, either pay the *jizya* or be killed (one assumes here that their status as dhimmis meant they have already rejected to convert to Islam). If they pay the *jizya*, then they are safe and Muslims can intermarry with them. As for those who lived outside the land of Islam (what Muslim jurists like al-Kulaynī often called *dār al-ḥarb* or 'the land of war'), Muslims cannot intermarry with them, and their choice is either to move to the land of Islam and pay the *jizya*, or to be killed. The third type of war is against the non-Arab polytheists, such as the Turkic and Daylam peoples and the Khazars (i.e., the inhabitants of historical Central Asia, Azerbaijan and the Caucasus). Their only choice is either to convert to Islam or be killed. Al-Kulaynī added a fourth type of war, albeit one that is suspended, against the evil dissenters and false exegetes,[26] which clearly signified errant Muslims. He also repeated several times that the warrior must first meet the requirements and ful-

24 Al-Kulaynī, *al-Kāfī*, Beirut: Manshūrāt al-Fajr, 2007, 5:5.
25 Ibid., 5:7.
26 Ibid., 5:8–9.

fill the duties that God has imposed on the believers before he can take part in *jihād*.[27] He quoted a ḥadīth attributed to the third Shīʿī imam al-Ḥusayn (d. 680) saying that war is forbidden except under the right leader (*imām*).[28]

Al-Kulaynī also addressed the conduct of war. On this topic, he sometimes provided contradictory views. In two ḥadīths, he quoted ʿAlī saying that the prophet Muḥammad prohibited poisoning the wells in the lands of the polytheists,[29] and that when waging war, the Muslims should not be excessive or mutilate the corpses, kill old people, children or women, or cut trees unless there is a necessity for that.[30] But in a ḥadīth attributed to the sixth Shīʿī imam Jaʿfar aṣ-Ṣādiq (d. 765), he is said to have allowed the burning of the enemy's town with its inhabitants, drowning it, or attacking it by mangonels even if this led to the death of women, children, old people, merchants and Muslim captives. However, aṣ-Ṣādiq did not approve directly fighting against non-combatant women, children, old people and the handicapped, because these groups are exempt from *jizya*.[31]

Enemy captives, according to al-Kulaynī, are to be treated according to two classifications. The first classification is if they were caught during the war, then the imam has the choice to kill them or amputate their limbs and let them die. The second classification is if they were caught after the war is over, then the imam has the right to free them, accept a ransom for their freedom, or enslave them.[32] If the Muslims are fighting evil Muslim dissenters, they should not chase them or kill their captives and wounded if they do not have a place to go back to in order to regroup with their comrades. But if they have comrades with whom they could regroup, then the captives must be killed, the runaway chased and the wounded slain.[33]

Al-Kulaynī was clear though that any Muslim can give an assurance of safety (*amān*), including the slave,[34] and that no enemy can be fought unless they are first summoned to Islam.[35]

These views are shared by the great Twelver Shīʿī scholar aṭ-Ṭūsī (d. 1068), who considered jihād a communal duty. He argued that every person who did

---

27 Ibid., 5:13.
28 Ibid., 5:15 and 17.
29 Ibid., 5:18.
30 Ibid., 5:17.
31 Ibid., 5:18.
32 Ibid., 5:20.
33 Ibid., 5:20–21.
34 Ibid., 5:18–19.
35 Ibid., 5:22–23.

not accept Islam and refused to admit the veracity of the *two shahādas*[36] must be fought. According to aṭ-Ṭūsī, they divide into two groups. The first group includes Jews, Christians and Zoroastrians, who must be fought in order to accept paying the *jizya* and abide by the conditions of the *dhimma*. The second group comprises all others, who must be fought until either they convert and proclaim the *shahādas* and perform all the religious obligations, or else if they are killed, their property is confiscated and their families are enslaved. Under no circumstances does the *jizya* apply to them.[37] Aṭ-Ṭūsī contended that it is the imam who calls for war and oversees its conduct, or it must be someone else delegated by the imam.[38] If the imam or his delegate is not present on the battlefield, it is not permissible to wage *jihād* against an enemy under the leadership of an illegitimate imam and those who insist on doing it commit a sin.[39]

Aṭ-Ṭūsī added a separate category for the evil dissenters (*ahl al-baghī*), whom he defined as any Muslim groups that refuse to accept the legitimate imam and rebel against him. It is the imam exclusively who gives permission to fight them, and once the war against them starts, it can only stop either by their death or by total repentance.[40]

The views of al-Kulaynī and aṭ-Ṭūsī on war actually bridge law and theology, in that it is clear that war is tied to the imam; he decides if it is needed and oversees its conduct. In other words, a just war is a war led by the imam or someone designated by him. Every other war is therefore unjust.

36 The two *shahādas* constitute the attestation of faith in Islam, and are generally uttered in one statement: "There is no god but God and Muhammad is the Messenger of God." For the formation of the *shahāda* and how the two *shahādas* came to form one statement, see Mourad, Suleiman A., "The Shahada and the Creation of an Islamic Identity," in: John Tolan (ed.), *Geneses: Comparative Study of the Historiographies of the Rise of Christianity, Rabbinic Judaism and Islam*, London: Routledge, 2019, 216–37.

37 Aṭ-Ṭūsī, *al-Iqtiṣād fīmā yajib ʿalā al-ʿibād*, ed. Muḥammad Qāsim al-Mūsawī, Qumm: Markaz Nūr al-Anwār, 2009, 597–599; and *an-Nihāya wa-nukatuha*, Qumm: Mu'assasat an-Nashr al-Islāmī, 1991, 2: 6–7.

38 Aṭ-Ṭūsī, *al-Iqtiṣād*, 597 and 599; and *an-Nihāya wa-nukatuha*, 2: 5.

39 Aṭ-Ṭūsī, *an-Nihāya wa-nukatuha*, 2: 5.

40 Aṭ-Ṭūsī, *al-Iqtiṣād*, 601–602; and *an-Nihāya wa-nukatuha*, 2: 11–12.

3 Doctrinal and Theological Arguments

3.1 Ibn ʿAsākir and the School of Ibn Taymīya

It is not always the case that scholars who wrote about war discussed its reasons, objectives and conduct. For instance, the great authority of ḥadīth Ibn ʿAsākir of Damascus (d. 1176) was asked by sultan Nūr ad-Dīn to write a treatise on *jihād*. This short book—entitled *al-arbaʿūn ḥadithan fī l-ḥathth ʿalā al-jihād* (The Forty Ḥadīths Inciting Jihad)—provides a different conceptualization of war than what we saw in the discussion above about Islamic law, in that Ibn ʿAsākir was not interested at all in the duty from a juridical point of view and focused exclusively on prophetic *ḥadīths*. These *ḥadīths* can be divided into four categories: 1) importance of the duty of waging *jihād*; 2) divine rewards for doing it; 3) divine punishments for not doing it; and 4) religious beliefs that should be attained before doing it. With respect to the last category, Ibn ʿAsākir cited a *ḥadīth* addressing the need that the Muslim who seeks to wage *jihād* against the enemy must be a good Muslim, otherwise his effort will not bring about any divine rewards.

> The Messenger of God said: "The slain dead are of three types. One is a believer who exerts his life and wealth waging *jihād* in the path of God—glory and greatness belong to Him—when he meets the enemy in battle he fights them until he is killed. He is a tested martyr whose abode will be the tent of God, underneath His throne; nothing separates him from prophets except their rank of prophethood. Another is a believer, having already committed transgressions and sins, who exerts his life and wealth waging *jihād* in the path of God, and when he meets the enemy in battle he fights them until he is killed. His transgressions and sins are cleansed, for the sword purifies from sins. He will also be admitted to Paradise from whichever gate he chooses, for Paradise has eight gates, and Hell has seven gates with some deeper than others. And a third is a hypocrite who exerts his life and wealth waging *jihād* in the path of God—glory and greatness belong to Him—and when he meets the enemy in battle he fights them until he is killed. He is in Hell, because the sword does not wipe out hypocrisy."[41]

What one understands from this *ḥadīth* is that participation in war requires a minimum proper belief and decent religious conduct that the Muslim must have. Otherwise, it earns the fighter no gains in the life to come. This reminds us of the point made above by aṭ-Ṭūsī, with the difference that Ibn ʿAsākir con-

---

41 See Mourad, Suleiman A./Lindsay, James E., *The Intensification and Reorientation of Sunni Jihad Ideology in the Crusader Period: Ibn ʿAsakir (1105–1176) of Damascus and His Age; with an edition and translation of Ibn ʿAsakir's* The Forty Hadiths for Inciting Jihad, Leiden: Brill, 2013, 182–183 (*ḥadīth* 40).

sidered Sunnism to be the proper belief and Shīʿism to be a heresy, whereas it was the other way with aṭ-Ṭūsī.

As said earlier, Ibn ʿAsākir's treatise on *jihād* was commissioned by sultan Nūr al-Dīn. The introduction offers us a very brief idea about its purpose:

> The just king ... expressed his desire that I collect for him forty *ḥadīth*s relating to *jihād* that have clear texts and uninterrupted sound chains of transmission so that they might stimulate the valiant *jihād* fighters, the ones with strong determination and mighty arms, with sharp swords and piercing spears, and stir them up to truly perform when they meet the enemy in battle, and incite them to uproot the unbelievers and tyrants who, because of their unbelief, have terrorized the land and proliferated oppression and corruption—may God pour on them all types of torture, for He is all-watching.[42]

This short introduction tells us that Ibn ʿAsākir understood *jihād* as a war to uproot unbelief and tyranny from earth. He does not specify if this applies to non-Muslims or if it includes errant Muslims. His animosity to Shīʿism was well known,[43] and consequently, it is possible to argue that he saw *jihād* from a doctrinal lens: a war against unbelief that requires the warrior to adhere to the right dogma.[44]

Ibn ʿAsakir was not unique in thinking of *jihād* along doctrinal terms, and this became much more mainstream in Sunnism with the Ḥanbalī jurist and theologian Ibn Taymīya (d. 1328) and his students, especially Ibn Qayyim al-Jawzīya (d. 1350). Ibn Taymīya argued that:

> Almighty God had allowed the killing of people for the well-being of humanity, as he said "driving people to unbelief is worse than killing" (Q. 2: 217), meaning that although killing may involve sins and corruption, unbelief is much more sinful and corrupting.[45]

Moreover, in two legal opinions (*fatwa*s) on fighting the Shīʿī inhabitants of Mount Lebanon, Ibn Taymīya contended that the war against them is an utmost form of obedience and fulfillment of religious obligation,[46] because they are "schismatic apostates and errant hypocrites who dissented from the Sunna of

42 See Mourad/Lindsay, *The Intensification and Reorientation*, 132–133.
43 On this, see Mourad, Suleiman A., *Ibn ʿAsakir of Damascus*, Oxford: Oneworld Press, 2021, chapter 3.
44 On this, see Mourad/Lindsay, *The Intensification and Reorientation*, 50–1.
45 Ibn Taymīya, *Sharḥ kitāb as-Siyāsa ash-sharʿīya li-shaykh al-islam Ibn Taymīya*, ed. Ṣāliḥ ʿU. al-Laḥḥām, Amman: ad-Dār al-ʿUthmānīyya and Beirut: Dar Ibn Ḥazm, 2004, 371.
46 Ibn Taymīya, *Majmūʿ al-fatāwa*, ed. Muṣṭafā ʿAṭā, Beirut: Dār al-Kutub al-ʿIlmīyya, 2000, 19 (pt. 35): 77.

the Prophet and the consensus of the Muslims, and strayed from Sharīʿa and the obedience [to the rightful caliphs]."[47]

Ibn Qayyim al-Jawzīya can help us understand the logic that informed such views as expressed by Ibn Taymīya. For instance, in the very influential *Zād al-maʿād* (What One Must Prepare for the Day of Resurrection), Ibn Qayyim argued that the Muslim must wage three types of wars: a war against the enemies of God (including the unbelievers and the Muslim hypocrites) to force them to adhere to Islam, a war against his own self to force it to comply with God's law, and a war against Satan.[48] The last two, Ibn Qayyim reasoned, are individual duties, whereas the first one is a communal duty.[49]

Ibn Qayyim divided warfare during the Prophet's time into three phases: the Meccan phase when *jihād* took the form of summoning the polytheists to Islam with preaching and persuasion; at this time, fighting was prohibited. Then in the early Medinan period warfare became a duty for the purpose of defense against those who attacked the Muslims. Then it became a duty against all polytheists, whether they attacked the Muslims or not.[50]

The doctrinal views of this cohort of Sunni scholars is to be contextualized with the challenging experiences of the Crusader and Mongol invasions (11th–14th century), a period which revived *jihād* preaching and propaganda, and by extension the discussion about war among the Muslims (more on this see below in section 6).

3.2 ʿAbd al-Jabbār

The Muʿtazila theologian ʿAbd al-Jabbār (d. 1025), who was also a notable jurist of Shafiʿī law, expressed some views that indirectly relate to war and help us understand how some Muʿtazila theologians understood the duty. Under the topic of *al-amr bi-l-maʿrūf wa-l-nahī ʿan al-munkar* ("commanding right and prohibiting wrong"), ʿAbd al-Jabbār argued that "prohibiting all types of wrong is a mandatory duty because they are all evil."[51] He then explained the logic for that:

---

47 Ibid., 16 (pt. 28): 180.

48 Ibn Qayyim al-Jawzīya, *Zād al-maʿād fī hadī khayr al-ʿibād*, Beirut: Muʾassasat ar-Risāla, 1994, 3: 6.

49 Ibid., 3:11 and 64.

50 Ibid., 3:64.

51 ʿAbd al-Jabbār, *Kitāb al-Uṣūl al-khamsa*, in Daniel Gimaret, "Les *Uṣūl al-Ḫamsa* du Qāḍī ʿAbd al-Ǧabbār et leurs commentaires," *Annales Islamologiques* 15 (1979), 82.

> It should be aspired, whenever possible, to reach a situation where the wrong does not occur easily and develop to something worse than it. For the goal is simply to eliminate the wrong. If the good can be realized through easy measures, then undertaking the hard measures is not permissible. Hence, the glorious and sublime God said: "If two groups of believers fight each other, make peace between them. If one group transgresses against the other, fight the transgressing group until it returns to the judgment of God" (Qur'ān 49:9). Therefore, it is incumbent to prohibit the wrong if it is determined that it does not lead to increase in sins and committing a greater harm. Otherwise, it is not permissible, and abstaining from it is more appropriate.[52]

Thus, one can surmise that ʿAbd al-Jabbār considered war as a necessary requirement only if it leads to ameliorating the situation to something better. If it leads to causing worse harm, then it is not permissible. He even absolved the individual from the duty of forbidding the wrong if it causes him any kind of harm: "If the person is able to do it and is not fearful for his person or possessions, and is convinced it will be accepted from him, then the duty is incumbent on him. In that case, if he does not pursue it, he becomes sinful."[53]

3.3 Sufism

Another theological approach to *jihād* and war is found in Sufism, where the teachings on war are also very complicated. There is a tendency to argue that the Sufis understood *jihād* purely as a tool to "fight" the soul and its inclination to seek the temptations of the world.[54] In all of Sufi literatures, *jihād* in the path of God meant warfare, and Sufis often pointed out that their own mystical path required a similar kind of struggle, which they also called *jihād* or *mujāhada*.

For example, the great Sunni Sufi authority al-Qushayrī (d. 1073) included *mujāhada* among the more than 45 mystical stations that the seeker of the mystical path must attain. In that short section, he spoke of how to fight the will, habit, desire, hunger, sleep, etc. The absence of any discussion of war is very normal, indeed expected, because the manual is focused on the individual and spiritual mystical formation, and not on state formation or physical defense.[55] But we see, for instance in his exegesis of the Qur'ān, that al-Qushayrī acknowledged

52 Ibid., 82.

53 Ibid., 94.

54 See for instance, Paul L. Heck, "Jihad Revisited," *Journal of Religious Ethics* 32.1 (2004): 95–128.

55 Al-Qushayrī, *al-Qushayri's Epistle on Sufism*, trans. Alexander D. Knysh, Reading: Garnet Publishing, 2007.

that *jihād* (as warfare) is necessary if the enemy does not heed the word or the threat.[56] In another instant, he contended that the Muslim should first start with fighting (*muqātala*) his own self, and after that, he could wage war (*mujāhada*) against the unbelievers.[57]

Similarly, the great al-Ghazālī (d. 1111) often likened *jihād* (warfare) in the path of God to fasting,[58] monotheism,[59] invocation of God,[60] hardship caused by caring for one's old parents and children,[61] charity,[62] and commanding right and forbidding wrong.[63] He also made the following interesting comparison:

> It is said that the mystical master must examine the novice's intelligence, for if he is not intelligent and astute, and does not command the manifest doctrine, he should not preoccupy him with remembrance and reflection. He should rather keep him focused on the standard practices and known prayers, or make him serve those who devote their lives for reflection in order for him to be touched by the grace they receive. For he who is incapable to wage *jihād* as warrior must fetch water for the warriors and take care of their beasts in order for him to be grouped with them on the day of resurrection, and for the grace they receive to extend to him even though he would not get their rank.[64]

Moreover, al-Ghazālī considered fighting as one of the necessary instruments that assure the preservation of society. In this respect, he said:

> Waging *jihād* and fighting against the unbelievers seeks to eliminate what they promote against the truth in terms of distortion to people's livelihood and religious observance, and which are the ways to reach the almighty God. As for the people of dissension, [fighting them] seeks to quell the disturbance caused by these apostates and their rejection to observe the religious responsibilities, which are administered, on behalf of the messenger of the Lord of creation, by the protector of the travelers [to God] and guarantor of the seekers of truth.[65]

---

56 Al-Qushayrī, *Laṭā'if al-ishārāt*, ed. Ibrāhīm al-Basyūnī, Cairo: al-Hay'a al-Miṣrīyya al-ʿĀmma li-l-Kitāb, 1981–1983, 2: 46.
57 Ibid., 2:74.
58 Al-Ghazālī, *Iḥyāʾ ʿulūm ad-dīn*, Beirut: Dār al-Maʿrifa, 1983, 1:237.
59 Ibid., 1:266.
60 Ibid., 1:294.
61 Ibid., 2:32.
62 Ibid., 2:308.
63 Ibid., 2:308.
64 Ibid. 3:78.
65 Al-Ghazālī, *Jawāhir al-qurʾān*, ed. Muḥammad Rashīd al-Qabbānī, Beirut: Dār Iḥyāʾ al-ʿUlūm, 1986, 33–34. I would like to thank Georges Tamer for pointing me to this work by al-Ghazālī.

Therefore, al-Ghazālī legitimized violence as a necessary tool to remove those who disrupt or derail the believers' journey to God. His language clearly underscored the two essential components of the journey: the physical one and the mystical one. We see this also emphasized in his discussion of the vital role jurists and theologians play in the maintenance of this world and the next. He contended:

> As for their relationship to the mystical path and goal, the relationship of the jurists is similar to the relationship of the builders of lodgings and water stations on the way to Mecca to the pilgrimage, and the relationship of the theologians is similar to the relationship of the armed soldiers and guardsmen on the pilgrimage route to the pilgrims. If they (theologians and jurists) enhance their profession with the journey on the path to almighty God by means of cutting the obstructions of the self, detachment from the world, and focus on almighty God, their eminence over others would be similar to the eminence of the sun over the moon. But if they do not, their rank is much lower.[66]

Here, al-Ghazalī essentially acknowledged that without the military guards, the pilgrims would not be able to fulfil the duty of journeying to Mecca to perform the rituals there and earn the rewards. In other words, the use of violence to protect pilgrims is essential because it makes the duty of pilgrimage possible and the rewards for doing it attainable. It is therefore a means to achieve a greater end.

There were also countless cases of mystics and ascetics joining battles. One notable case is the band of ascetics who came from central Asia and joined the garrisons of Anatolia to fight against the Byzantines. Out of this milieu came the famous early Muslim scholar Ibn al-Mubārak (d. 797), who authored the first books on *jihād* and asceticism, which in his opinion represented the two most important facets of the Islamic persona.[67]

Moreover, when Saladin captured the town of Tiberius after his victory at Ḥaṭṭīn in 1187, he asked the scholars and mystics in his army to kill the captives, each person to kill one captive. Some of them, we are told, obliged.[68] Similarly, the Ottoman army used to feature a band of mystics leading the way with tambourines and trumpets in order to stimulate the troops and terrify the enemy, which is the origin of military marching bands.

---

66 Al-Ghazālī, *Jawāhir al-qur'ān*, 41.

67 On the involvement of some mystical groups in *jihād* and warfare, see Sizgorich, *Violence and Belief in Late Antiquity*; and Tor, Deborah G., *Violent Order: Religious Warfare, Chivalry, and the* ʿAyyār *Phenomenon in the Medieval Islamic World*, Würzburg: Ergon, 2007.

68 ʿImād ad-Dīn al-Iṣfahānī, *al-Fatḥ al-qussī fī l-fatḥ al-qudsī*, Cairo: Dār al-Manār, 2004, 53.

The fact that we do not possess many books on *jihād* as warfare written by Sufis does not mean that Sufism was not interested in it. The nature of Sufi literature tended to focus on the individual struggles to attain union with the divine for which they often borrowed the terminology and imagery of warfare or compared it to warfare. In the few occasions when they did discuss war, directly or tangentially, they conveyed their understanding of its need to eliminate greater threats that hinder the Muslims from living in this world the life that earns them divine rewards and allows them to seek the path to the divine and reach him.

4 Philosophy

4.1 Al-Fārābī

Some Muslim philosophers addressed the issue of war and often tied it to a greater goal that, once attained, allows the society to reach the utmost level of progress and comfort. For instance, the noted philosopher al-Fārābī (d. 950) contended that, if it is needed, war is a tool for disciplining (*taʾdīb*) humanity and must be delegated to an individual who possesses professional and rational virtues and who complies with the objective of the leader. The delegated person "must have under his command an army to use to discipline people, either through consent or by force."[69] Al-Fārābī also included competence in the administration of war as one of the six fundamental expertises that the leader of the perfect society must exhibit, saying that: "He must possess excellent personal stamina when initiating warfare and the war machine must be under his authority and in his service."[70]

4.2 Al-ʿĀmirī

The idea that war is essential for disciplining society can also be attested in the words of the philosopher al-ʿĀmirī (d. 992). He divided war into three categories: *jihād*, national or ethnic conflicts, and pillaging. *Jihād*, according to al-ʿĀmirī, is the only form of warfare that has a virtue; the other two are forms of brute vio-

69 Al-Fārābī, *Kitāb Taḥṣīl as-saʿāda*, ed. ʿAlī Bū-Milḥim, Beirut: Dār wa-Maktabat al-Hilāl, 1995, 80.

70 Al-Fārābī, *Ārāʾ ahl al-madīna al-fāḍila wa-muḍādātuhā*, Cairo: Muʾassasat al-Hindāwī, 2013, 77.

lence. *Jihād* is to be undertaken by the rulers for the defense of religion and to maintain social order, and it is praised by people of discernment, unlike the other two.[71] Al-ʿĀmirī contended that if one were to examine the military career of the prophet Muḥammad, it becomes apparent that his objective from war was for people to admit God's oneness and his revelation. Once they did, he stopped fighting them and protected them. He compared the Prophet's wars to the physician who is obliged to amputate a limb or an organ in order to save the patient's life. Hence, al-ʿĀmirī asserted that:

> [The prophet Muḥammad] during his raids killed a number of people in order to save the multitude from perdition and degeneration. For he was certain that those forced at first to follow religion, once they realize its true merits having been enlightened by its glow, they would be immensely thankful to him.[72]

This gives us a clear idea about how al-ʿĀmirī understood the purpose of war: it is a necessary lesser evil employed in order to ensure that humanity worships God and accepts his guidance. It is God's worship and guidance that exclusively assure humanity true salvation.

5 The Qurʾān

War is a reality in the Qurʾān. The text regularly reminds its audience of their duty to fight in God's way and of the rewards they will attain. For instance,

> Do not imagine those killed in the path of God to be dead. Rather, they are alive with their Lord, enjoying his bounty, jubilant at what God has granted them from his grace, eagerly expecting those who have not yet followed, to come after them. In truth, no fear shall fall upon them, nor shall they grieve. They look forward with joy to bliss from God and to his bounty. In truth, God does not neglect the reward of believers. (Qurʾān 3:169 – 79)[73]

> God has purchased from the believers their souls and their wealth and, in exchange, the Garden shall be theirs. They fight in the cause of God, they kill and are killed—a true promise from him in the Torah, the Gospel and the Qurʾān. Who is more truthful to his promise than God? So be of good cheer regarding that business deal you transact. That is the greatest of triumphs. (Qurʾān 9: 111)

---

71 Al-ʿĀmirī, *al-Iʿlām bi-manāqib al-islām*, ed. Aḥmad Ghurāb, Cairo: Dār al-Kitāb al-ʿArabī, 1967, 156.

72 Ibid., 156 – 7.

73 All translations from the Qurʾān are generally based on Khalidi, Tarif (trans.), *The Qurʾan*, New York: Penguin, 2008.

Yet at no point does the Qur'ān lay out a clear vision about war that might allow us to precisely outline its view of just war. As noted earlier, Muslim scholars realized the inconsistency of the Qur'ān regarding many issues, including the question of war, and adopted hermeneutical tools in order to resolve the contradictions (e. g., the notion of abrogation, linguistic theories, etc.). More importantly, as far as we can tell, the Qur'ān was often not the starting point of Islamic thought regarding war, or any topic for that matter. It gradually gained importance after many views have been established, and scholars would go to the Qur'ān in order to validate them vis-a-vis others. Also, it is not always the case that they would adopt what the Qur'ān says unconditionally. For instance, Ibn Qayyim al-Jawzīya argued, as mentioned earlier, that *jihād* with the heart, tongue and wealth are obligatory individual duties (*farḍ ʿayn*), whereas *jihād* with one's body is an obligatory communal duty (*farḍ kifāya*).[74] He quoted in support of his argument two passages from the Qur'ān, 9:41 and 61:10–2, both of which say to the believers: "wage *jihād* in the path of God with your wealth and bodies." My question is how one can conclude from such a pronouncement that the *jihād* of wealth is an obligatory individual duty, whereas the *jihād* of the body is an obligatory communal duty? The distinction is not made in either verse, or in the Qur'ān for that matter. It is made outside the Qur'ān, by recourse to *ḥadīth*, to the views of early scholars (the founding fathers), or to hermeneutical tools intended to impose a coherence on the Qur'ān, which allowed each scholar to reach conclusions in line with the dogmatic tenets of his sect or school.

In what follows, I will try to give some examples about the complexity of the subject in the Qur'ān. My objective is to show that the Qur'ān does not take a single position on war, its objectives and its conduct, and that is due to the inherent struggle in the text between God's mercy, on the one hand, and war as a tool to force humanity to worship and obey God, on the other hand. In other words, the text hesitates between firmness and leniency, war and negotiation. This tendency in the text of the Qur'ān will be made apparent in the examples below.

If one were to look for verses that might reflect a position on just war, we find several examples, which we can divided into three types: verses that speak of war caused by God as a punishment, verses that speak of war as a tool to convert others to Islam, and verses that speak of war as a test to demon-

74 Ibn Qayyim al-Jawzīya, *Zād al-maʿād*, 3: 64. For a discussion of *jihad* as a collective duty (*fard kifaya*), see Adnan Zulfiqar, *Collective Duties (Farḍ Kifāya) in Islamic Law: The Moral Community, State Authority and Ethical Speculation in the Premodern Period*, Ph.D. Dissertation, University of Pennsylvania, 2018, Chapter 2.

strate one's belief and reliance on God. For example, the following verses speak of God permitting violence as a punishment of the ancient Israelites:

> We decreed in Scripture to the Children of Israel: "You shall corrupt the earth twice, and shall soar to a great height. When the time of the first promise came, we sent against you servants of ours, very ferocious, and they marched across your territory to slaughter you. The promise was fulfilled. ... When the second promise arrived, we sent against you servants of ours, to abase your faces, to break into the temple as they did once before and to destroy utterly whatever they laid their hands upon. ...." (Qur'ān 17:4–7)

Thus, in order to punish the Israelites for their corruption, God unleashed against them servants of his to destroy them (the Qur'ān might be alluding here to the Babylonians invasion under Nebuchadnezzar in 587 BC and to the destruction of the Temple of Jerusalem by the Romans under Titus in 70).

Similarly, war is a punishment for the unbelievers as in the following verses:

> In God's sight, the worst creatures are the unbelievers for they have no faith; those with whom you contract an obligation and they break their word, every time, without fear of God. When you meet them in battle, scatter them utterly as a lesson to those coming after them, perhaps they will reflect. If you fear treachery from a group, renounce your compact with them on equal terms for all, for God loves not the treacherous. Let it not be thought that the unbelievers have the upper hand, for they shall not escape. Prepare against them whatever force and war cavalry you can gather to frighten therewith the enemy of God and your enemy, and others besides them whom you do not know but God does. Whatever you expend in the cause of God will be returned in full to you, and you shall not be wronged. (Qur'ān 8:55–60)

> The punishment of those who make war against God and his messenger and spread corruption in the earth is to be killed or crucified, or have their hands and feet cut off, alternately, or be exiled from the land. This would be their shame in the present life, and in the next a terrible torment awaits them, except those who repented before you defeated them. Know that God is forgiving and merciful. O believers, fear God and seek to draw close to him, and wage *jihād* in his cause, so that you might succeed. (Qur'ān 5:33–5)

War in the Qur'ān is also a religious duty and a test of belief and steadfastness imposed on the believers, as the following verses stipulate:

> Fighting has been imposed on you as a duty even though you hate it. For you might hate something which is good for you, and you might like something which is harmful to you. God knows and you do not. They ask you about the Sacred Month: is there fighting in it? Say: 'Fighting in it is a grave sin. But obstructing the path to God and blasphemy against him and the Sacred Mosque, and the expulsion of its inhabitants from it, is a graver sin with God. (Qur'ān 2:216–17)

Likewise, the following verse describes the conduct of war:

> When you encounter the unbelievers blow their necks until, once you have routed them, you are to tighten their fetters. Thereafter, it is either gracious bestowal of freedom or holding them to ransom until war has laid down its burdens. Yet, had God willed, he could himself have vanquished them, but it was so in order that he might test some of you through others. (Qur'ān 47:4)

Moreover, war is a tool to force unbelievers to obey and worship God, as the following verses proclaim:

> Tell the unbelievers: if they desist, past sins will be forgiven them, but if they persist, the lesson of the ancient nations shall come to pass. Therefore, fight them so that there will be no discord and the whole of religion belongs to God. If they desist, God sees best what they do. If they turn away, know that God is your patron: how excellent a patron, how excellent a champion! (Qur'ān 8:38–40)

The motive for war is, therefore, to punish those who rebel against God and make a lesson of them to others, to frighten the unbelievers and the enemies of God—the known ones and the unknown—and force them to obey him. War is equally a test to those who obey God and the Prophet.

Sometimes the Qur'ān ties the injunction to fighting with physical threat against the believers. That is, the believers are commanded to defend themselves as in verse 2:190: "Fight in the path of God those who fight you, but do not commit aggression. God loves not the aggressors."[75] But as we saw earlier (e.g., verse 8:38–40), physical threat to believers is not always the case, and the command is often tied to unbelief.

What is left out in this dry presentation is the actual context that gave rise to these verses, which is not always clear in the Qur'ān. It is equally unclear whether the command to do war is meant to be only applicable to the specific situation that the verse raised or is supposed to become the norm to follow in all subsequent cases. Neither of these problems is resolvable with the historical information at our disposal. Muslim scholars tried, as noted earlier, to settle some of these difficulties in the text of the Qur'ān by proposing a chronology for its verses and occasions for their revelation (the genre called *asbāb an-nuzūl*). But they are not in agreement on the chronology or occasions, which led to disagreement over which verse came before which, and whether or not the later ones abrogated the earlier ones.

---

75 There is disagreement whether verse 2:190 was abrogated by the verses in Chapter 9, especially 9:1–5 and 36. See aṭ-Ṭabarī, *Tafsīr aṭ-Ṭabarī – Jāmi' al-bayān fī ta'wīl al-qur'ān*, Beirut: Dār al-Kutub al-'Ilmīyya, 1999, 2: 195–7; and aṭ-Ṭabrisī, *Majma' al-bayān fī tafsīr al-qur'ān*, ed. Hāshim al-Maḥallalātī, Beirut: Mu'assasat at-Tarīkh al-'Arabī, 2005, 2: 369.

Additionally, a verse is often read partially. One famous case is verse 5:32: "He who kills a soul neither in revenge for another nor to prevent corruption on earth, it is as if he killed the whole of mankind; whereas he who saves a soul, it is as if he saved the whole of mankind." What is left out is the first line, which reads: "It is for this reason that we decreed to the Children of Israel that …." Clearly, God is not imposing this duty on Muḥammad and his followers, and the language does not indicate whether it should define the Muslims' own understanding of war. Moreover, we are not sure what "prevent corruption on earth" means in order to deduce the exact message it is supposed to convey, especially if corruption intends or includes religious worship, and consequently if war is to be waged against every form of corruption.

Indeed, the discussion of war in the Qur'ān is very complicated on account that the text itself seems to be unsure whether to promote war or restrict it. Verse 9:5 (known as the 'sword verse') explicitly shows this struggle not only within the text of the Qur'ān, but even within a single verse. It reads:

> Once the sacred months are shorn, kill the polytheists wherever you find them, arrest them, imprison them, besiege them, and lie in wait for them at every site of ambush. If they repent, perform the prayer and pay the alms, let them go on their way: God is all-forgiving, compassionate to each.

Verse 9:5 is a complicated verse. It starts by stating: "Once the sacred months are shorn, kill the polytheists wherever you find them." One assumes that the divine decree has been delivered: to seek and kill the polytheists wherever the Muslims find them. But then, the next part of the verse proceeds to say: "arrest them, imprison them, besiege them, and lie in wait for them at every site of ambush." The question is how can one group arrest, imprison, besiege and lie in wait for another group if they already killed them? Or are these to be understood as different forms of treatment for the polytheists? The remaining part of the verse only adds more confusion: "If they repent, perform the prayer and pay the alms, let them go on their way: God is all-forgiving, compassionate to each." It gives the impression that the only condition for releasing a polytheist is if they repent, perform the prayer and pay the alms. Does this imply submission or conversion? It is not clear, although conversion does not seem to be the case, since the polytheists are still treated as polytheists and permitted to "go on their way." Additionally, why start with an injunction to kill, and then proceed to offer other forms of treatment that range from imprisonment to releasing?

Verse 9:6 complicates matters even more. It reads: "If a polytheist seeks your protection, grant him protection until he hears the speech of God, then escort him to where he feels safe. For they are a people of no understanding."

According to verse 9:6, the polytheists should be left alive, and the Muslims should only read to them the Qur'ān and let them go in peace. Here as well, the puzzling question is why fight the polytheists if the final verdict is to let them go and keep practicing polytheism? Are verses 9:5–6, therefore, a decree for the treatment of polytheists or simply a wavering rhetorical pronouncement? There is no way to know, and whatever conclusion we come up with is simply an understanding that we as readers impose on the text by reading part of it and not all of it.

It is relevant to point out here that some Muslim exegetes "found" a solution for the problematic language of verses 9:5–6, by either proposing that there is transposition of word order and that what is mentioned first must go last: hence, "wherever you find the polytheists, arrest them ... and kill them," or that the believers will decide (*takhyīr*) what is most suitable.[76] Others argued that verse 9:5 abrogated verse 9:6.[77] Some even suggested that verse 9:5 abrogated all other verses in the Qur'ān that address peace and averting war with the polytheists.[78] Still, some contended that the language starts with what is at hand (the issue of killing the polytheists), but then moves to engage related issues, including preserving the life of the polytheists to give them one more chance, which, for the famous theologian Fakhr ad-Dīn ar-Rāzī (d. 1210 CE), shows how intricately complicated the whole discussion is and the need to apply rational inquiry to discern the true intension of verses 9:5–6.[79]

I mentioned that my objective is to show that the Qur'ān is uncertain about war, and I think this is due to the inherent struggle in the text between the mercifulness of God and war as a tool to force humanity to worship and obey him. Verses 9:5–6 are an excellent case. On the one hand, we have a clear command to kill the polytheists, without even any pretext. On the other hand, we have clear injunction not to harm them. We also have a range of treatments between the two.

---

76 See for example, al-Māwardī, *an-Nukat wa-l-ʿuyūn – Tafsīr al-Māwardī*, 6 vols., ed. as-Sayyid ʿAbd ar-Raḥīm, Beirut: Dār al-Kutub al-ʿIlmīyya, 1992, 2: 340; and aṭ-Ṭabrisī, *Majmaʿ al-bayān*, 5: 13.

77 See for example, az-Zamakhsharī, *Tafsīr al-kashshāf ʿan ḥaqāʾiq ghawāmiḍ at-tanzīl*, ed. Muḥammad Shāhīn, Beirut: Dār al-Kitāb al-ʿArabī, 2009, 2: 241. Az-Zamakhsharī attributed this view to the early exegetes as-Suddī (d. 745 CE) and aḍ-Ḍaḥḥāk b. Muzāḥim (d. 723 CE).

78 See for example, ath-Thaʿlabī, *al-Kashf wa-l-bayān fī tafsīr al-qurʾān*, ed. Sayyid K. Ḥasan, Beirut: Dār al-Kutub al-ʿIlmīyya, 2004, 3: 168; and aṭ-Ṭabrisī, *Majmaʿ al-bayān*, 5: 13.

79 See, for instance, ar-Rāzī, *Mafātīḥ al-ghaybat – Tafsīr al-kabīr*, Beirut: Dār Iḥyāʾ at-Turāth al-ʿArabī, 1990, 15: 529–30.

One can say as well that the treatment of the People of the Book is equally perplexing. If we take the infamous *jizya* verse (Qur'ān 9:29), which reads:

> Fight those who do not believe in God and the Last Day, and who do not hold illicit what God and His messenger hold illicit, and who do not follow the religion of truth from among those given the Book, until they offer up the *jizya*, by hand, in humble mien.

According to this verse, the objective of waging war against the People of the Book is to impose on them the *jizya*. Even though the text mentions that the cause of the war is their unbelief and disobedience to God's law (e.g., verses 9:30–35), the objective of the war is not to correct any of that. Moreover, if we read verse 9:29 alongside verse 5:69, it becomes clear that they take us in opposite directions. Verse 5:69 equates the Muslims and other religious communities, as all believers in God earning his protection and rewards:

> Those who believe, and the Jews, and the Sabeans, and the Christians—that is those who believe in God and the Last Day and do righteous deeds—they should not worry about their fate or grieve.

One might surmise here that war against them therefore is not possible. The only way to reconcile them together (if we were to impose such a reconciliation) is that those among the People of the Book who are unbelievers must be fought to pay the *jizya*, whereas those who are believers are equal to the Muslims and therefore should not be fought and should not pay the *jizya*.

There is one final point to raise regarding a justification given repeatedly in the Qur'ān for launching a war, which I did not yet mention. It relates to fighting those who displace the believers and cause them injustice. This is mentioned in relation to the biblical Israelites (Qur'ān 2:246), and to the followers of Muḥammad (Qur'ān 9:13, 22:39–40, 60:9). For example, verse 22:39 reads:

> Permission is granted to those who fight, for they were wronged, and God is assuredly capable of making them victorious. They are those who were unjustly driven out of their homes, only because they said: "Our lord is God".

One can say therefore that injustice as tied to displacement is an issue that justifies war. Nevertheless, the question of this chapter remains unresolved. If we were to construct a just war theory on the basis of the Qur'ān, what material can we use to do so? First, we need to ignore all the complexity and contradiction in the text, as we have seen, and also forget about the contested meanings. We can select a few verses that might help define a theory of just war, as many modern scholars have done.[80] But any conclusion based on such an exercise will not be about the Qur'ān's view of just war. It is rather the matter of the selective usage of some verse of the Qur'ān in order to construct a theory about just war.

6 The Historical Practice: The Crusader Period

The Crusader period is generally hailed as a prominent example of the "inevitable" clash of civilizations between Muslims and Christians.[81] Some historians even consider the overall relation between the members of the two major religious traditions as inherently violent.[82] No doubt, there were countless battles between Muslims and Crusaders. Moreover, as we have seen with the examples of Ibn ʿAsākir, Ibn Taymīya and Ibn Qayyim al-Jawzīya discussed earlier, *jihād* propaganda and warfare literature witnessed a kind of resurgence at the time.[83]

However, violence and hostile rhetoric and preaching was not the only feature of Muslim-Crusader relations. The period also witnessed a heightened level of active diplomacy between the various Muslim rulers in Syria, Egypt and Mesopotamia, and the different Crusader leaders in the Middle East and Europe.[84] This diplomacy engaged a variety of issues that needed to be resolved, such as conflicts, ransoming of captives, commercial and financial grievances. The justifications Muslim scholars gave for peace with the Crusaders have not

---

80 See, for instance, Blankinship, Khalid Yahya, "Parity of Muslim and Western Concepts of Just War," *The Muslim World* 101.3 (2011): 412–26; and Takim, Liyakat, "War and Peace in the Islamic Sacred Sources," *Journal of Shiʿi Islamic Studies* 4.1 (2011): 5–22.

81 Any survey of the Crusades focuses almost exclusively on the series of wars and battles between European Christians and Muslims in the Middle East. See, for example, Saʿīd ʿĀshūr, *al-Ḥaraka aṣ-ṣalībiyya: ṣafḥa mushriqa fī tārīkh al-jihād al-ʿarabī fī l-ʿuṣūr al-wusṭā*, Cairo: Maktabat al-Anglū al-Miṣrīyya, 1963; Hillenbrand, Carole, *The Crusades: Islamic Perspectives*, Edinburgh: Edinburgh University Press, 1999; Madden, Thomas F., *The New Concise History of the Crusades*, New York: Rowman & Littlefield, 2005; and Riley-Smith, Jonathan, *The Crusades: A Short History*, New Haven: Yale University Press, 2005.

82 The late historian and political analyst William R. Polk made the clash of civilizations a hallmark of Muslims' relations with all those around them, especially people in what he called "the Global North": see his *Crusade and Jihad: The Thousand-Year War between the Muslim World and the Global North*, New Haven: Yale University Press, 2018.

83 On this, see Mourad/Lindsay, *The Intensification and Reorientation*; and Kenneth A. Goudie, *Reinventing Jihād: Jihād Ideology from the Conquest of Jerusalem to the End of the Ayyūbids (c. 492/1099–647/1249)*, Leiden: Brill, 2019.

84 On this, see Köhler, Michael, *Alliances and Treatises between Frankish and Muslim Rulers in the Middle East: Cross Cultural Diplomacy in the Period of the Crusades*, trans. P.M. Holt, rev. and ed. Konrad Hirschler, Leiden: Brill, 2013.

been studied in modern scholarship in any serious manner. It is an aspect that requires an extensive inquiry. Nevertheless, the few examples discussed below give us some ideas of how truces and treatises concluded between Muslim and Crusader rulers were explained and their legal bases, which help us introduce a different component of just war, namely limitations on war and "just" peace.

One concept that was often invoked by Muslims to justify peace with an enemy was the notion of *maṣlaḥa*, which means something done in the best interest of the Muslims. For instance, the Damascene Ḥanbalī jurist Ibn Qudāma (d. 1223) argued that, even though truces have a maximum limit of ten years, the notion of *maṣlaḥa* allows the renewal of a truce beyond ten years.[85] Truces were constant recourses for Muslim and Crusader leaders in order to avoid war between them and were often invoked by either party if the other side violated their terms.[86]

Some Muslim leaders, generals and jurists also appealed to the concept of the "wellbeing" of Muslims to prevent or end war with the Crusaders. This is often stated or alluded to in the recorded deliberations among Muslim religious and military elites regarding peace treatises or truces with the Crusaders. For instance, in 1191, Saladin's advisors urged him to conclude a truce with King Richard the Lionheart because "the troops are exhausted and discontent with fighting, and they have consumed or lost most of their arms, rides and wages."[87] Chronicler Ibn Wāṣil (d. 1298) quoted the letter Richard wrote to Saladin asking for peace, in which the King made it a point that he was not doing so out of weakness, but rather he was seeking what is in the best interest of both parties, and that it is not permissible for either monarch to insist on war and risk killing or wounding his own followers.[88] Similarly, at the end of the Fifth Crusade, the generals of the Ayyūbid sultan al-Kāmil (r. 1218–1238) pressured him to attack and slaughter the helpless Crusader army. Al-Kāmil, however, refused, explain-

---

85 Ibn Qudāma, *al-Mughnī*, eds. Ṭaha M. az-Zaynī and Muḥammad Fāyid, Cairo: Maktabat al-Qāhira, 1968–1970, 297.

86 For specific cases, see Mourad, Suleiman A., "Crusader-Muslim Relations: The Power of Diplomacy in a Troubling Age," in: Howard Williams (ed.), *The Palgrave Handbook in International Political Theory*, London: Palgrave Macmillan, 2021 (in press).

87 Ibn al-Athīr, *al-Kāmil fī t-Ta'rīkh*, ed. 'Umar 'Abd-as-Salām Tadmurī, Beirut: Dār al-Kitāb al-'Arabī, 1997, 10: 111; ídem, *The Chronicle of Ibn al-Athir for the Crusading Period from* al-Kamil fi'l-Ta'rikh, trans. D. S. Richards, Farnham: Ashgate, 2006–2008, 2: 401–2.

88 Ibn Wāṣil, *Mufarrij al-kurūb fī akhbār Banī Ayyūb*, eds. Jamāl ad-Dīn ash-Shayyāl and Ḥasanayn M. Rabi', Cairo: Dār al-Kutub, 1957–1977, 2: 390–91.

ing that letting them go was a better strategy because it is in the best interest of the Muslims:

> These here are not all the Franks. If we were to kill them, we would not be able to liberate Damietta except after prolonged fighting. Their kings beyond the sea and their Pope would get the news of what happened to them and will dispatch against us manifold the number of these ones. Our troops are discontented of war and exhausted.[89]

Theoretical discussions in Islamic law manuals from the period give the legal basis that sanctioned such views, which would have been known to the actors involved. As seen earlier, Ibn Qudāma allowed the extension of truces beyond the ten-year limit. He also argued that peace with the enemy is permissible and can be achieved on the basis of a mutual agreement without payment of money, and can also entail money paid by the enemy to the Muslims. As for money paid by the Muslims to the enemy, he contended that:

> It is only permissible if necessity (*ḍarūra*) requires it, such as fear that war might lead to Muslims being killed or taken hostages. For paying money to the enemy is a humiliation, which might be tolerated in order to avoid a worse humiliation, such as killing, imprisonment, or enslavement which leads to disbelief.[90]

Here, like with the notion of maṣlaḥa, Ibn Qudāma appealed to the notion of ḍarūra (necessity) in order to justify Muslims paying money to the enemy in order to guarantee peace. The same view is also endorsed by the Ḥanafī jurist Zayn al-Dīn ar-Rāzī (d. after 1267), who lived in Egypt and Syria. He argued that the leader of the Muslims has the authority to conclude peace with the enemy, either for no money, for money paid to the Muslims or by the Muslims. He also argued that it is not permissible to sell the enemy weapons and horses, even during peacetime, but it is permissible to sell them food and clothes.[91]

It is important to emphasize that such juristic views constituted scholarly studies of the legality of war and peace in Islam similar to what we might call today scholarly research. They were not written in direct reference to or because of the Crusades. Yet, one should assume that they formed part of the legal knowledge of contemporary jurists who were involved in diplomacy and negotiations of truces and treatises at the time and furnished the textual basis of their legal reasoning.

---

89 Ibn Wāṣil, *Mufarrij al-kurūb*, 4: 97.
90 Ibn Qudāma, *al-Mughnī*, 9:297–98.
91 Zayn ad-Dīn ar-Rāzī, *Tuḥfat al-mulūk fī fiqh madhhab al-imām Abī Ḥanīfa an-Nuʿmān*, ed. ʿAbdallāh N. Aḥmad, Beirut: Dār al-Bashāʾir, 1997, 181.

Aside from the notions of *maṣlaḥa* and *ḍarūra*, verse 8:61 of the Qur'ān was often invoked to legitimize and substantiate not fighting the Crusaders. The verse reads: "If they seek peace, accept and put your trust in God." For instance, when Saladin decided in 1179 to attack a Crusader fortress in northern Palestine, his advisors told him: "If they ask you for a truce, agree, for God said: 'If they seek peace, accept'."[92] Saladin, however, did not heed their advice. In another instance, he obliged. It was in 1188 when Prince Bohemond of Antioch proposed a peace to Saladin, and the generals and jurists urged him to accept it by invoking the said verse, even though he was inclined to the contrary.[93] Similarly, during the negotiation with King Richard, Saladin's court advisors pushed him to accept peace, by saying:

> It is more advisable that we accept what God had said in the verse which he revealed, namely "If they seek peace, accept it." For only then people could go back to their lands and raise crops. Troops could replenish their supplies and get respite from the vicious conflict. Should war resume, we will be ready and well prepared, with food and fodder, not exhausted or penniless. For it is during the days of peace that we get ready for war and prepare the instruments of fighting. It is not an abandonment of religious duties, but rather a period of renewal and improvement. As for the Franks, they are deceitful and do not observe their oaths. Make truce with their leaders so that they leave and disperse.[94]

It is important to reproduce the full text of verses 8:61–62, for those who invoked part of verse 8:61 understood it in the broader context of trusting God even in matters that might involve treachery: "If they seek peace, accept it and put your trust in God. He is all-hearing, omniscient. But if they intend to deceive you, God is your helper, for he made you victorious and rallied the believers around you." It is also interesting that many early Qur'ān exegetes considered verse 8:61 as abrogated by verse 9:5.[95] This brings up another issue, namely that Muslim scholars—here and elsewhere—generally invoked individual qur'ānic verses in support of their arguments, irrespective of what the field of qur'ānic exegesis stipulated. Citing a qur'ānic verse or a prophetic *ḥadīth* in justification of war or peace was, therefore, a matter of convenience. The need to deploy verse 8:61 in order to lend religious sanction and legitimacy for truces and peace with the Crusaders required that the issue of abrogation be ignored.

---

92 Abū Shāma, *Kitāb ar-Rawḍatayn fī akhbār ad-dawlatayn an-Nūrīyya wa-ṣ-Ṣalāḥīyya*, ed. Ibrāhīm az-Zaybaq, Beirut: Mu'assasat ar-Risāla, 1997, 3:19.

93 'Imād ad-Dīn al-Iṣfahānī, *al-Fatḥ al-qussī fī l-fatḥ al-qudsī*, Cairo: Dār al-Manār, 2004, 141.

94 Ibid., 315.

95 See, for example, aṭ-Ṭabarī, *Tafsīr aṭ-Ṭabarī*, 6:278–79; and ath-Tha'labī, *al-Kashf wa-l-bayān*, 3: 154. Aṭ-Ṭabarī rejected the view that it is abrogated.

6.1 Muslims' Tendency for War

The Crusader period was not an exception in Islamic history. Many other examples can be quoted in relation to the complexity of war and peace for the Muslims, and its formative effect on scholarly arguments. From the early conquests in the seventh century to modern times, the Muslims have always found ways to legitimize their tendency to wage war or refrain from war, be they legal, theological, philosophical, etc. Or even to differ among themselves as to which course should be adopted: war or peace.[96] One can even point out that the Muslims' rejection of participation in warfare, which became more widespread starting in the 9th century, forced most Muslim rulers to opt to buy slaves and train them for military purposes. The aversion to war on the part of many Muslims was not necessarily a rejection of warfare or violence per se. Some could have been against war as such, but others were simply motivated by the preservation of life and livelihood, or had other priorities than war.

The tendency to purchase slaves and use them as military forces became customary in the ninth century. Many ʿAbbasid caliphs (750–1258) had units of Turkic soldiers purchased from Central Asia. The Fāṭimid caliphs (969–1171) too had African troops employed in their army. There was also the option to recruit non-Muslim mercenaries, as in the case of the Armenian troops hired by the Fāṭimids.[97] Gradually, these slaves or mercenaries converted to Islam. The most celebrated outcome of this policy was the rise of the Mamluk Empire (1250–1517), which emerged on the ruins of the Ayyūbid Sultanate (1174–1250) when slave soldiers united to form their own state in Egypt, Syria and most of the Arab Middle East. Similar practices were adopted by the Ottomans.

7 Modern Debates

7.1 Maududi

In his *Book on Jihad*, the Indian-Pakistani thinker Abu Aʿla Maududi (d. 1979 CE) argued that:

---

96 On the complexity of the early Conquests, see Hoyland, Robert G., *In God's Path: The Arab Conquests and the Creation of an Islamic Empire*, Oxford: Oxford University Press, 2015.
97 On the Fāṭimid Armenians, see Dadoyan, Seta B., *The Fatimid Armenians: Cultural and Political Interaction in the Near East*, Leiden: Brill, 1997.

> Islam is a revolutionary ideology and programme that seeks to alter the social order of the whole word and rebuild it in conformity with its own tenets and ideal. ... And 'Jihad' refers to that revolutionary struggle and utmost exertion that the Islamic Party brings into play to achieve this objective.[98]

Maududi's description of Islam as a revolutionary ideology and program set to alter world society and rebuild it in ways that conform to its tenets is to be contextualized in modern Islamic reforms. It is not a familiar language that we encounter in classical Islamic texts. It brings to mind the language of the Communist Manifesto, and even though he and many Muslim religious reformers like him saw Communism as the most dangerous foe to Islam, nonetheless they borrowed its vocabulary. Similarly, defining *jihād* as the revolutionary tool that brings about this change is also something unheard of in the classical literature on *jihād*. Nevertheless, Maududi's words leave no ambiguity that he believed Islam employs violence as a necessary tool in order to achieve its objectives.

Although Maududi refused to use the term war in a traditional meaning, he essentially called for a war to capture political authority around the world, taking it away from those who usurped it.[99] The call of Islam, he alleged,

> Loudly proclaimed 'Sovereignty belongs to no one except Allah.' No one has the right to become a self-appointed ruler of men and issue orders and prohibitions on his own volition and authority. To acknowledge the personal authority of a human being as the source of commands and prohibitions is tantamount to admitting him as the sharer in the powers and authority of God.[100]

Thus, the problem of modern governments is that they are man-made systems, and as such they are inherently a rebellion against God's sovereignty because they replace God and assume his role. Worse, they cause the exploitation of God's creation.[101] One can grasp the epistemological rationale that informs Maududi's logic. The duty of humans is to worship God and God alone. If they worship each other, then they not only rebel against God. They replace him with one of his own creation. But God's rule is not only meant to assure the sole worship of God (as in the qur'ānic verse 2.21: "O People! Offer worship to that God alone who created you").[102] It was equally meant to liberate humans

98 Maududi, Abul A'la, *Jihad in Islam*, Beirut: The Holy Koran Publishing House, 1980, 5.
99 Ibid.,19.
100 Ibid., 11–2.
101 Ibid., 12.
102 Ibid.,11.

from the bondage to this world. Thus, *jihād* is the struggle that assures that the rebellion against God is crushed and humanity is not exploited.

7.2 Sayyid Quṭb

Similarly, Sayyid Quṭb (d. 1966) built on Maududi's ideas and developed the slogan of "the parting of ways," which is meant to say that the true Muslims must leave their societies because they are cultures of unbelief (*kufr*) and must wage war against them in order to force true Islam on them. In his *ʿAlāmāt ʿalā ṭ-ṭarīq* (Milestones), Quṭb declared that "the whole world today lives in *jāhilīya*," which represents "an attack against God's sovereignty on earth."[103] He added: "Only in the Islamic way of life do all men become free from the servitude of some men to others and devote themselves to worshiping God alone, deriving guidance from him alone, and bowing before him alone."[104]

The way Quṭb employed the notion of *jāhilīya* is very interesting. Literally, the term is a reference to pre-Islamic Arabia and its society. Quṭb, however, used it as the diametrical opposite of Islam (as he understood Islam), thus pre-Islamic *jāhilīya* was a society that lived by all the opposite values and tenets to those of Islam: absence of God, worship of nondivine beings, barbarism, exploitation, absence of dignity and morality, etc. If the entire world today is living in *jāhilīya*, as Quṭb contended, then the Muslims too are in *jāhilīya*, hence the need for the use of violence against them, in similar way to what the Prophet did, in order to force them to return to Islam and bring about an Islamic revival.

How can this Islamic revival begin? This is a question that Quṭb actually posed himself.[105] His answer is that the Islamic revival needs a "vanguard" to lead the war to eradicate the *jāhilīya* of the modern age. This group of Islamist pioneers must keep themselves "somewhat isolated, on the one hand, and somewhat in contact, on the other hand, with this all-encompassing *jāhilīya*" around them.[106] Such a group existed only once in Islamic history: the companions of the prophet Muḥammad, who Quṭb nicknamed "the unique qurʾānic generation."[107] They were formed by the message of the Qurʾān alone,[108] which allowed

103 Sayyid Quṭb, *Maʿālim fī ṭ-ṭarīq*, Cairo: Dar ash-Shuruq, 1979, 8; and idem, *Milestones: Maʿalim fi'l-tareeq*, ed. A.B. al-Mehri, Birmingham: Maktabah Booksellers, 2006, 26–7. The book was written in 1964.
104 Quṭb, *Maʿālim*, 8; *Milestones*, 26–7.
105 Quṭb, *Maʿālim*, 9; *Milestones*, 27.
106 Quṭb, *Maʿālim*, 9; *Milestones*, 28.
107 Quṭb, *Maʿālim*, 11–9; *Milestones*, 29–35.

them to break with the *jāhilīya* and fight it without having to remove themselves completely from it.

The corruption, according to Quṭb, started when later Muslim generations were lured by other cultures, such as "Greek philosophy and logic, ancient Persian legends and their ideas, Jewish scriptures and traditions, Christian theology, ...,"[109] which distanced them from the Qur'ān and corrupted their Islam. He contended that:

> People are conditioned by innate laws which God had fashioned. They govern their birth and growth, health and disease, and life and death. They are also conditioned by these laws in their collective choices and the consequences of their voluntary actions. They are incapable of changing God's decree with respect to the laws of the universe which govern and control it. It is therefore essential that they recover their senses by returning to Islam in those aspects of their life that are voluntary, making God's law the arbiter in all manners of their life. They should also establish a harmony between the voluntary aspect and the innate aspect, as well as their entire existence in both aspects and that of the universe. *Jāhilīya*, however, rests on people's lordship over one another. It is an aberration against the universe and brings the voluntary aspect of human life into conflict with the innate aspect.[110]

In these words, we realize the epistemic foundation of Quṭb's thought. Everything in the universe comes from God, and everything is set up to function according to God's plan. Birth and growth, life and death, health and disease, all the laws that govern the way things function, etc., are determined by God. If humans reject to follow God's comprehensive and perfect system in the universe that assures the happiness and freedom of humanity, and substitute other systems in its place, then it is imperative on the Islamic vanguard to fight them until they accept God's system. Quṭb further contended that:

> Islam has no choice but to spread in the earth and remove the status quo which is in violation of this general declaration of freedom. It does that by preaching and action, striking hard at all political powers, which force people into servitude to anyone other than God, rule them by a law other than God's law and his sovereignty, and prevent them from listening to the preaching and adopting the creed freely without intimidation from those powers.[111]

This last point completes Quṭb's epistemic rationale about war in that it delineates what is to be done if humans reject God's system: they must be fought

---

108 Quṭb, *Ma'ālim*, 12–3; *Milestones*, 30.
109 Quṭb, *Ma'ālim*, 14; *Milestones*, 30.
110 Quṭb, *Ma'ālim*, 47; *Milestones*, 57.
111 Quṭb, *Ma'ālim*, 63; *Milestones*, 70.

until they accept it unconditionally. This war under the banner of *jihād* seeks to accomplish several objectives:

> To assert God's divinity on earth, affirm his way in human affairs, cast out demons and Satanic systems, and destroy the human system that forces people into servitude. People are the servants of God alone, and it is not permissible for them to be ruled over by one of God's servants who imposes on them his own power and arbitrary law. These reasons give enough justification for proclaiming *jihād*.[112]

Jihād, therefore, becomes the war that assures that God's plan for humanity functions as God meant it to be, and no other competing systems are in existence to divert or lure humans away from God. In other words, *jihād* seeks to guarantee that God's sovereignty is not replaced by other forms of sovereignty. It is also a preemptive struggle, never a passive one, because, according to Quṭb, the nature of Islam "necessitates that it takes initiative to free humans throughout the earth from servitude to anyone other than God."[113]

In all of these arguments, it is rather clear that Quṭb considered the modern Muslims to have substituted God's system for *jāhilīya* systems, which means that they are now in a state of rebellion against God and must be fought to force them to return to Islam. This is exactly what is called *takfīr*, that is the declaring of Muslims to be unbelievers. It is the doctrine that justifies and legitimizes killing fellow Muslims because they ceased to be Muslims.

7.3 Hasan al-Bannā

The views of Quṭb were echoed in an earlier book entitled *Kitāb al-Jihād* (Book of Jihad) by Ḥasan al-Bannā (d. 1949), the founder of the Muslim Brothers. Al-Bannā declared that "*jihād* was imposed by God on every Muslim as an obligatory and binding duty that cannot be evaded."[114] He added that the teachings of Islam promote the most ideal system of *jihād* intended to protect the truth.[115] He further contended that:

---

112 Quṭb, *Ma'ālim*, 74; *Milestones*, 81.
113 Quṭb, *Ma'ālim*, 78; *Milestones*, 84.
114 Ḥasan al-Bannā, *Risālat al-Jihād*, in *Thalāth rasā'il fī j-jihād: Abū l-A'lā al-Mawdūdī, Ḥasan al-Bannā, Sayyid Quṭb*, Amman: Dār 'Ammār, 1991, 69; and idem, *Kitab ul Jihad*, in Sayyid Qutb, *Milestones: Ma'alim fi'l-tareeq*, ed. A.B. Mehri, Birmingham: Maktabah Booksellers and Publishers, 2006, 220.
115 Al-Bannā, *Risālat al-Jihād*, 70; and idem, *Kitab ul Jihad*, 220.

> God did not ordain *jihād* for the Muslims so that it be used as a tool of oppression or to further personal gains, but rather to safeguard the mission of spreading Islam, guarantee peace and proclaim the supreme message, whose implementation the Muslims bear. This message is to guide humanity to truth and justice. For Islam did not only impose fighting as a duty but also praised peacemaking.[116]

The language of al-Bannā largely agreed with what we saw with Maududi and Quṭb, but he was more evasive and apologetic. He was trying to walk a tightrope between the revivification of the duty of *jihād* and the eagerness to portray Islam in the most favorable light. That is why he did not go anywhere near the kind of total-war mentality that we came across in the words of Maududi and Quṭb. Nevertheless, all three shared a similar conviction that allows us to draw the conclusion that the only "just" war is a war to spread Islam, guarantee an "Islamic" peace, and guide humanity to God according to the teachings of Islam (as they understood it).

This way of thinking about the purpose of war is clearly tied to the challenges of modernity and the "popularity" of revolutionary ideologies that promised to improve and liberate people from the yoke of such systems as colonialism and capitalism. As noted earlier, the language that we find in Maududi and Quṭb is similar in some ways to that employed by Communist thinkers, which points to its perceived popularity and appeal. Thus, they gave the purpose of war a new dimension in Islamic thought.

7.4 Maḥmūd Shaltūt

The time during which the likes of al-Bannā, Maududi and Quṭb wrote also featured other scholars who argued that *jihād* in today's world was only possible for the purpose of defense. For instance, in an influential treatise entitled *al-Qur'ān wa-l-qitāl* (The Qur'ān and Combat), Maḥmūd Shaltūt (d. 1963), who was the Sheikh of al-Azhar between 1958 and 1963, wrote the following about the way the Qur'ān discusses warfare:

> The purpose of warfare according to the Qur'ān is limited to repelling aggression, protecting the summon to Islam, and liberty of practicing religion. ... When one looks into these verses from the book of God, one finds they establish for the Muslims general principles, out of which a tangible law of combat can be formed that is superior to any other in modern times and in advanced civilizations. This tangible law of combat for a nation seeking pride and dignity stands on three elements: the first element is the strengthening of the morale of

116 Ḥasan al-Bannā, *Risālat al-Jihād*, 97; and idem, *Kitab ul Jihad*, 236.

> the nation, the second element is the preparation of the physical force, and the third element is the practical planning for war. The Qur'ān, which outlines for people the contours of good life, discussed these three elements in a comprehensive manner that encompasses all that has been said about them across the ages and cultures. It does not ignore any element or engage it only briefly. Moreover, given their intensity and extensiveness, they possess people's hearts and fill them with mercy and compassion. They also infuse them with the spirit of devotion and the desire for God's approval by way of purifying the earth from corruption and cleansing it from the means of tyranny and aggression. These meanings are exhibited in each of the three elements.[117]

It is clear from the discussion above that Shaltūt limits warfare to three cases: 1) repel aggression, 2) protect the preaching to Islam, 3) assure the freedom of religious practice. We can, therefore, construe his words to mean that a just war can only be pursued under one of these causes. Otherwise, it cannot be just.

Shaltūt also discussed how to put the laws of the Qur'ān on warfare into practice. He contended that the Prophet and the first two caliphs were the only Muslim leaders who executed them properly. After that time, however, the Muslims allowed internal and external circumstances to steer them away from these laws and rules that God has legislated about warfare.[118] He concluded that:

> People must return to the legislation of the Qur'ān about the treatment of the people of treatises and *dhimmis*. They must also read the history of the rightly guided caliphs and the just rulers and the way they dealt with those who do not profess Islam. ... Then they can learn ... how lenient Islam is in the treatment of its non-Muslim subjects and how it loves universal peace and human solidarity. They will also learn how exalted its universal human laws are ....[119]

Thus, Shaltūt argued that the Qur'ān provided a comprehensive road map for all the elements of warfare, both the planning and execution. The Muslims need simply put it into application. But as we have seen earlier with the discussions of several Muslim scholars who tried to involve the Qur'ān in their theories of war, the text is neither clear nor coherent, so that they often resorted to quoting single verses instead of giving it a comprehensive reading. Furthermore, Shaltūt was eager, like many Muslim modernists, to present Islam as superior to all other systems when it comes to war and peace. This obsession reflected an inferiority

---

117 Maḥmūd Shaltūt, *al-Qur'ān wa-l-qitāl*, Cairo: Dār al-Kiṭāb al-ʿArabī, 1951, 41–2; idem, *The Qur'an and Combat*, trans. Lamya al-Khraisha, Amman: The Royal Aal al-Bayt Institute for Islamic Thought, 2012, 53–4.
118 Shaltūt, *al-Qur'ān wa-l-qitāl*, 59; idem, *The Qur'an and Combat*, 77.
119 Shaltūt, *al-Qur'ān wa-l-qitāl*, 67; idem, *The Qur'an and Combat*, 85.

complex on the part of some Muslim modernists regarding the hegemonic Western culture and its proclaimed values.[120] They were impressed by them and eager to demonstrate that Islam promotes them too.

7.5 Mahmoud Ṭaha

The modernist Mahmoud M. Ṭaha (d. 1985) distinguished himself from both Muslim militants and moderates. In his *The Second Message of Islam*, he argued that "Islam's original view is that a person is free until it is known, in practice, that he or she is unable to properly discharge the duty of such freedom."[121] He added that God enacted "fighting with the sword in order to curtail the freedom of those who abuse it, so that the sword brings them to their senses."[122] "In justifying the use of the sword," Ṭaha surmised, "we may describe it as a surgeon's lancet and not a butcher's knife. When used with sufficient wisdom, mercy, and knowledge, it uplifted the individual and purified society."[123] This language reminds us of what al-ʿĀmirī said, but again the similar vocabulary should not confuse the fact that each one of them was writing and thinking in a different historical moment and responding to dissimilar challenges.

The novel thing in Ṭaha's reasoning is his argument that *jihād* "signifies a descent from the level of *al-islām* to the level of *al-imān*,"[124] which led him to say that "*jihād* is not an original precept of Islam."[125] Thus, the perfect Muslim society that practices the highest level of Islam does not need warfare. This highest form of Islam, which Ṭaha defined as exhibiting external and internal submission, is to be contrasted with the lowest form of Islam, which he defined as exhibiting external submission only.[126] It was only the prophet Muḥammad, as Ṭaha contended, who could practice the highest form of Islam. When the Prophet, as Ṭaha argued, realized that his followers could not grasp it, he replaced it with the lowest form of Islam. One can conclude, therefore, that

120 I say proclaimed values because they (e. g., human rights, freedom, rule of law) are mostly rhetorical and academic, and selectively applied, as the West has also been a leading violator of human rights, freedom and the rule of law.
121 Ṭaha, Mahmoud M., *The Second Message of Islam*, trans. Abdullahi A. An-Naʿim, Syracuse: Syracuse University Press, 1987, 132.
122 Ibid., 135.
123 Ibid., 134.
124 Ibid., 136.
125 Ibid., 132.
126 Ibid., 45.

such original and unprecedented views about *jihād* and war are tied to the condition of the Muslims themselves and the level of Islam they practice, rather than to the nature of their relation with their enemies. Consequently, Ṭaha was doing a critique of modern Islamic thought and practice, and which, like in the case of Shaltūt, was partly shaped and informed by the "values" of Western modernity.

This context allows us to better understand the motives of these scholars to say what they said about the issue of war in Islam. Even though the language used by them might be similar, and it might resonate as well with the language we find in premodern treatises on *jihād*, yet they all differ in a major way in that it was the context that gave specific meanings to what each one said. Therefore, Shaltūt was in fact saying something very different from what al-Bannā (or Maududi and Quṭb) said, even if they all used similar phrases about the nobility of Islam in the way it treats non-Muslims, its eagerness for world peace and happiness of humanity, etc. Moreover, some tried to express this in the form of a revolutionary language, others in the form of a "humanitarian" modernity.

7.6 Bin-Laden and al-Qaeda

Thinkers like Maududi and Quṭb were inspirational for a generation of Muslims who were shaped by a renewed interest in *jihād* and warfare, especially following the invasion of Afghanistan by the USSR in 1978 and the Iranian revolution in 1979. From this context emerged the organization known as al-Qāʿida (anglicized as al-Qaeda, which means the Base). Its former leader Usama bin Laden (d. 2011) issued on 23 August 1996 a declaration of war against the US and the Saudi regime. The reasons for the declaration are listed as such:

> The aggression, iniquity and injustice imposed on them by the Zionist-Crusader alliance and their collaborators, to the point where Muslim blood has become the cheapest and their wealth as loot in the hands of their enemies. ... The latest and the greatest of the aggressions inflicted on Muslims since the death of the Prophet (peace be upon him) is the occupation of the Land of the Two Holy Places [Saudi Arabia]—the foundation of the house of Islam, the place of the Revelation, and the place of the noble Kaʿba, the qibla of all Muslims.[127]

127 Usama Bin Laden, "Declaration of War against the Americans Occupying the Land of the Two Holy Places," in: Roxanne Euben/Muhammad Qasim Zaman (eds), *Princeton Readings in Islamist Thought*, Princeton: Princeton University Press, 2009, 436–37.

The declaration justifies war on the grounds that it is needed to defend the Muslims and protect their religion from "the aggression, iniquity and injustice" caused by the West and Israel (which is what the expression "Zionist-Crusader" means). This grievance can easily comply with the required conditions for permissible war set forth by Shaltūt, as we have seen earlier. The point is not to exonerate a militant organization like al-Qaeda, but rather to clarify the type of religious arguments it and similar organizations employ to legitimize their war and violence, especially for their supporters.

What is more important are the reasons the declaration listed for war against the Saudi regime, which include suspension of Islamic law and persecution of religious scholars, the inability of the Saudi regime to protect the country, and the permission it gave to the enemy (the US in particular) to occupy the country.[128] But for Bin Laden and his audience, this was not enough to justify war. Hence, the declaration goes into the details of all the efforts that were done to bring the issue repeatedly to the attention of the Saudi authorities in order to convince them to change course, and the fact that these efforts were all rejected.[129] It says: "Advocates of the reform movement have been intent on using peaceful means to protect the unity of the country and to prevent bloodshed," but "the regime closed off all peaceful routes [of expression], pushing the people toward armed action as the only remaining choice to implement righteousness and justice."[130] Thus, it is only after all the attempts at warning and counseling have been exhausted that war could be declared.

8 Modern Scholarship

The topic of just war in Islam has received some attention in modern scholarship. In an article entitled "The Evolution of Just War Theory in Islamic Law," Ahmad Atif Ahmad alleged that "[a]n Islamic just war theory, therefore, stands on both a correct reading of authoritative texts and a correct reading of early Muslim history."[131] This brazen claim is misleading in that Ahmad took the modern definition of just war theory, looked for verses in the Qurʾān that support it, however vaguely, and concluded that Islam promotes it.

128 Ibid., 439.
129 See the discussion in Bin Laden, "Declaration of War," 441.
130 Ibid.
131 Ahmad, Ahmad A., "The Evolution of Just War Theory in Islamic Law: Texts, History, and the Purpose of "Reading," *American Foreign Policy Interests* 28.2 (2006),107.

This questionable method is widespread in modern Islamic studies (and in other fields as well). We find it in John Kelsay's *Arguing the Just War in Islam.* In order to prove that Islam has a "just war" theory, Kelsay analyzed a selective number of arguments made by the notable early jurist ash-Shaybānī, and presented them as Islam's view on just war.[132] It would have been more scholarly and historically accurate to label them as some of the views of ash-Shaybānī on war and its legitimacy, for ash-Shaybānī was not always as coherent on these issues as Kelsay made him to be.

The tendency to treat the views of ash-Shaybānī as reflective of Islam's position on the relations between nations and on the laws of war became popular after his book was translated into English in 1966. It led to many misreading and erroneous conclusions about what he meant, and the intellectual and physical context of ash-Shaybānī's views. For instance, on the basis of a *ḥadīth* quoted by ash-Shaybānī, James T. Johnson argued that:

> This charge establishes the proper order of the mission of the Islamic community. It is most desirable that people accept Islam. While this acceptance must be "without compulsion" (Qur'ān 2:256), where "polytheists" are concerned, they must in fact accept the religion of Islam or be killed.[133]

Let us look at the *ḥadīth* in question in order to realize that some widespread ideas in modern scholarship about Islam and its concept of war might be simply the result of misreading of classical texts due to an eagerness to show Islam in a positive light:

> Whenever the Apostle of God sent forth an army or a detachment, he charged its commander personally to fear God, the Most High, and he enjoined the Muslims who were with him to do good [i.e., to conduct themselves properly]. And the [Apostle] said: "Fight in the name of God and in the 'path of God' [i.e., truth]. Combat [only] those who disbelieve in God. Do not cheat or commit treachery, nor should you mutilate anyone or kill children. Whenever you meet your polytheist enemies, invite them [first] to adopt Islam. If they do so, accept it, and let them alone. You should then invite them to move from their territory to the territory of the *émigrés* [Madīna]. If they do so, accept it and let them alone. Otherwise, they should be informed that they would be [treated] like the Muslim nomads (Bedouins) [who take no part in the war] in that they are subject to God's orders as [other] Muslims, but that they will receive no share in either the *ghanīma* (spoil of war) or in the *fay'*. If they refuse [to accept Islam], then call upon them to pay the *jizya* (poll tax); if they do, accept it and leave them

132 Kelsay, John, *Arguing the Just War in Islam*, Cambridge: Harvard University Press, 2007, 99–109.

133 Johnson, James T., *The Holy War Idea in Western and Islamic Traditions*, University Park: Pennsylvania State University Press, 2002, 70.

> alone. If you besiege the inhabitants of a fortress or a town and they try to get you to let them surrender on the basis of God's judgment, do not do so, since you do not know what God's judgment is, but make them surrender to your judgment and then decide their case according to your own views. But if the besieged inhabitants of a fortress or a town asked you to give them a pledge [of security] in God's name or in the name of His Apostle, you should not do so, but give the pledge in your names or in the names of your fathers; for, if you should ever break it, it would be an easier matter if it were in the names of you or your fathers."[134]

As this *ḥadīth* clearly shows, the two options that the Prophet identified for his army are that they should offer the people they fight the chance to convert to Islam, or to pay the *jizya*. It does not say anything at all about killing them if they refuse to convert, as Johnson alleged. Equally significant is that the Prophet did not define in this *ḥadīth* a law for the Muslim fighters to follow. Actually, he insisted that they should make their own judgment on the way they determine the treatment of a besieged town, the terms of surrender and assurance or pledge of security (*amān*). In addition, there are two issues here that must be distinguished: what the Prophet meant by *ḥadīth*s like this and their precise context, and what the generation of Muslim scholars later on thought he had meant. These are two different things, and given what we know of Islamic history, it is impossible to assert what the Prophet meant exactly, and whether he intended this to be universal or something valid for one time only.

Johnson also contended that: "The invitation to Islam is to be issued before fighting begins, to allow them to exercise this choice. The *jihād* of the sword, then, takes, second place to that of the tongue, the call to Islam."[135] But as made very clear by many Muslim scholars, including ash-Shaybānī, this was not a policy that the prophet Muḥammad systematically promoted, and scholars disagreed on whether to summon the enemy to Islam before the war is needed. Ash-Shaybānī himself was fine either way. He also found commendable, as we saw earlier, that the Muslims destroy everything on their way as they march to fight the army of the enemy, which I am not sure fit within the Prophet's enjoining his followers to conduct themselves properly during wars.

We see as well this tendency of misreading or carefully editing the complex web of views and laws about war in Islam and deducing from that specific answers in the article written by Justin Parrott. In order to prove that *jihād* is only

---

134 Ash-Shaybānī, *Kitāb as-Siyar*, 93; idem, *The Islamic Law of Nations*, 75–7. The translation here is that of Khadduri.
135 Johnson, *The Holy War Idea*, 70.

defensive, Parrott examined a carefully selected set of qur'ānic verses, prophetic *ḥadīth*, and a few random opinions by Muslim scholars, and proclaimed that:

> The mainstream view of *jihād* in Islam is consistent with modern international norms of non-violence. The Quran and Sunnah permit Muslims to defend themselves from aggression, while also limiting warfare to the purpose of preserving security, freedom, and human rights. Clarity on this issue should help remove the misperception that Islam is, by nature, an aggressive political ideology that threatens the West, as well as reduce the discrimination, suspicion, and hostility experienced by Muslim citizens in western countries.[136]

The words of Parrott leave no doubt about the motivation of many scholars and researchers who write about Islam and just war. Their efforts are driven by an eagerness to correct the "misperception" about Islam that exists in the West as a violent religion, and which causes hostility towards the Muslims.

The renowned scholar of Islamic legal thought, Wael Hallaq, also addressed *jihād*. But for some reason, he insisted that it is a legal concept, thus implicitly faulting all other articulations of *jihād* and warfare in Islam. He even contended that "*jihād* is a theory that belongs to the past," and that books "on *jihād* sharply declined after the 3rd century,"[137] which is absolutely not the case. In fact, the literary output increased dramatically in the Crusader period, and *jihād* was regularly invoked by some Muslim scholars across the centuries.

Nevertheless, the major problems with Hallaq are his inability to realize the complexity of Islamic thought about *jihād*, his insistence that *jihād* in Islam is a juristic concept, and his narrow view of its conditions. As demonstrated by the diversity of opinions on *jihād* that were expressed over the centuries by Muslim scholars from all professions (some of which were examined above), *jihād* is equally a philosophical, doctrinal, theological, mystical and political concept, and not only a juristic one. Moreover, Hallaq's contention that *jihād* "theory is narrowly driven by a single concern, namely the conversion of unbelievers to the Islamic faith"[138] is also false because, as we saw clearly in many examples above, this was simply one of several concerns and was not always the main one. Another controversial claim he makes is that *jihād* "theory is partial in

---

136 Parrott, Justin, "Jihād as Defense: Just-War Theory in the Quran and Sunnah," Yaqeen Institute for Islamic Research website (16 October 2016) <https://yaqeeninstitute.org/justin-parrott/jihad-as-defense-just-war-theory-in-the-quran-and-sunnah/#.XXAznH1yVUl> (accessed 4. September 2019).

137 Hallaq, Wael B., *Sharīʿa: Theory: Practice, Transformations*, Cambridge: Cambridge University Press, 2009, 324.

138 Ibid., 333.

that it deals only with conflict between Muslim and non-Muslim sovereignties. Nowhere in the entirety of juristic discourse do the legists deal with wars and conflict between and among Muslim principalities ...."[139] As we have seen in the discussion on Islamic law, jurists and non-jurists alike spoke of fighting and waging *jihād* against errant Muslims as one of the valid causes of war.

These problems in Hallaq's discussion of *jihād* resulted from the nature of modern legal thinking, and not necessarily from a lack of knowledge about Islamic history on his part. Modern legal thinking insists on harmonizing things in order to deduce from them coherent and applicable laws. Islamic legal thought, however, does not function in this way. It is by nature contradictory and is more concerned with listing all the views and positions, however incoherent and conflicting, and leaves it to the judge to decide which one to apply. In other words, Hallaq was reading classical Islamic thought on war backward, from the vantage point of a modern scholar of jurisprudence who thinks according to specific scholarly and professional conventions. Instead of allowing the many voices of Muslims on this topic to be expressed, he decided that the only ones that matter are the legal opinions (those expressed by Sunnis specifically), and the only way to present them is to impose on them a certain coherence.

9 Concluding Remarks

To understand "just war" in Islam, we need to understand how Muslims across the centuries have understood war and what makes it just. This cannot be done by maintaining the specific connotations and parameters of just war theory (be they Christian or in modern international law) and expecting the Islamic tradition to provide a precise answer about it. Therefore, since the Muslim scholars did not use the category as such (they only gradually started to do so in the twentieth century), we can only examine the way they have argued in a variety of scholarly fields (law, philosophy, theology, etc.), as well as in the Qur'ān for the legitimate causes and motives of war and its conducts and laws.

The examination of this chapter has shown that Muslims did not and do not agree on anything specific about war. They gave different arguments and justifications for its purpose and the way it is to be done. There are also doctrinal distinctions and different historical contexts in which they expressed their views,

139 Ibid.

meaning that even in those cases where we have similar language, it does not necessarily indicate the same intention.

Below is a summary of the main views that they expressed, divided into three categories: 1) valid causes and motives of war, 2) valid conducts of war, and 3) valid truces. I should emphasize that the summary does not constitute a theory of just war in Islam, for the simple reason that there is absolutely no agreement on it. What some might have considered valid, others have considered invalid. Equally important is the fact that these views were expressed over a large span of time, different historical circumstances, and varied influences and doctrinal differences. One cannot, therefore, impose a unity on them. Additionally, classical Islamic thought on war is no more relevant in our world of today in that modernity has triggered a major disruption between modern Islamic thought and pre-20th century Islamic thought, so much so that modern Muslim thinkers who write about war and peace (or any other topic for that matter) cannot be said to represent any structural continuity with their pre-modern peers. It is for this reason that I have added a section on "Islamic Modernism and the Validity of War."

9.1 Valid Causes and Motives of War

Probably the only thing Muslim scholars agreed upon in this connection is that war is a necessary thing. But what exactly it is meant to address, is a different matter. The most notable motives they gave for it are four: summoning or conversion of non-Muslims to Islam, levying the *jizya* tax from the People of the Book, protecting the lands of Islam, or fighting errant Muslims. There was disagreement between those who specified that war can proceed only after the enemy was summoned to Islam and refused to do so (as argued by Ibn Rushd and al-Kulaynī), and those who did not make the summoning a condition for war (as seen in some of the arguments made by Abū Yūsuf, ash-Shaybānī and aṭ-Ṭūsī). Similarly, one of the motives of war is to levy the *jizya* from the People of the Book, but here the category itself (who exactly are the People of the Book) is not clearly defined. Some scholars (such as aṭ-Ṭūsī) considered it to include exclusively Jews, Christians and Zoroastrians, while other scholars, however, extended it to other groups living under the rule of Muslims or in adjacent territories (Ethiopians, Turkic peoples, Indians, etc.), as is made amply clear in the analysis of Ibn Rushd. It is worthwhile to note that some Arab Christian tribes, such as the Banū Taghlib, benefited from a preferential treatment of paying a *zakāt* like the Muslims, which was likely due to their contributions alongside Muslim armies.

Some scholars tried to make a clear distinction that the People of the Book are not fought for the purpose of conversion but only for the purpose of accepting to pay the *jizya*. Ibn Rushd was of the opinion that it was both, but al-Kulaynī and aṭ-Ṭūsī argued that it was only for *jizya*.

Some scholars (aṭ-Ṭūsī, al-Qushayrī, Ibn ʿAsākir, etc.) raised the issue that war cannot be waged by errant Muslims, thus conditioning valid war on proper Islamic doctrine and belief. Some tied it to the individual condition: if the Muslim has the means, he must do it otherwise he sins, and if not he should avoid it, such as in the argument of ʿAbd al-Jabbār. He emphasized, however, that it is only to be done if it is certain that it does not lead to committing a worse harm than the one being fought.

There was also a difference regarding whether war is to be waged against a physical or conceptual enemy. Ibn ʿAsākir, for instance, argued that *jihād* was a war against unbelief and tyranny. ʿAbd al-Jabbār referred to eliminating the "wrong," which is broader than unbelief, and al-Fārābī spoke of war as a tool to discipline humanity. These conceptual frameworks are different from specifying the enemy as unbelievers or People of the Book. Al-Ghazālī introduced another angle, namely that the rationale of war against unbelievers is to disrupt the distortion and confusion they cause to believers, thus tying war not to conversion and *jizya* but rather to a conceptual threat to the spiritual wellbeing of the Muslims and their livelihood. Al-ʿĀmirī too compared valid warfare to a surgical operation, which necessarily causes a lesser harm but saves from a worse harm.

Fighting errant Muslims, often called people of dissent or evil dissenters, was also one of the causes of valid warfare. But disagreements here were much more pronounced than in other topics. The fragility of Muslim society was at stake, which likely led some who believed in its merit and value to still argue for not doing it, such as al-Kulaynī.

The issue of *jihād* being a personal versus communal duty is important. The Shīʿīs, who often labeled it as communal, insisted nevertheless that the individual choosing to do it must only do it under the leadership of the true imam (as we saw with aṭ-Ṭūsī), thus, bringing into it an obligatory personal component. Sunnis generally spoke of it as a communal duty, but they did not always specify whether the decision to launch war is exclusively that of the leader. As we saw with Ibn ʿAsākir, he avoided the issue altogether, and that is partly explained by the fact that heightened *jihād* propaganda at his time intended to sway people to fight, and therefore he intentionally avoided the hair-splitting details that we commonly find in legal manuals about *jihād* and warfare.

Finally, the Qurʾān also discusses the issue of valid war, and ties it to several motives: a punishment for unbelief and rebelling against God, a mechanism to force others to convert to Islam or pay the *jizya*, and a test to the believers to show their devotion to God.

9.2 Valid Conducts of War

Muslim scholars equally disagreed pretty much on every issue relating to the conducts of war. The discussion in both Ibn Rushd and al-Kulaynī leave no doubt that the differences were sometimes sharp and do not allow any coherent conclusions to be drawn. The reason for that, as Ibn Rushd admitted, was a combination of contradictions and differences within the Qurʾān, ḥadīth, and the historical practice of Muslims. They are all authoritative sources, and scholars gave them equal weight, which made the divergences impossible to resolve. A verse in the Qurʾān was on par with the Sunna of the Prophet, the practice of a Muslim leader or general, and the opinion of a jurist.

The issue of the enemy the Muslims are allowed to kill also received no agreement. As made evidently clear by Ibn Rushd and al-Kulaynī, aside from enemy fighters, scholars disagreed on whether women, children, the elderly, the handicapped, and the clergy can be killed too. This problem was triggered by a conceptual disagreement over whether the killing is necessitated on the basis of unbelief or ability to fight. If the former, then everyone is to be killed, if the latter, then only fighters can be killed. Even in the former case, it was permissible to kill non-combatants (as in the opinion attributed to imam Jaʿfar aṣ-Ṣādiq) only if this occurred as a result of war activities (something like the modern concept of 'collateral damage'), but the Muslim fighters should not directly fight them and kill them.

The same applies to causing damage to the homes and farms of the enemy and whether the use of weapons such as mangonels are allowed (as recorded by Ibn Rushd). Some allow cutting trees and burning homes and homesteads (the view attributed to aṣ-Ṣādiq and Ibn Taymīya), some ban it unless there is necessity for it (al-Kulaynī).

As for captives, some approve of their torture and mutilating their bodies, but others ban that and only permit burning. But there seems to be an agreement that only the leader/imam has the authority to free unconditionally, free for a ransom, free on condition of *jizya*, enslave, or kill the hostages (as argued by al-Kulaynī and Ibn Rushd). And there seems to have been an agreement that when it comes to errant Muslims, if they are to be fought, the duty must be followed to its ultimate conclusion: the complete elimination of their threat.

They equally disagreed on whether it is permissible to give the enemy an assurance of safety (*amān*), and if so who can issue it: the leader only or any Muslim other than a slave (as we saw in Ibn Rushd), or even the slave (as argued by al-Kulaynī).

Some Muslim scholars pointed out the historical development of the concept of war, and the important changes it underwent. As we saw earlier, they argued for different phases: the phase of the life of the prophet Muḥammad when he was in Mecca, the phase when he was in Medina, and the phase after his death. But this distinction was invariably tossed aside and ignored when scholars quoted verses from the Qur'ān or prophetic *ḥadīth* without any regard to the three phases, and sometimes without regard to the internal contradiction in each corpus (contradiction among the verses of the Qur'ān, and contradiction among the *ḥadīth*s of the Prophet).

9.3 Valid Truces

Scholars generally did not agree on the permissibility of truces and their condition. As recorded in Ibn Rushd, the divergence was over whether they are made on the basis of the clemency of the Muslims or their necessity to the Muslims. Some allowed truces on condition that the enemy pays the Muslims but not the other way. Others allowed that the Muslims pay the enemy. There is also disagreement over the length of a truce; some put the maximum at three years, others at ten years. But as we saw, historical circumstances infused energy into the argument about the need for truces. The Crusader period is one notable case, and it witnessed both a heightened increase in *jihād* and war propaganda, and ironically too it featured a widespread policy of peacemaking justified by recourse to legal arguments such as the notions of the "best interest" (*maṣlaḥa*) of the Muslims and "necessity" (*ḍarūra*) to preserve Muslim lives and resources. It was also during this time, as we saw with Ibn Qudāma and Zayn ad-Dīn ar-Rāzī, that legal arguments were made allowing the extension and renewal of truces beyond the 10-year maximum limit, which effectively meant legitimizing open peace.

9.4 Islamic Modernism and the Validity of War

Modern Islamic thought about war varies dramatically from that of the premodern period. The circumstances, challenges and inspirations were very different, and led the Muslims to develop new ways of thinking about war. As it was made abundantly clear with the likes of Maududi and Quṭb, valid war is an Islamic revolution to free humanity from bondage to ungodly systems and make the world a better place. It must be led by a vanguard who take their cue from the teachings of Islam exclusively, especially the Qur'ān and the career of the prophet Muḥammad. Needless to say, it was a specific and partial reading of the Qur'ān, prophetic career and Islamic history that they advocated.

Other modern thinkers, such as Shaltūt, were eager to see Islam advocate for the same principles of Western modernity. Thus, their language about warfare in Islam echoed its vocabulary: valid war is for defensive reasons, to repel aggression, and safeguard freedoms. Yet thinkers like Ṭaha went beyond this, arguing that *jihād* and warfare are hallmarks of an inferior Islam. For humanity to attain its highest potential, this inferior Islam must be replaced and superseded by the highest form of Islam, which has no use for war and violence.

The closing decades of the twentieth century brought a change to the language of war among militants. Even though they were inspired by ideologues like Maududi and Quṭb, nevertheless, they had no use for the language of warfare as a world revolution. They were more concerned with universal ideals such as human suffering, economic exploitation, poverty, etc., and their discussion of war featured those issues. In other words, militant organizations like al-Qaeda consider valid war as a war to defend against and repel "aggression, iniquity and injustice" caused by the West and its cronies.

9.5 Practical Applicability of the Concept of Just War in Islam

The discussion about the practical applicability of the concept of just war in Islam today is very problematic, mostly because there is no one concept about the validity of war. Equally important is the fact that the issue of applicability depends exclusively on the Muslims today seeking to pursue a theory about just war. But as this chapter has shown, the Muslims' own thinking of war, its causes and motives, and its conducts was never static and reflected a wide range of views and convictions. Moreover, the sources of inspiration for some positions on valid warfare sometimes came from outside the Islamic tradition. Modernity is an obvious case. It was the values and ideals of Western modernity (as we saw with Shaltūt and Ṭaha) that prompted some to look into the Islamic foundational sources and tradition for examples that would allow the construction of a modern and humane Islamic theory of war. It was the competition with Communism that inspired some militant thinkers (as we saw with Maududi and Quṭb) to borrow its language and redesign a theory of the validity and purpose of warfare in Islam. Even the early Muslims could have been inspired by some

Christian Byzantine views that valorized warfare and the rewards warriors would attain if war was conducted for the triumph of religion.[140]

Another serious challenge is the fact that Islamic law is not practiced any more, except for a minor branch that deals with family law. Muslims live in nation-states and follow modern constitutions and legal systems based on them. These constitutions often have their own definitions of valid war and its conduct and limitations. Likewise, Muslim countries are invariably signatories to international agreements and conventions on war and peace, which means that what Islam says about war and peace is not necessarily relevant. It might be rhetorically relevant and some rulers might seek supportive religious *fatwā*s or opinions in order to placate the popular mood. Add to this that the exercise to write about just war in Islam is generally done by some Muslims in order to legitimize international agreements and conventions. For instance, the peace between Israel and Egypt (signed at the Camp David Accord in 1979) was legitimized by the Sheikh of al-Azhar and the great mufti of Egypt as compliant with Islam, and they based their reasoning on verse 8:61 ("If they seek peace, accept it"), the peace treaties the prophet Muḥammad concluded with his enemies, and the notion of *maṣlaḥa* (best interest of the Muslims).[141]

Finally, Islam (and this might be applicable to other world religions as well) lacks and has always lacked a central religious authority that can issue religious directives and circulars binding on all Muslims. As such, Islam is unlike Christianity, especially the Catholic Church, which often streamlines its theological teachings and positions on many questions. Islam is also unlike modern legal systems where once a decision is adopted, it becomes legally binding. What this means is that a view expressed by any Muslim scholar is "Islamic", but it is not Islam, whereas a view expressed by a Catholic person does not represent the teachings of Catholic Christianity unless the Vatican accepts it. Therefore, the applicability of any study on just war in Islam is only consultative and temporary. New circumstances, new experiences and new needs might render any conclusions mute or irrelevant.

---

140 More on this point see Tesei, Tommaso, "Heraclius' War Propaganda." I should say that Tesei might be forcing the issue.

141 On this, see Ramadan, Abdel Azim, "Fundamentalist Influence in Egypt: The Strategies of the Muslim Brotherhood and the Takfir Group," in: Martin E. Marty/ R. Scott Appleby (eds), *Fundamentalisms and the State: Remaking Polities, economies, and Militance*, Chicago: University of Chicago Press, 1993, 169; and Yūsuf Ḥ. Yūsuf, *al-Ittifāqāt wa-l-muʿāhadāt fī ḍawʾ al-qānūn ad-duwalī*, Amman: Markaz al-Kitāb al-Akkādīmī, 2017, 303.

Bibliography

Primary Sources

ʿAbd al-Jabbār, *Kitāb al-Uṣūl al-khamsa*, in Daniel Gimaret, "Les *Uṣūl al–Ḫamsa* du Qāḍī ʿAbd al-Ǧabbār et leurs commentaires," *Annales Islamologiques* 15 (1979), 79–96.
Abū Shāma, *Kitāb ar-Rawḍatayn fī akhbār ad-dawlatayn al-Nūrīyya wa-l-Ṣalāḥīyya*, 5 vols., ed. Ibrāhīm az-Zaybaq, Beirut: Muʾassasat ar-Risāla, 1997.
Abū Yūsuf, *Kitāb al-Kharāj*, ed. Iḥsān ʿAbbās, Beirut: Dār ash-Shurūq, 1985.
Al-ʿĀmirī, *Kitāb al-Iʿlām bi-manāqib al-islām*, ed. Aḥmad Ghurāb, Cairo: Dār al-Kitāb al-ʿArabī, 1967.
Al-Bannā, Ḥasan, *Risālat al-Jihād*, in: *Thalāth rasāʾil fī j-jihād: Abū l-Aʿlā al-Mawdūdī, Ḥasan al-Bannā, Sayyid Quṭb*, 67–105, Amman: Dār ʿAmmār, 1991.
Al-Bannā, Ḥasan, *Kitab ul Jihad*, trans. A. B. Mehri, in: Sayyid Qutb, *Milestones: Maʿalim fi'l-tareeq*, ed. A.B. Mehri, Birmingham: Maktabah Booksellers and Publishers, 2006, 217–40.
Bin Laden, Usama, "Declaration of War against the Americans Occupying the Land of the Two Holy Places," in: Roxanne Euben and Muḥammad Qasim Zaman (eds), *Princeton Readings in Islamist Thought*, Princeton: Princeton University Press, 2009, 436–59.
Al-Fārābī, *Kitāb Taḥṣīl as-saʿāda*, ed. ʿAlī Bū-Milḥim, Beirut: Dār wa-Maktabat al-Hilāl, 1995.
Al-Fārābī, *Ārāʾ ahl al-madīna al-fāḍila wa-muḍadatuha*, Cairo: Muʾassasat al-Hindāwī, 2013.
Al-Ghazālī, *Iḥyāʾ ʿulūm ad-dīn*, 4 vols., Beirut: Dār al-Maʿrifa, 1983.
Al-Ghazālī, *Jawāhir al-qurʾān*, ed. Muḥammad Rashīd al-Qabbānī, Beirut: Dār Iḥyāʾ al-ʿUlūm, 1986.
Ibn ʿAsākir, *al-Arbaʿūn ḥadīthan fī l-ḥaththʿalā al-jihād*, in: Suleiman A. Mourad/James E. Lindsay, *The Intensification and Reorientation of Sunni Jihad Ideology in the Crusader Period: Ibn ʿAsakir (1105–1176) of Damascus and His Age*, Leiden: Brill, 2013, 130–203.
Ibn al-Athīr, *al-Kāmil fī t-Taʾrīkh*, 10 vols., ed. ʿUmar ʿAbd-as-Salām Tadmurī, Beirut: Dār al-Kitāb al-ʿArabī, 1997.
Ibn al-Athīr, *The Chronicle of Ibn al-Athir for the Crusading Period from* al-Kamil fi't-Taʾrikh, 3 vols., trans. D. S. Richards, Farnham: Ashgate, 2006–2008.
Ibn Qayyim al-Jawzīya, *Zād al-maʿād fī hadī khayr al-ʿibād*, 5 vols., Beirut: Muʾassasat ar-Risāla, 1994.
Ibn Qudāma, *al-Mughnī*, 10 vols., eds Ṭaha M. al-Zaynī and Muḥammad Fāyid, Cairo: Maktabat al-Qāhira, 1968–1970.
Ibn Rushd, *Bidāyat al-Mujtahid wa-nihāyat al-muqtaṣid*, 4 vols., ed. Muḥammad Ṣ. Ḥ. Ḥallāq, Cairo: Maktabat Ibn Taymiyya, 1994.
Ibn Rushd, "The Chapter on Jihad from Averroes' Legal Handbook al-Bidāyah," in: Rudolph Peters, *Jihad in Medieval and Modern Islam*, Leiden: Brill, 1977, 9–25.
Ibn Rushd, *Faṣl al-maqāl fī taqrīr ma bayn ash-Sharīʿa wa-l-ḥikma min ittiṣal*, ed. Muḥammad-ʿĀbid al-Jābirī, Beirut, Markaz Dirāsāt al-Wiḥda al-ʿArabīyya, 1997.
Ibn Taymīya, *Majmūʿ al-fatāwa*, 22 vols. (36 pts), Ed. Muṣṭafā ʿAṭā, Beirut: Dār al-Kutub al-ʿIlmiyya, 2000.
Ibn Wāṣil, *Mufarrij al-kurūb fī akhbār Banī Ayyūb*, 5 vols., eds, Jamāl ad-Dīn ash-Shayyāl and Ḥasanayn M. Rabiʿ, Cairo: Dār al-Kutub, 1957–1977.
ʿImād ad-Dīn al-Iṣfahānī, *al-Fatḥ al-qussī fī l-fatḥ al-qudsī*, Cairo: Dār al-Manār, 2004.

Al-Kulaynī, *al-Kāfī*, 8 vols., Beirut: Manshūrāt al-Fajr, 2007.
Al-Māwardī, *al-Ḥāwī al-kabīr*, 19 vols., ed. ʿAlī Muʿawwaḍ and ʿĀdil ʿAbd al-Mawjūd, Beirut: Dār al-Kutub al-ʿIlmiyya, 1999.
Al-Māwardī, *an-Nukat wa-l-ʿuyūn – Tafsīr al-Māwardī*, 6 vols., ed. as-Sayyid ʿAbd ar-Raḥīm, Beirut: Dār al-Kutub al-ʿIlmīyya, 1992.
Maududi, Abul Aʿla, *al-Jihād fī sabīl allāh*, in: *Thalāth rasāʾil fī j-jihād: Abū l-Aʿlā al-Mawdūdī, Ḥasan al-Bannā, Sayyid Quṭb*, 5–66, Amman: Dār ʿAmmār, 1991.
Maududi, Abul Aʿla, *Jihad in Islam*, Beirut: The Holy Koran Publishing House, 1980.
Al-Qushayrī, *Laṭāʾif al-ishārāt*, 3 vols., ed. Ibrāhīm al-Basyūnī, Cairo: al-Hayʾa al-Miṣrīyya al-ʿĀmma li-l-Kitāb, 1981–1983.
Al-Qushayrī, *al-Qushayri's Epistle on Sufism*, trans. Alexander D. Knysh, Reading: Garnet Publishing, 2007.
Quṭb, Sayyid, *Maʿālim fī ṭ-ṭarīq*, Cairo: Dār ash-Shurūq, 1979.
Qutb, Sayyid, *Milestones: Maʿalim fi'l-tareeq*, ed. A. B. al-Mehri, Birmingham: Maktabah Booksellers, 2006.
Ar-Rāzī, *Mafātīḥ al-ghayb – at-Tafsīr al-kabīr*, 32 vols., Beirut: Dār Iḥyāʾ at-Turāth al-ʿArabī, 1990.
Ash-Shāfiʿī, *The Epistle on Legal Theory*, ed. and trans. Joseph E. Lowry, New York: New York University Press, 2013.
Shaltūt, Maḥmūd, *al-Qurʾān wa-l-qitāl*, Cairo: Dār al-Kiṭāb al-ʿArabī, 1951.
Shaltūt, Maḥmūd, *The Qurʾān and Combat*, trans. Lamya al-Khraisha, Amman: the Royal Aal al-Bayt Institute for Islamic Thought, 2012.
Ash-Shaybānī, *Kitāb as-Siyar*, ed. Majid Khadduri, Beirut: Dār al-Muttaḥida li-n-Nashr, 1975.
Ash-Shaybānī, *The Islamic Law of Nations: Shaybānī's Siyar*, trans. Majid Khadduri, Baltimore: Johns Hopkins Press, 1966.
Aṭ-Ṭabarī, *Tafsīr aṭ-Ṭabarī – Jāmiʿ al-bayān fī taʾwīl al-qurʾān*, 12 vols., Beirut: Dār al-Kutub al-ʿIlmīyya, 1999.
Aṭ-Ṭabrisī, *Majmaʿ al-bayān fī tafsīr al-qurʾān*, 10 vols., ed. Hāshim al-Maḥallalātī, Beirut: Muʾassasat at-Tarīkh al-ʿArabī, 2005.
Ṭaha, Mahmoud M., *The Second Message of Islam*, trans. Abdullahi A. An-Naʿim, Syracuse: Syracuse University Press, 1987.
Ath-Thaʿlabī, *al-Kashf wa-l-bayān fī tafsīr al-qurʾān*, 6 vols., ed. Sayyid K. Ḥasan, Beirut: Dār al-Kutub al-ʿIlmīyya, 2004.
Aṭ-Ṭūsī, *al-Nihāya wa-nukatuha*, 3 vols., Qumm: Muʾassasat an-Nashr al-Islāmī, 1991.
Aṭ-Ṭūsī, *al-Iqtiṣād fīmā yajib ʿalā al-ʿibād*, ed. Muḥammad Qāsim al-Mūsawī, Qumm: Markaz Nūr al-Anwār, 2009.
Az-Zamakhsharī, *Tafsīr al-kashshāf ʿan ḥaqāʾiq ghawāmiḍ at-tanzīl*, 4 vols., ed. Muḥammad Shāhīn, Beirut: Dār al-Kitāb al-ʿArabī, 2009.
Zayn ad-Dīn ar-Rāzī, *Tuḥfat al-mulūk fī fiqh madhhab al-imām Abī Ḥanīfa an-Nuʿmān*, ed. ʿAbd Allāh N. Aḥmad, Beirut: Dār al-Bashāʾir, 1997.

Modern Scholarship

Abdel Haleem, M.A.S., "Qur'ānic '*Jihād*': A Linguistic and Contextual Analysis," *Journal of Qur'ānic Studies* 12 (2010), 147–66.

Abou El Fadl, Khaled, "Islamic Law, Jihad, and Violence," *Journal of Islamic and Near Eastern Law* 16 (2017), 1–27.

Afsaruddin, Asma, *Striving in the Path of God: Jihād and Martyrdom in Islamic Thought*, New York: Oxford University Press, 2013.

Ahmad, Ahmad A., "The Evolution of Just War Theory in Islamic Law: Texts, History, and the Purpose of 'Reading'," *American Foreign Policy Interests* 28.2 (2006), 107–15.

ʿĀshūr, Saʿīd, *al-Ḥaraka aṣ-ṣalībiyya: ṣafḥa mushriqa fī tārīkh al-jihād al-ʿarabī fī l-ʿuṣūr al-wusṭā*, 2 vols., Cairo: Maktabat al-Anglū al-Miṣriyya, 1963.

Bakircioglu, Onder, *Islam and Warfare: Context and Compatibility with International Law*, London: Routledge, 2016.

Blankinship, Khalid Yahya, "Parity of Muslim and Western Concepts of Just War," *The Muslim World* 101.3 (2011), 412–26.

Boisard, Marcel A., *Jihad: A Commitment to Universal Peace*, Plainfield: American Trust Publications, 1988.

Calasso, Giovanna/Lanioni, Giuliano (eds), *Dar al-islam / dar al-harb: Territories, People, Identities*, Leiden: Brill, 2017.

Cook, David, "Fighting to Create the Just State: Apocalypticism in Radical Muslim Discourse," in: Sohail Hashmi (ed.), *Just Wars, Holy Wars, & Jihads: Christian, Jewish and Muslim Encounters and Exchanges*, New York: Oxford University Press, 2012, 364–82.

Cook, David, *Understanding Jihad*, Oakland: University of California Press, 2015.

Dadoyan, Seta B., *The Fatimid Armenians: Cultural and Political Interaction in the Near East*, Leiden: Brill, 1997.

Freedman, Lawrence, "Defining War," in: Yves Boyer and Julian Lindley-French (eds), *The Oxford Handbook on War*, Oxford: Oxford University Press, 2012, 17–29,.

Goudie, Kenneth A., *Reinventing Jihād: Jihād Ideology from the Conquest of Jerusalem to the End of the Ayyūbids (c. 492/1099–647/1249)*, Leiden: Brill, 2019.

Hallaq, Wael B., *Sharīʿa: Theory: Practice, Transformations*, Cambridge: Cambridge University Press, 2009.

Hashmi, Sohail H. (ed.), *Just Wars, Holy Wars, & Jihads: Christian, Jewish, and Muslim Encounters and Exchanges*, New York: Oxford University Press, 2012.

Hillenbrand, Carole, *The Crusades: Islamic Perspectives*, Edinburgh: Edinburgh University Press, 1999.

Hoyland, Robert G., *In God's Path: The Arab Conquests and the Creation of an Islamic Empire*, Oxford: Oxford University Press, 2015.

Johnson, James T., *The Holy War Idea in Western and Islamic Traditions*, University Park: Pennsylvania State University Press, 2002.

Köhler, Michael, *Alliances and Treatises between Frankish and Muslim Rulers in the Middle East: Cross Cultural Diplomacy in the Period of the Crusades*, trans. P.M. Holt, rev. and ed. Konrad Hirschler, Leiden: Brill, 2013.

Kelsay, John/Johnson, James Turner (eds), *Just War and Jihad: Historical and Theoretical Perspectives on War and Peace in Western and Islamic Traditions*, New York: Greenwood Press, 1991.

Kelsay, John, *Arguing the Just War in Islam*, Cambridge: Harvard University Press, 2007.

Kepel, Gilles, *Jihad: The Trail of Political Islam*, Cambridge: The Belknap Press of Harvard University Press, 2002.

Madden, Thomas F., *The New Concise History of the Crusades*, New York: Rowman & Littlefield, 2005.

Mourad, Suleiman A., "What Inspires Non-Violence and Violence in Islam? Some Religious and Historical Factors," in: Sudhir Chandra (ed.), *Violence and Non-Violence across Time: History, Religion and Culture*, London: Routledge, 2018, 53–77.

Mourad, Suleiman A., "The Shahada and the Creation of an Islamic Identity," in: John Tolan (ed.), *Geneses: Comparative Study of the Historiographies of the Rise of Christianity, Rabbinic Judaism and Islam*, London: Routledge, 2019, 216–37.

Mourad, Suleiman A., "Crusader-Muslim Relations: The Power of Diplomacy in a Troubling Age," in: Howard Williams (ed.), *The Palgrave Handbook in International Political Theory*, London: Palgrave Macmillan, 2021, (In Press).

Mourad, Suleiman A./Lindsay, James E., *The Intensification and Reorientation of Sunni Jihad Ideology in the Crusader Period: Ibn ʿAsākir (1105–1176) of Damascus and His Age; with an edition and translation of Ibn ʿAsākir's* The Forty Ḥadīths for Inciting Jihad, Leiden: Brill, 2013.

Oppenheim, Lassa, *International Law: A Treatise. Vol. II: War and Neutrality*, ed. Ronald F. Roxburgh, London: Longmans, Green and Co. 1921.

Parrott, Justin, "Jihād as Defense: Just-War Theory in the Quran and Sunnah," Yaqeen Institute for Islamic Research website (16 October 2016), <https://yaqeeninstitute.org/justin-parrott/jihad-as-defense-just-war-theory-in-the-quran-and-sunnah/#.XXAznH1yVUl> (accessed 4. September 2019).

Peters, Rudolph, *Jihad in Classical and Modern Islam: A Reader.* Princeton: Marcus Wiener, 1996.

Polk, William R., *Crusade and Jihād: The Thousand-Year War between the Muslim World and the Global North*, New Haven: Yale University Press, 2018.

Ramadan, Abdel Azim, "Fundamentalist Influence in Egypt: the Strategies of the Muslim Brotherhood and the Takfir Group," in: Martin E. Marty/R. Scott Appleby (eds), *Fundamentalisms and the State: Remaking Polities, economies, and Militance*, 144–75, Chicago: University of Chicago Press, 1993.

Riley-Smith, Jonathan, *The Crusades: A Short History*, New Haven: Yale University Press, 2005.

Roy, Olivier, *Holy Ignorance: When Religion and Culture Part Ways*, New York: Columbia University Press, 2010.

Sizgorich, Thomas, *Violence and Belief in Late Antiquity: Militant Devotion in Christianity and Islam*, Philadelphia: University of Pennsylvania Press, 2009.

Takim, Liyakat, "War and Peace in the Islamic Sacred Sources," *Journal of Shiʿi Islamic Studies* 4.1 (2011), 5–22.

Tesei, Tommaso, "Heraclius' War Propaganda and the Qurʾān's Promise of Reward for Dying in Battle," *Studia Islamica* 114 (2019), 219–47.

Tor, Deborah G., *Violent Order: Religious Warfare, Chivalry, and the* ʿAyyār *Phenomenon in the Medieval Islamic World*, Würzburg: Ergon, 2007.

Yūsuf, Yūsuf Ḥ., *al-Ittifāqāt wa-l-muʿāhadāt fī ḍawʾ al-qānūn ad-Duwalī*, Amman: Markaz al-Kitāb al-Akkādīmī, 2017.

Zawati, Hilmi, *Is Jihad a Just War? War, Peace and Human Rights under Islamic and Public International Law*, Lewiston: Edwin Mellen Press, 2001.

Zulfiqar, Adnan, *Collective Duties (Farḍ Kifāya) in Islamic Law: The Moral Community, State Authority and Ethical Speculation in the Premodern Period*, Ph.D. Dissertation, University of Pennsylvania, 2018.
Zulfiqar, Adnan, "Claiming Jurisdiction over Jihād: Islamic Law and Its Duty to Fight," *West Virginia Law Review* 120 (2018), 427–68.

Suggestions for Further Reading

The following titles give the interested reader a focused access into the major debates and scholarly conventions regarding the topics of war and peace in Islam. They are furnished as suggested further reading, which is not an evaluation of their worthiness or lack thereof.

Abdel Haleem, M.A.S., "Qur'ānic '*Jihād*': A Linguistic and Contextual Analysis," *Journal of Qur'ānic Studies* 12 (2010), 147–66.
Afsaruddin, Asma, *Striving in the Path of God: Jihād and Martyrdom in Islamic Thought*, New York: Oxford University Press, 2013.
Boisard, Marcel A., *Jihad: A Commitment to Universal Peace*, Plainfield: American Trust Publications, 1988.
Calasso, Giovanna/Lanioni, Giuliano (eds), *Dar al-islam / dar al-harb: Territories, People, Identities*, Leiden: Brill, 2017.
Cook, David, *Understanding Jihad*, Oakland: University of California Press, 2015.
Kelsay, John, *Arguing the Just War in Islam*, Cambridge: Harvard University Press, 2007.
Mourad, Suleiman A./Lindsay, James E., *The Intensification and Reorientation of Sunni Jihad Ideology in the Crusader Period: Ibn ʿAsākir (1105–1176) of Damascus and His Age; with an edition and translation of Ibn ʿAsākir's* The Forty Ḥadīths for Inciting Jihad, Leiden: Brill, 2013.
Shaltūt, Maḥmūd, *The Qur'ān and Combat*, trans. Lamya al-Khraisha, Amman: the Royal Aal al-Bayt Institute for Islamic Thought, 2012.
Ṭaha, Mahmoud M., *The Second Message of Islam*, trans. Abdullahi A. An-Naʿim, Syracuse: Syracuse University Press, 1987.
Zawati, Hilmi, *Is Jihad a Just War? War, Peace and Human Rights under Islamic and Public International Law*, Lewiston: Edwin Mellen Press, 2001.
Zulfiqar, Adnan, "Claiming Jurisdiction over Jihād: Islamic Law and Its Duty to Fight," *West Virginia Law Review* 120 (2018), 427–68.

Georges Tamer and Katja Thörner

Epilogue

1 Introduction

What could be just about war? Could there ever be good reasons for razing cities to the ground, depriving people of their homes, killing soldiers and even children, old women and men? Today, it is quite possible that the majority of people would say no, but equally, they would likely confess that there has never been a time in history without war, and that "good" reasons to wage war have very often been easily found. But what was seen as good reasons by one side has almost always been seen as bad by the other. Yet, might it still be possible to find criteria for a just war that anyone could agree with? For example, it seems plausible that the protection of one's homeland is a good reason to wage war, while attacking a nation to plunder resources is by no means a good one. But what if these resources prove necessary for survival and the force of arms has been found only as a last resort after a long period of negotiation? Admittedly, the example is quite abstract; while the distribution of resources is often an important cause of waging war, there is almost always a bundle of multiple causes that lead to war, rather than a single cause. And religious beliefs are commonly among these causes.

Therefore, following the classical distinction between *jus ad bellum* and *jus in bello*, we can ask: what have been considered reasons for the legitimization of war in Judaism, Christianity and Islam? And what do religious sources say about rules of the permissible and the forbidden in war, in relation to warriors and military leaders?

In the following, we will approach these and other questions attempting ultimately to determine commonalities and differences among the three religions in relation to the obviously problematic concept of just war.

2 The Concept of Just War from a Jewish Perspective

Since there is nothing in the Jewish tradition that would offer a fully elaborated theory of just war, one has to instead extract a concept of just war in Judaism from the foundational texts of this religion.

https://doi.org/10.1515/9783110733136-005

At first glance, Judaism may appear to be a thoroughly pacifistic religion: the key term in worship and Jewish liturgy is "peace" – *shalom*, not war, which is never mentioned as desirable in this context. The same impression arises from a casual reading of rabbinic literature. But to understand *shalom* here as peace in the sense of the absence of military conflict is misleading. *Shalom* can be used as the opposite of war; however, it often means, more generally, the absence of any conflict, or rather inner tranquility.[1] At the same time, the need to wage war under certain circumstances was never denied in the Jewish tradition.

In the Hebrew Bible, war seems to be accepted as a part of human life. The scripture expresses high estimation for successful military leaders like King Saul or David, and even describes God himself as a warrior. From a theological perspective, war in the biblical context can be seen as an instrument to enforce God's justice, who does not back off from violence and total extinction of the enemy. In this respect, the biblical approach to war seems to be dependent on the cultural environment from which it emerged. However, at the same time one can find in the biblical scriptures the beginnings of opposing tendencies showing elements of what we today call a theory of just war. For example, one condition for waging war is that fighting is commanded by God, and is grounded on God's promise to the people of Israel to live peacefully within the borders of the Promised Land. In Deuteronomy in particular, there are several passages that contain rules of conduct in war that can be considered as a rudimentary version of *jus in bello*, such as how to treat women and children in the besieged cities of the enemy.

In the rabbinic literature, different categories of war were developed and brought together into a hierarchy of approbation. Whereas divinely commanded wars (*milchemet mitzvah*) and obligatory wars (*milchemet chovah*) were considered as justified, the attitude towards discretionary wars (*milchemet hareshut*) was more cautious. While there is no clear definition of the three categories, it can be said that the rabbis accepted wars to protect territorial integrity and in relation to self-defense, but questioned the right to wage war in order to expand territory and gain spoil.

In medieval writings like those of Rashi or Maimonides, the categories were reduced to two: commanded wars and discretionary wars. Like the rabbis, Rashi and Maimonides were not concerned with current wars or the applicability of the rules of the Torah to the present. However, the position of Maimonides shows

1 Cf. Alick Isaacs, "The Concept of Peace in Judaism," in: Georges Tamer (ed.), *The Concept of Peace in Judaism, Christianity and Islam*, Berlin/Boston: De Gruyter, 2020, 1–44, here: 4.

two significant innovations in his approach to war: first, he is more tolerant in regard to discretionary wars fought in order to enlarge the borders of Israel and second, he seems to view wars waged to eliminate idolatry as commanded wars. But this view was not adopted by his contemporaries, a fact that is perhaps attributable, as Daniel Polish assumes, to the fact that Maimonides spent most of his life in an Islamic environment and, to some extent, incorporated the idea of *jihād* into his own thinking. For the leading scholar and near contemporary of Maimonides, Moses ben Nahman, who is better known by his acronym Ramban, the narratives of wars in the Bible have no implications for other wars in later times. The rules and criteria of just war that the rabbis extracted from the biblical text can only be applied to the specific circumstances of war that were waged for the literal conquest of the land of Israel and are to be fought again in the Messianic time.

The preconditions for thinking about warfare changed dramatically with the foundation of the State of Israel on Palestinian territories with its own army. From this point on, the question of legitimizing war became no longer an issue of abstract thinking, but rather an urgent question needing to be resolved. In the first place, however, it was not a religious task to formulate the condition under which war should be waged, so that it could be justified, but rather the task of politics and the military. It turns out, however, that statements on the legitimacy of war reflect some religious elements, even in the twentieth century. From the early times of Jewish settlement in Palestine, Jewish scholars and thinkers tried to relate current acts of violence and armed conflicts, initially waged under the British mandate and then under Israeli leadership from the 1948 War of Independence onwards, to the ancient sacred texts of Judaism. Even the concept of "holy war" (*milchamah qedosha*), which was never mentioned in classical texts, was used in the context of the "Arab Revolt" (1916–18) to legitimize Jewish settlement as a morally pure type of waging war. The crucial aim was to extend the narrative of the Land of Israel up to the present day and apply it to the current political reality. The Ashkenazi Chief Rabbi of Israel, Isaac Halevi Herzog, considered it mandatory to conquer the land of Israel. And the first Chief Rabbi of the Israel Defense Forces stated that the "integration of the sword and the book [is] a continuous thread in Jewish history."[2] But one can also find modern voices that resemble Ramban in arguing that the biblical commandment of conquest is limited to the particular circumstances of the time of Joshua. And perhaps it can be seen as an essential characteristic feature of Jewish thought on *jus ad bellum* that it eschews generalizations, since the specific circumstances

2 See footnote 48 in Polish, cited in Eisen, *Religious Zionism*, 87.

from which wars emerge are far too complex to be subjected to general rules of legitimation.

3 The Concept of Just War from a Christian Perspective

From a sociological point of view, Christianity began in small communities of converted Jews who lived in the Roman Province Judea. Expecting the return of the Messiah and the kingdom of peace to begin, they were surrounded by armed revolts and threatened with persecution. As with most of Jewish history, there was no need for early Christians to ponder the justification to wage war. The sacred scriptures of Christianity reflect that situation clearly and urge the faithful to accept the political order and to separate it from the things that are God's (Mark 12:17). But that does not mean that all early Christians were pacifists. As soldiers, they were engaged in wars, and it even seems that this was largely accepted, although it was also subjected to criticism, e. g. by the converted Christian author Tertullian.

In order to answer the question whether Christians were allowed to participate in military combat or wage war, Augustine in the fourth century formulates some criteria that allow to distinguish between an unjust and a just war. The historical background of his thought is the threat of the decline of the Roman Empire due to the attacks of external enemies such as the Visigoths and Vandals. The metaphysical background of Augustine's statements concerning a concept of just war is the idea that everything in the world is striving for peace, and the highest degree of peace is in God. But there is a flaw in human nature: human beings are prone to evil. This implies that people have evil desires; conquering countries, devasting the homes of the inhabitants and killing them are among these evil desires. Hence, it is not possible to end violence and wars in this world, but rather, the power and authority of the state are needed to avoid anarchy. Punitive force by the state is legal if it serves to reduce sin in one's own community and, from a metaphysical point of view, in the world as a whole. According to this line of thought, a war is just when it is—as last resort—waged to overcome sin in the world, but it is unjust if it is based on an evil desire to conquer and to destroy.

At the beginning of the 12th century, the Bolognese compiler of Canon Law Gratian collected statements on the question of just war and organized them according to systematic criteria. He also compiled Augustine's statements on the subject, which are contained in several of his writings and letters. Thomas Aquinas used this collection to develop his approach to the problem of just war. The theological context in which Thomas formulated his concept of just war is the treatise *de bello*, in which he tried to answer the question whether waging war is against Christ's command to love your neighbor. According to Thomas, political leaders (*principes*) should govern according to the natural law, and the political community should serve to prevent individuals from sin and allow them to live in devotion. In this context, "war" means the use of lethal force against evildoers in one's own community to prevent internal disturbances and the use of weapons to defend the community against external enemies. But what Thomas had in mind when he spoke of the need to defend the community (*res publica*) against outer enemies is not the concept of a war between two sovereign states. For Thomas it is the *orbis christianus* as the worldly side of the community of all faithful—i. e. the church—that must be rescued from the attacks of the enemies of Christianity. Concretely, those enemies were for Thomas the Albigenses, who led the faithful away from the true belief of the church, or Muslim authorities in Palestine who did not allow Christians to practice their faith. Thomas also addresses the question of *jus in bello*, i. e., the question of rules and regulations in the case of war, when he states that war should be fought with the right intention—a criterion that has been subsequently elaborated over time.

Just as it is possible to legitimize war on the basis of just war theory, it is also possible to withdraw the legitimation in the same way. This was precisely the strategy of Francisco de Vitoria, a Spanish Dominican known as one of the fathers of international law, in his rejection of the Spanish colonialism of the "new world". With reference to Augustine and Thomas, he comes to the conclusion that the Spanish conquest of America must be unjust because none of the conditions to legitimize war existed in that case.

The Thomasian line of just war theory remained predominant until the 20th century. The terrible atrocities of World War I and II triggered a turning point towards the establishment and institutionalization of a functional international law. This methodical shift was underscored by the transition from "just war theory" to guidelines of "just peace" in the 1980s. The new programmatic thinking of the churches—especially in Germany—emphasizes the inextricable interdependence of justice and peace, the reliance of global peace on (international) law and the need for post-conflict care (peacebuilding). The main dilemma, however, remains: is it possible to achieve an objective assessment of the *jus ad bellum* question? Does it not remain so that, in all cases, war is considered as "just war on both sides"?

4 The Concept of Just War from an Islamic Perspective

In general, the Qur'ānic assertions related to thought about just war can be divided according to three aspects: wars initiated by God for punishment, wars that express a special reliance on God, and wars waged to cause non-Muslims to convert to Islam. Wars that can be subsumed under the first category are always just because they are intended by God. The second aspect implies an inner duty to demonstrate one's own strong belief by fighting in the path of God. Regarding the third aspect, the question arises whether it is always permissible, or even commanded, to wage war against non-Muslims. The Qur'ān presents different answers to this question. In sura 22:67, the Qur'ānic speaker commands the Muslims to enjoin non-Muslims to believe in the Lord, and not to wrangle with them but to trust in God's wisdom. Sura 9:5–6 also emphasizes the duty to let them know the word of God and to invite them to Islam; however, it also commands Muslims to coerce them even with violence to believe. Therefore, it seems that the Qur'ān struggles with the tension between God's mercifulness, on one hand, and the need of the community to bring unbelievers to the true faith for their own sake, be it by weapons, on the other.

The same problem arises when one consults the *ḥadīth* literature, which does not offer a unified harmonious answer to whether God's messenger Muḥammad attacked the polytheists only under certain preconditions or not.

Because of these internal tensions in the Qur'ān and *ḥadīth*, it is not possible to simply apply some isolated assertions to other situations. It is necessary to elaborate and use several tools of exegesis in order to be able to draw conclusions that apply to other contexts with recourse to the holy text. One of the central questions in the legal tradition is whether it is permissible to attack polytheists without first inviting them to Islam. Influential jurists like Abū Yūsuf ash-Shaybānī of the Ḥanafī school, but also the Shāfiʿī jurist al-Māwardī, distinguish between different conditions for war. For example, ash-Shaybānī taught that it is not necessary to first call the enemy to Islam if the enemy had already heard about Islam—it can be done but it must not to be done. Three centuries later, the philosopher Ibn Rushd, who is also a Mālikī jurist, denies that view without mentioning ash-Shaybānī. He even stated that all jurists agree that Muslims had always first to invite their enemies to Islam before fighting them.

In addition to the two main categories concerning just war– i.e. the question of its just reasons and objectives, and the conduct in war–, the concept of *jihād* implies the idea of earning divine rewards for fighting just wars or earning punishment for abandoning it. The pleasures of those who have fought and were killed in the path of God are described in the Qur'ān (e.g. in sura 3:160 – 79). According to the influential Ḥanbalī scholar Ibn Qayyim al-Jawzīya, for example, a Muslim has to wage three types of war in his life in order to earn eternal rewards: the war against the enemies of God, which includes also Muslim hypocrites; the war against his own self; and the war against Satan. That does not mean, however, that the Muslim community is always obliged to fight against non-Muslims. For instance, the Muʿtazilī theologian ʿAbd al-Jabbār limits the right to wage war only to situations in which one can expect that this will lead to a better situation. One can also find the view—even during the crusader period—that, under certain circumstances, it might be better for Muslim society to make peace with the enemy and to prevent future wars. Thus, striving for peace is not merely a marginal attitude in Islam, one that is often ascribed to Sufism. Although the Sufi literature emphasizes the meaning of *jihād* as an inner spiritual struggle, even Sufis are also aware of the fact that sometimes spiritual duties cannot be fulfilled without the protection of armed soldiers. Particularly the pilgrims had sometimes to be guarded by military forces on their way to Mecca; in general, Sufis were no pacifists, and were even involved sometimes in combat.

To sum up, one can observe that even the most intelligent and scholarly thinkers in the Islamic tradition could not harmonize Qur'ānic assertions about war in a single consistent teaching. Rather, they developed different concepts of *jihād* against the background of their social and historical environment, and in accordance with their wider thought, in order to legitimize war with recourse to the Qur'ān and the hadīth.

This can be observed in the tradition, and down into the modern period. However, some features that were not found in traditional Islam have been transferred from political theories of the 19th and 20th century into Islamic thought. Protagonists of fundamentalist Islam like the Indian-Pakistani thinker Abul Aʿla Maudūdī and the Egyptian theorist of the Muslim Brotherhood, Sayyid Quṭb, consider *jihād* as a revolutionary struggle to overcome the ungodly state of the present world and rebuild an Islamic society.

On the contrary, the former Sheikh of al-Azhar, Maḥmūd Shaltūt, emphasizes the peaceful and humanizing side of Islam by claiming that the Qur'ān restricts warfare to the purpose of self-defense and the protection of the freedom to practice religion. By means of interpreting the Qur'ān in this way, he tries to bring Islamic thought on just war into harmony with the principles of "just war" in the Western world.[3]

5 Common Features and Differences

All three traditions represent the view that wars are just if they are waged against the right enemy. God himself mandates wars against his enemies and the enemies of his people. However, neither Judaism nor Christianity nor Islam portray God primarily as the God of war. War remains a means to overcome evil and bring eternal peace, which is the essence and ultimate goal of the three religions.

War is not only armed combat, but also a state of emergency—even if it lasts several years. This becomes obvious on the juridical level: martial law overrides the common law in sensitive issues. Even one of the most horrible deeds that a person can do to another person, i. e. killing, is no longer murder if it is done in the battlefield. Therefore, all three traditions agree that the duration of war should be limited to the shortest possible time. However, on a metaphysical level, war is an exceptional state of emergency: no one dares to think of eternal

3 According to Ella Landau-Tasseron one can observe a tendency that she terms a "strategy of covert analogy" with regard to the relationship between international law and the concept of *jihād* among prominent representatives of political Islam, (al-Qaraḍāwī and Muṭahharī respectively). She claims that with regard to the arguments used to justify war many scholars present their apologetics in terms of shaping "*jihād* [...] according to just war and international law." Ella Landau-Tasseron, "Jihād and Just War: Overt and Convert Analogies," *Jerusalem Studies in Arabic and Islam*, 48 (2000), 1–48, here. A major problem of this enlightening elaboration on modern *jihād*-conceptions referring to just war conceptions is that it is unclear which position she means when speaking of "civilized" "Western just war" (7) and "just war tradition" (9). General juxtapositions like "The just war tradition developed over time, but its goal has always been to limit warfare. This is not the goal of *jihād*" (13) do not consider the developments in the concept of just war as a whole. The major goal at least in the beginning of this tradition was to legitimatize warfare within Christianity in the face of the commandment to love your neighbors. Another problem is that the author fails to mention the historical 'frame' within which a scholar like al-Qaraḍāwī was writing and the programmatic objectives of his very influential two-volume work *Fiqh al-Jihād*. Al-Qaraḍāwī, who wrote his work in 2009, as militant Islam had reached a new peak of violence, classifies the theoretical approaches to *jihād* into three categories (Landau-Tasseron, "Jihād and Just War," 25), one may describe these as: the position of quietists that reduce *jihād* to a purely spiritual undertaking, the position of radical activists that want to declare *jihād* against the whole world, both of which he rejects, and a third middle position (hence his *waṣatīya*) that stipulates that *jihād* is a complex matter that only the learned may decide, thus taking the decision to launch war out of the authority of the populous. Programmatically, or discursively, al-Qaraḍāwī is trying to delegitimize the prevalent and populous forms of *jihād* that spiraled out of control in the social context he is addressing.

war, but (almost) all people (not only Jews, Christians and Muslims) would strive for eternal peace. This deep desire for heavenly peace lies at the bottom of Judaism, Christianity and Islam. They share the perspective that war can only be just if it is waged in order to reconstitute the cosmological balance or, more properly, in order to return God's creation to its original state of peace and justice.

War and devastation have never been considered as the only or primary means of God's action in the world; rather his willingness to forgive, his patience and mercy characterize and distinguish his dealings with human beings. From this perspective, thought about just war in Judaism, Christianity and Islam can be considered as a critical and even humanizing authority in the face of rampant raids and looting and can even serve as a legal tool to criticize one's political leaders as the case of Francisco de Vitoria illustrates.

But, of course, this is only one side of the coin. In general, religious reflections on the normative dimensions of war do not emerge until religion gains political influence. In contradistinction to Judaism and Christianity, Islam was confronted with the question of warfare at an early formative stage, and thus it is not surprising that these questions were tackled more often and more vigorously in the Qur'ān and other early authoritative writings than in Judaism and Christianity. To conclude from that that Islam is more warlike than Judaism and Christianity would be an essential hermeneutical mistake. What differentiates Islam from Judaism and Christianity in this regard is mainly the idea that fighting in war will be rewarded in afterlife. This idea can be found in the Qur'ān, but not in the Bible. However, eschatological rewards were promised by Byzantine Emperors to Christian soldiers who would die while defending the territory of the Empire against the enemies of God, thus granting Christians and the Christian faith a secure existence.

Generally speaking, it can be observed that under certain conditions, there is only a narrow distinction to be drawn from the claim that it is justified from a religious point of view to wage war under the given circumstances (like self-defense), to the statement that war is warranted on religious grounds (holy wars). The enemy, or the hostile world, consists of the world outside one's own religious community—may this be called *bne Yisra'el*, *orbis christianus* or *dār al-islām*. Such a position can be seen in Maimonides as well as in Augustine, Thomas and al-Ghazālī.

In modern times, there have been strong efforts to institutionalize "just war principles" through international law without reference to religious ideas. At the same time, "holy war propaganda" is used in the context of political ideologies. Yet it remains a dilemma that the identification of the aggressor against whom one has to fight in order to return to the state of just order, remains in the eye of the beholder.

Yet this dilemma is incorporated into the concept of just war in Judaism, Christianity and Islam. Indeed, all three religions represent an absolute concept of God as the God of peace, love and mercy, who knows no compromises, no half-truths. How then could war be justified out of faith in him? With the concept of just war, religious thought in Judaism, Christianity and Islam attempts to reconcile the absolute concept of the good God with the reality of the *conditio humana*. These religions must take into account 1) that war is part of the human reality and that the state of eternal peace, according to their faith, is not to be expected until the age to come, and 2) that self-defense against aggression is essential in certain circumstances to maintain one's own existence. The concept thus appears as an expression of the tension between the ideality of faith and the reality of life, in which monotheistic religions always find themselves. In regards to our current topic, this tension is felt particularly clearly in Christianity. For in neither of the other two religions is the believer urgently required not to react to violence with violence (Luke 6:29). And in neither of the other two religions is self-sacrifice out of love at the center of the believer's way of life. It is probably due to this strained situation that the theological justification of just war is more pronounced in Christianity than in Judaism and Islam. In the same sense, the Orthodox Church knows the practice of preventing participants in the holy war from partaking of the Holy Communion until they have spent a time—sometimes several years—in penance.

With the concept of just war, Judaism, Christianity and Islam demonstrate the effort not to let cruel phenomena of human existence—such as war—be unrestrained, but rather to delimit them through religious restrictions, since they cannot be abolished. All three religions have in common the view that justified war is an unavoidable evil towards a better world. For the realization of a better world, Jews, Christians and Muslims should work resolutely and in every temporal and spatial context by non-violent means. This is also the view of Muslim thinkers, who see the early spread of Islam by means of violence as a historically and regionally conditioned phenomenon that does not have universal validity.

Finally, we should be aware that the determination of which war is just is subject to historical conditions set and validated by rulers and authorities who may be guided more by power-political interests than by theological considerations. Here it is the responsibility of faithful Jews, Christians and Muslims to stand vehemently against arbitrariness and the manipulation of religion, and to work together to ensure that just peace prevails instead of just war.

List of Contributors

Heinz-Gerhard Justenhoven is director of the Institute for Theology and Peace in Hamburg and since 2010 Adjunct Professor at the Theological Faculty of Theology of the University of Freiburg. He studied Theology and Philosophy at the St. Georgen Jesuit Graduate School of Philosophy and Theology in Frankfurt/Main as well as at the Marquette University in Milwaukee, USA. In 1990 he received his Ph.D. at Sankt Georgen Jesuit Graduate School of Philosophy and Theology on the "Peace Ethics of Francisco de Vitoria." He completed his habilitation in 2006 in Moral Theology at the University of Freiburg i.Br. on "International Arbitration between Ethics and Law." He was visiting Professor at the Catholic Theological Union, Chicago (2006) und at Hekima College, Nairobi / Kenya (2007/2009). His recent publications include *Kampf um die Ukraine. Ringen um Selbstbestimmung und geopolitische Interessen* (Nomos 2018), together with Mary Ellen O'Connell *Peace Through Law: Reflections on 'Pacem in Terris From Philosophy, Law, Theology and Political Science* (Nomos 2016) and with William Barbieri, *From Just War to Modern Peace Ethics* (De Gruyter 2012).

Suleiman Mourad, Suleiman A. Mourad is historian of Islam and the Middle East and Professor of Religion at Smith College, Northampton (USA). He was the director of the Nantes Institute for Advanced Study (France). He received his Ph.D (2004) from Yale University in Arabic and Islamic Studies, and holds an M.A. (1996) in History from the American University of Beirut. His research focuses on Muslims as makers and interpreters of their own religious, historical and legal traditions, with a special attention on Qur'anic Studies, Jerusalem, Jihad ideology, the Muslim world during the Crusader Period, and on the challenges of modernity that led to major changes in Muslims' perception of and attitude towards their own history and classical thought. His publications include *The Intensification and Reorientation of Sunni Jihad Ideology in the Crusader Period* (Brill 2013), *The Mosaic of Islam* (Verso 2016), and *Ibn ʿAsakir of Damascus: Champion of Sunni Islam in the Time of the Crusades* (Oneworld 2021).

Daniel F. Polish Daniel F. Polish is the rabbi of Congregation Shir Chadash of the Hudson Valley in LaGrange New York. He is also a college teacher. He earned his rabbinic ordination from the Hebrew Union College-Jewish Institute of Religion in 1968 and his Ph.D. in History of Religion from Harvard University in 1974. He is the author of two books about the Psalms: *Bringing the Psalms to Life* and *Keeping Faith with the Psalms;* and of *Talking about God: Exploring the Meaning of Religious Life with Kierkegaard, Buber, Tillich and Heschel.* He has co-authored a number of articles about the Jewish—Hindu conversation and is currently working on a book on that subject.

Georges Tamer holds the Chair of Oriental Philology and Islamic Studies and is founding director of the "Baverian Research Center for Interreligious Discourses" and speaker of the Centre for Euro-Oriental Studies at the Friedrich-Alexander-University Erlangen-Nuremberg. He received his Ph.D. in Philosophy from the Free University Berlin in 2000 and completed his habilitation in Islamic Studies in Erlangen in 2007. His research focuses on Qu'rānic hermeneutics, philosophy in the Islamic world, Arabic literature and interreligious discourses. His Publications include: *Zeit und Gott: Hellenistische Zeitvorstellungen in der altarabischen Dichtung und im Koran*, 2008, and the edited volumes *Islam and Rationality. The Impact of al-*

Ghazālī (2015) and *Hermeneutical Crossroads: Understanding Scripture in Judaism, Christianity and Islam in the Pre-Modern Orient* (2017).

Katja Thörner is managing director of the "Baverian Research Center for Interreligious Discourses" at the Friedrich-Alexander-University Erlangen-Nuremberg. She studied Philosophy and German Literature in Trier, Würzburg and Berlin and received her Ph.D. in Philosophy at the Munich School of Philosophy in 2010. She is author of *William James' Konzept eines vernünftigen Glaubens auf der Basis religiöser Erfahrung*, 2011 and published with Martin Turner, *Religion, Konfessionslosigkeit und Atheismus*, 2016 and in collaboration with Trutz Rendtorff, *Ernst Troeltsch: Schriften zur Religionswissenschaft und Ethik (1903–1912), 2014.* Her research focuses on the philosophy of religion, theories of interreligious discourses and comparative studies of concepts of the hereafter in Islam and Christianity.

Index of Persons

Aaron 3
ʿAbd al-Jabbār 107 f., 138, 155
Abdel Haleem, M.A.S. 147
Abel 7
Abraham 6, 8
Absalom 20
Abū Bakr 100
Abū Ḥanīfa 98, 100
Abū Yūsuf 96–99, 137, 154
Afsaruddin, Asma 147
Ahitophel 20
Ahmad, Ahmad Atif 132
Akhan 35
al-ʿĀmirī 111 f., 130, 138
al-Bannā, Ḥasan 127 f., 131
al-Bāqir, Abū Jaʿfar Muḥammad 102
al-Fārābī 111, 138
al-Ghazālī 109 f., 138, 157
al-Ḥusayn 103
al-Kāmil 120
al-Kulaynī 102–104, 137–140
al-Māwardī 98, 117, 154
al-Qushayrī 108 f., 138
Alarich 47
Albright, Madeleine 74
ʿAlī ibn Abī Ṭālib 102 f.
Amalek 10, 25 f., 38
Amiel, Moshe Avigdor 31
Amos 10, 14
Annan, Kofi 75
ar-Rashīd, Hārūn 96, 98
ar-Rāzī, Fakhr ad-Dīn 117, 121
Asfaw, Semegnish 67, 91
ash-Shāfiʿī 100
ash-Shaybānī 96, 98 f., 133 f., 137, 154
ʿĀshūr, Saʿīd 119
aṭ-Ṭabarī 115, 122
aṭ-Ṭabrisī 115, 117
aṭ-Ṭūsī 96, 102–106, 137 f.
ath-Thaʿlabī 117, 122
Athanasius the Great 49 f.
Augustine 1, 43, 45–49, 51, 53, 55, 59, 61 f., 71, 74, 76, 84, 93, 152 f., 157
az-Zamakhsharī 117

Bainton, Roland H. 45
Bar Kochba, Simon 15, 32
Bartholomé de Las Casas 55
Basil the Great 50, 61
Beestermöller, Gerhard 52 f., 63, 74, 76
Ben Yehoyada, Benayahu 20
Benedict XV, Pope 64
Berlin, Naftali Tzvi Yehudah 22, 43 f., 56, 61, 77, 83, 91, 150
Bethke Elshtain, Jean 74 f.
Biggar, Nigel 59, 65, 70
Bin Laden, Usama 131 f.
Blankinship, Khalid Yahya 119
Bleich, David 28 f.
Bohemond of Antioch 122
Boisard, Marcel A. 147
Bonifatius 46
Bos, Hildo 49 f.
Brachtendorf, Johannes 47 f.
Brennecke, Hans Christof 44 f.
Broyde, Michael 17 f., 21 f., 37 f.
Brunstetter, Daniel R. 43
Buchbender, Ortwin 73
Bush, George W. 77, 82

Cain 7
Calasso, Giovanna 147
Calvin, John 54, 59–62
Cassidy, Richard J. 44
Charney, Jonathan I. 75
Cicero 43, 45 f.
Coates, Anthony J. 72 f.
Cole, Darrell 72, 76
Cook, David 147
Cornelius the Centurion 44
Cortés, Hernán 57
Crossley, Robert N. 60

Dadoyan, Seta B. 123

David 8f., 19–22, 27f., 30, 50, 59, 70, 72, 142, 147, 150
Delgado, Mariano 55

Ecclesiastes 5
Eisen, Robert 22, 31, 33f., 41, 151
Elijah 7f.
Elisha 8
Enns, Fernando 81f.
Esau 29, 38
Esther 7, 12
Evyatar 20
Ezekiel 9

Faber, Eva Maria 62
Firestone, Reuven 12, 30, 33, 41
Ford, John C. 71
Francisco de Vitoria 54–60, 63, 71f., 153, 157
Freedman, Lawrence 94
Fuchs, Stephan 70

Gillner, Matthias 57
Good, Robert M. 9f., 54, 60
Goren, Shlomo 32–34, 36
Goudie, Kenneth A. 119
Gratian from Bologna 51, 93, 153
Gritsch, Kurt 75
Grube, Falko 75

Habermas, Jürgen 74
Hallaq, Wael 135f.
Hamilton, Bernice 58
Harnack, Adolf von 45
Harries, Richard 67
Herbert, Bob 74
Herzog, Isaac Halevi 31f., 151
Hillel 3
Hillenbrand, Carole 119
Hobbes, Thomas 11
Höffe, Otfried 73f.
Hofheinz, Marco 61
Hornus, Jean Michel 45
Hoyland, Robert G. 123
Huber, Wolfgang 66, 68
Hussein, Saddam 72

Ibn al-Athīr 120
Ibn al-Mubārak 110
Ibn ʿAsākir of Damascus 105
Ibn Qayyim al-Jawzīya 106f., 113, 119, 155
Ibn Qudāma 120f., 140
Ibn Rushd 96, 99–101, 137–140, 154
Ibn Taymīya 99, 105–107, 119, 139
Ibn Wāṣil 120f.
ʿImād ad-Dīn al-Iṣfahānī 110, 122
Ingham, Michael 67
Innocence III, Pope 53
Isaacs, Alick 150
Isaiah 2, 4f., 9
Ivo of Chartres 51

Jacob 29, 38
Jaʿfar aṣ-Ṣādiq 103, 139
Jesus 43f., 52, 76, 80f., 91
Joel 5f., 10, 17f., 41
John, Apostle 63, 71, 80, 84, 91, 99, 104, 133, 147
John Paul II, Pope 65f.
John XXIII, Pope 65
Johnson, James Turner 43, 70f., 133f.
Joshua 8–12, 19, 21, 24–26, 34f., 151
Justenhoven, Heinz-Gerhard 43, 47, 51f., 54–56, 65f., 83, 91

Kany, Roland 51
Keller, Andrea 46
Kelsay, John 133, 147
Kimchi, David 27
Kirchschlager, Bernd 75
Koch, Bernhard 78, 80
Koheleth 5
Köhler, Michael 119
Krisch, Nico 77
Kronenberg, Ulrich 66

Laiou, Angeliki 50
Landau-Tasseron, Ella 156
Lederach, John Paul 84
Leibowitz, Yeshayahu 38
Leo XIII, Pope 64
Leppin, Hartmut 44
Levi 7
Lienemann, Wolfgang 70, 91

Lindsay, James E. 105 f., 119, 147
Loew, Judah 29
Luther, Martin 6, 54, 59–62, 91
Lutz, Dieter S. 74
Luzzatto, Samuel David 30

Maccabeus, Judah 15
Madden, Thomas F. 119
Maimonides 25–28, 150 f., 157
Mālik b. Anas 100
Maududi, Abul A'la 123–125, 128, 131, 140 f.
McMahan, Jeff 78–80, 84
McNeil, Particia F. 71
Me'iri, Menachem 28
Micah 2, 4 f.
Missalla, Heinrich 70
Montesinos, Pedro de 55
Moses 7, 25, 28, 34, 151
Mourad, Suleiman A. 93, 104–106, 119 f., 147
Muḥammad 95–104, 107, 109, 112, 115–118, 120, 125, 129–131, 134, 140–142, 154
Muldoon, James 57

Nahmanides 28, 34, 151
Nahum 14
Nebuchadnezzar 114
Noah 7, 27
Nūr ad-Dīn 105

Oppenheim, Lassa 93 f.
Overbeck, Franz Josef 68 f., 91

Pacelli, Eugenio 64
Parrott, Justin 134 f.
Paul, Apostle 44, 61, 70 f., 81, 84, 108
Pecci, Vincenzo 64
Pérez de Cuéllar, Javier 72
Pius XII, Pope 65
Pizzaro, Francisco 57
Polish, Daniel F. 1, 7, 151
Polk, William R. 119

Quṭb, Sayyid 125–128, 131, 140 f., 155

Rabbi Akiva 32
Rabbi Judah 18 f., 29
Rabbi Simeon bar Yohai 32
Rabbi Yocḥanan 19
Rabbi Yose 17
Rabinowitz, Nahum 34
Rad, Gerhard von 13
Ramadan, Abdel Azim 142
Ramsey, Paul 70 f.
Rashi 24 f., 27, 150
Rav Yehudah 18
Rav Yosef 20
Rava 19 f.
Ravitzky, Aviezer 34
Reed, Charles 59
Regout, Robert H.W. 43
Reichberg, Gregory M. 43, 91
Reuter, Hans Richard 66, 68 f.
Richard the Lionheart 120
Riley-Smith, Jonathan 119

Saladin 110, 120, 122
Salmān al-Fārisī 97
Samuel 7, 9 f., 12, 20, 23, 28, 30
Saul 8, 10, 23, 27 f., 150
Scattola, Merio 58
Schiffman, Lawrence 6, 17, 22, 36, 41
Schlabach, Gerald 82–84
Schockenhoff, Eberhard 46 f., 69
Schrage, Marco 64
Sepúlveda, Juan Ginés de 54
Shaltūt, Maḥmūd 128 f., 131 f., 141, 147, 155
Shatz, David 22, 38
Simeon 7, 32
Simma, Bruno 75
Sizgorich, Thomas 96, 110
Sokolow, Moshe 36, 38
Solomon, Norman 30 f., 37
Stümke, Volker 59 f., 62

Ṭaha, Mahmoud M. 120, 130 f., 141, 147
Takim, Liyakat 119
Taparelli d'Azeglio, Luigi 63
Tertullian 45, 152
Tesei, Tommaso 96, 142

Thomas Aquinas 46, 50–54, 58 f., 61–63, 71, 77, 81, 84, 153
Thumfart, Johannes 56
Titus 114
Troeltsch, Ernst 61

ʿUmar 100, 120
Uriah the Hittite 27

Waldenberg, Eliezer Yehudah 21
Walters, LeRoy 59
Walzer, Michael 26, 28 f., 78
Weber, Max 81
Webster, Alexander 49, 91
Weissenberg, Timo 48
Weizsäcker, Carl Friedrich von 83
Wellhausen, Julius 8 f.
Williams of Canterbury, Rowan 77
Wilson, Woodrow 64

Yisraeli, Shaul 34
Yoav 20
Yoder, John Howard 80 f., 83, 91
Yūsuf, Yūsuf Ḥ. 142

Zawati, Hilmi 147
Zayn ad-Dīn ar-Rāzī 121, 140
Zephaniah 9
Zulfiqar, Adnan 113, 147

Index of Subjects

al-Qaeda 131f., 141
Arabia 1, 97, 125, 131
authority 19, 22, 32, 34, 44, 48, 50, 52f., 58–61, 63–65, 71–76, 82, 100f., 105, 108, 111, 113, 121, 124, 139, 142, 152, 156f.

Catholic Church 60, 62, 70, 82, 142
Christians 1, 44f., 47, 49f., 54, 60, 62, 83f., 100, 104, 118f., 137, 152f., 157f.
civilians 23, 31f ., 34, 39, 59, 69f., 76, 83
civilization 13, 35f., 55, 119, 128
combatants 18, 34f . 39, 69, 79, 101
commanded war(s) 18f., 21, 24–27, 33, 150f.
common good 58, 62, 65, 72, 81
companions 97f., 125
criterion of discrimination 71
criterion of proportionality 71
Crusade 53, 105, 107, 119–123, 131f., 135, 140, 147, 155
– Crusaders 49f., 107, 119f., 122

dār al-ḥarb 102
defensive war 17, 19, 25, 32f., 50, 61
discretionary war 18–21, 23–28, 32, 150f.

Eastern Orthodox Churches 49, 52
Europe 70, 72, 93, 119
Evangelical Churches 66
Evangelical Church in Germany 66, 68–70
evil 5, 36f., 47f., 52–54, 60, 62, 82f., 97, 102–104, 107, 138, 152, 156, 158

God 2f., 6, 8–12, 20, 23, 27, 36f., 44, 47–49, 52f., 55, 60, 62, 67, 71, 76, 81–83, 95, 97, 99, 102–110, 112–118, 122–130, 133f., 138f., 147, 150, 152, 154–158
government(s) 31, 60, 63, 67f., 72–77, 124

halacha 29, 32, 36, 39
Huguenots 62
humanitarian intervention 52f., 57, 69, 73, 75, 79, 82

idolatry 22, 27f., 151
imām 100, 103, 121
injustice 13, 46, 52–54, 58, 60f., 66, 79, 118, 131f., 141
intention 19, 54, 79, 81, 137
international common good 65, 72, 75, 77, 83
international law 36, 54, 56f., 64, 68f., 71f., 74–77, 83, 93, 136, 147, 153, 156f.
international policing 82–84
Israel 2f., 5, 9–15, 19–21, 24–26, 28, 30–33, 35–38, 114, 116, 132, 142, 150f.
– Israelites 9–14, 28, 114, 118
ius ad bellum 71
ius in bello 58, 71, 78

jāhilīya 125–127
Jerusalem 114, 119, 156
Jews 1, 4, 15, 18f., 23, 27, 29–31, 34, 36, 44, 104, 118, 137, 152, 157f.
jihād 27, 98f., 102–114, 119, 124f., 127f., 130f., 134–136, 138, 140f., 147, 151, 155f.
jizya 97, 100, 102–104, 118, 133f., 137–139
just authority 73
just cause 54, 58, 61, 63, 70f., 74, 76, 79, 81, 94
justice 3, 6, 9, 29, 32, 37, 44, 46, 62f., 66f., 71f., 76f., 94, 128, 132, 150, 153, 157
just policing 82–84
just war on both sides 70, 72, 154

last resort 37, 48, 60–62, 77, 81, 83, 149, 152
legitimate authority 48, 52, 61–63, 81
lesser evil 82, 112
Lutheran Churches 59

Mecca 107, 110, 140, 155
Medina 98, 107, 140
Messiah 4, 15, 27–29, 32, 152
Middle East 119, 123
Muslim Brothers 127
Muslims 1, 94–97, 99–103, 106 f., 111, 116–121, 123, 125, 127–129, 131–142, 154 f., 157 f.

national interest 58, 74, 77, 83
nationalism 15, 49, 63
NATO 69, 73–75
natural law 7, 52, 56, 153
non-combatants 13 f., 23, 27, 29, 35 f., 39, 139
nonconformity 80 f.
nonviolent 69, 80 f.
– non-violence 47, 135

obligatory war 18 f., 21, 150
offensive war 48
Ottoman Empire 29

pacifism 43, 45, 48, 66, 82 f.
Palestine 29 f., 35, 53, 122, 151, 153
peace 2–6, 13, 17, 26, 28 f., 36 f., 40 f., 43, 46–54, 57–71, 75 f., 81 f., 84, 91, 93, 108, 117, 119–123, 128 f., 131, 137, 140, 142, 147, 150, 152 f., 155–158
– just peace 66–70, 91, 153, 158
Peace Churches 44, 80–83
People of the Book 100, 118, 137 f.
Pietist Churches 80
polytheists 97, 100, 102 f., 107, 116 f., 133, 154
protection 23, 32, 68, 76, 82, 116, 118, 149, 155
punishment 7–9, 11, 22, 28, 105, 113 f., 138, 154 f.

Rabbinic Literature 3, 16, 150
Reformed Churches 59 f.
responsibility 37, 54, 58, 62, 71 f., 76, 78 f., 81 f., 158
right intention 58 f., 61, 76, 81, 153
Russian Orthodox Church 62 f.

Sabbath 4, 7, 19, 31 f.
Second Temple Judaism 15
self-defense 17 f., 22, 33, 35, 38, 65, 69, 74, 76, 150, 155, 157 f.
shahāda(s) 104
shalom 2–4, 66, 150
Shīʿī 102 f., 106, 138
– Shīʿism 96, 106
Successors 59, 97 f.
Sufism 108, 111, 155
– Sufis 108, 111, 155
Sunni 98, 102, 105, 107 f., 136, 138, 147
– Sunnism 99, 106

terror, terrorist, terrorism 13, 39, 75–77, 82, 94
threat 34, 60, 67, 70 f., 75, 78 f., 109, 111, 115, 138 f., 152
tranquility 4, 47, 71, 76, 150

United Nations 31, 65, 67, 71 f., 83

zakāt 100, 137
Zoroastrians 100, 104, 137

www.ingramcontent.com/pod-product-compliance
Lightning Source LLC
Chambersburg PA
CBHW031402230426
43670CB00006B/620
9783110738056